Sheryl Sandberg, China & Me

An ordinary woman moves her family to China for her
career, watches her career implode, and with it,
her life – or so she thought.

J.T. Gilhool

JG_ink

a division of Pink Streak Ink

www.pinkstreakink.us
www.facebook.com/JenniferGilhoolInk

Variations between the original blog posts and the published versions herein are due to editing for clarity and comprehension in book format. The events depicted are based on the author's actual experiences and are recounted from the author's perspective. All locations, dates and people are real; names have been changed to protect the privacy of individuals. The "Salt Mine" is not the real name of any company known to the author and is used to represent a real corporation.

Cover Illustration: Randa Mansour
Publisher: JG_ink
Editor: Lisa Wilder
Photos courtesy Fife's Photography

ISBN 978-0-615-94958-1
Printed in the United States of America

Praise for Sheryl Sandberg, China & Me

"Jennifer Gilhool doesn't just talk conceptually about the challenges women face in the corporate world. She lets the reader into her mind, heart and home as she seeks success in a world that too often fails to value women's contributions. Jennifer finds a new sense of self that is energizing and inspirational!"

Janet Hanson
Founder 85 Broads Unlimted, LLC, and former Managing Director Lehman Brothers

"Through her first-hand account of journeying into corporate leadership, Jennifer Gilhool gives readers a unique look into the hearts and minds of many ambitious career women who sacrifice more than they care to admit in hopes of fulfilling career goals that too often remain out of reach. It's an inspiring story."

Gail Evans
Best-selling author of Play Like A Man, Win Like A Woman, *CNN Executive Vice President (retired), Former Member of President Johnson's White House Staff, Office of the Special Counsel*

"I'm a big Jennifer Gilhool fan – in part because Jennifer's life and career are proof that real growth happens when we risk and make ourselves uncomfortable. Her professional and personal experiences are woven together with humor, grit, and honesty, all of which make for fascinating reading. Regardless of your level, you'll be glad you read this helpful, reassuring book of life lessons."

Selena Rezvani
Author of PUSHBACK: How Women Ask—And Stand Up— For What They Want *and columnist for The Washington Post*

"*Lean In's* Sheryl Sandberg has nothing on this woman! What a delight to read the real heart and soul of a woman warrior in a leadership role. This is a can't-put-it-down book for a great summer read – an entrée into a woman's family room, kitchen counter and a fly on the wall in the boardroom all at once. Jennifer is the hero in her own story – but so are her family, colleagues and friends. This is about humor, satire, revenge, ego AND family. This real life story makes you question "leaning in" but also captures the need to bring more women onto a mentoring platform. We got the vote in 1920 but we still get the shaft."

Gail M. Romero, CFRE
CEO, Collective Changes – Mentoring Women
Globally to Build Business and Jobs

"Where Sheryl Sandberg may have opened the lid of Pandora's Box with *Lean In*, Jennifer Gilhool has been living inside the Box for years. Sandberg shines a flashlight on the issues and challenges for professional women in today's workplace, but Gilhool drags them out of the box and into the full light of day.

Jennifer combines keen analytic skills and the sensibilities of a working mother and spouse. She bares her soul and raw feelings in her daily fight to create the delicate balance between the often-conflicting demands of work, of family and of being true to herself – in a world where the deck is still heavily stacked against women who just want to be themselves.

Gilhool's words and poignant images will leave you breathless and wanting more . . . more of her unique ability to describe the struggle that too many women still face today – and that too many of us men still allow to endure. Read this book. It will wake you up and move you to action."

Bob Kantor
Executive Coach, Kantor Consulting Group, Inc.

Dedication

I am fortunate to be surrounded by wonderful women and men. But without the two men who have been the predominant forces in my life, I would never have come to this point in my journey. A point where I am beginning to feel my feet underneath me again.

For my father and my husband
and, of course, the three Defectors,
who bring me more happiness than I deserve.

Autobiographies are only useful as the lives you read about and analyze may suggest to you something that you may find useful in your own journey through life.

- Eleanor Roosevelt

Table of Contents

Author's Note

I never expected to share my story. I also never expected to move to China. But, I did move to China with a husband, three children and a dog. I also wrote a blog to "journal" our family's adventures and keep our families at home up to date on their grandchildren, cousins, nieces and nephew.

Family and friends shared my postings with their friends and families and so on. Then, Sheryl Sandberg published *Lean In*. Some commentators criticized Ms. Sandberg for suggesting that women needed to do more to "lean in" to their careers. Others suggested Ms. Sandberg was ignoring the "sticky floor." And, some even suggested that Ms. Sandberg didn't have standing to enter the discussion because she was "too" successful and has "too many" resources at her disposal to be credible on the issue of women and equality in the work place.

Odd. Sheryl Sandberg lacking standing to tell her story because she is too successful. Okay, I thought, if that is the case, then maybe I should tell my story. I'm no Sheryl Sandberg. But I did lean in, long before the term was coined.

Gloria Steinem said any movement takes at least 100 years and we are only 50 years into the feminist movement. So, with this in mind, I decided to share my story. Why? Because I have daughters and nieces and I hope to have granddaughters one day. I also have a son and nephews and, if I am lucky, I may even get a grandson someday.

My story is one of an ordinary woman who moved her family to China for her career, saw her career implode and, with it, her life — or so she thought. This story is told as it unfolded through the actual blog posts. It is unvarnished. I decided not to self-censor because I wanted to share the raw emotions associated with trying to balance the competing priorities of home and career, as well as the roadblocks that I set for myself and those set for me by others.

It is my story. Perhaps, it is our shared story.

Prologue

The Beginning

Well, it isn't really the beginning. Maybe it is the middle. I want it to be the end.

When I wake up each night at 3 a.m., all I can think about is tequila. I don't even like tequila, actually. Still, the only thought running through my head is the mixture of pills and tequila. How many shots of tequila will it take to down all the painkillers, sleep aids and other assorted prescription pills in the house to guarantee myself a nice long sleep? As I stare at the ceiling, this same loop runs over and over in my head. Is that disturbing?

When I board a plane for a business trip, I calculate the benefit that my life insurance will pay if the plane crashes and I die. Then, I look around to be sure there aren't too many children on board and that the plane isn't full, and I silently wish for a crash. You probably don't want to fly with me. That is disturbing, isn't it?

On my latest trip to Australia, I walked the Sydney Harbor Bridge several times. Was it high enough? How much would the impact with the water hurt or would it knock me out immediately? What were the chances of my falling body hitting a ferry or other vessel? Drowning seems like a bad way to go. Don't you think?

I didn't share these thoughts aloud. At least, not at first. But they were there lurking in the dark. And, it was getting darker every day until one day it just became overwhelming. The man who has loved me for more than half my life intervened, asking "Do you really think I can't hear you crying in the shower?"

Actually, yes.

And, so the unraveling began. The beginning.

A Word About The Unravelling

I wish I could say that my unravelling was simply an over-reaction to a rough day or week or month at the office or that moving to China was a rougher transition than I expected, but that would not be true. I had no idea — until later — that I *was actually reacting* to something. It wasn't China or work. It would be months before I would understand.

This is the story of my coming to that understanding and being pushed to the brink by my obsessive devotion to my work and the promise of reaching ever-increasing heights within the management structure. Today, Sheryl Sandberg might say this is my story of "leaning in." But, when I started this journey, Sheryl Sandberg and *Lean In* were not yet on the radar screen.

My story is not just about leaning in at the office. It is also the story of coming to terms with my personal demons and insecurities. Everyone has them. Everyone has secrets. It's how you handle them that often determines how things work out for you.

This is the story of my awakening. It is the story of a woman who overcame the obstacles that clutter each of our lives and nearly lost herself in the process. It is the story of a woman who dove headfirst into her career and nearly drowned. It is the story of a woman who found herself, her purpose and her worth through that experience and the mixture of her demons with her devotion.

It all happened just like this . . . in China.

———————————

Part One:
An American Family
Moves to China

Shanghai skyline at night - view from the Bund in Puxi looking toward Pu Dong.

Five For Chinese

August 2011
Detroit to Shanghai

A journey of a thousand miles begins with a single step.

~ *Confucius*

If you are flying Delta Airlines to Shanghai, a wise first step might be to the airline counter next to you. I've made this little journey a few times now and, while I am no Arthur Frommer, I am not a novice either. I know how weather, broken cockpit glass and flight crews beyond their flight limit can delay a flight for hours and even days. So, when I booked our family's trip from the States to China, I insisted on a direct flight. No connections in Tokyo, Seoul or Los Angeles for my crew. I wanted a straight shot to the Middle Kingdom.

Get 'em on the plane just once.

Yep. That was my plan.

I left the States 10 weeks ago to start my new assignment with the Salt Mine in Shanghai, China. I left my husband, Jack, and our three children — Jane (13), Henry (10) and Bella (9) — and the dog, Wrigley, in the States for the summer. Two of those kids have never been on a plane and the youngest keeps asking if there are enough parachutes on board for all the passengers. (I think she has watched Leo and Kate on the Titanic one too many times.)

Get 'em on the plane once.

In accordance with the terms and conditions of their international travel tickets, the traveling band of wild emotions arrived at the airport 2 hours before their scheduled departure and took up residence in the business class lounge. As luck would have it, the flight board indicated an on-time departure. Cookies and soda in hand, the gang sat down and got cozy with their iPads.

Right on schedule, they were called to the gate only to be turned back around instantly. A water leak. The nervous 9-year-old must have been conjuring images of Leo on that fated cruise because she unleashed her very own gusher. Certain this meant disaster, she insisted on a parachute count before she would step foot on that plane! Cookies. Dad's best hope was more cookies.

Nearly 2 hours later, they were called to the gate again and this time they made it on-board. For first-time flyers, business class isn't bad and the kids' nerves began to ease as their attention turned to the seat features, dining options and movie selections. Dad just wanted his pre-flight cocktail that wasn't coming, which made him nervous. Sure enough, Dad's cocktail delay was telling. The passengers were de-planed.

Get 'em on the plane *once.*

First, the good news. The 9-year-old had moved from tears to anger. The bad news, it took another hour before they would get on the plane again and . . . then get off the plane, again.

Yep, get 'em on the plane *once.*

The third time did the trick and when they were finally on the plane, they were stuck there. As in stuck on the plane, sitting at the gate, for 3 hours. The airline had altered the flight route. So, of course, this required more fuel. Fuel adds weight and, naturally, the plane was now overweight. Needing a diet, cargo was removed from the belly of the beast. As would be expected, that left the plane unbalanced. A careful and thorough balancing process ensued until, finally, the plane was cleared for takeoff.

The flight was not much better. No cocktails, soggy chicken nuggets, and unfriendly service. Now on the plane, they just wanted off. Eight hours later than scheduled, it landed in Shanghai.

Now, we just need to get the dog here . . .

Dog Gone Shanghai . . .

August 2011
Shanghai

Well, you may have heard by now that our dog racked up the frequent flier miles. Depending on the story, and it changes daily,

Wrigley has flown from the States to Amsterdam and back, and then on to China. He arrived here on the 18th or 19th of August, again depending on the story.

Along his travels, his paperwork was lost. And if the Chinese love anything, it's their paperwork. Thus, Wrigley remains confined at the airport. He has not cleared customs and is in quarantine. This is the worst possible scenario.

On the bright side (and it isn't all that bright), the Salt Mine's Government Affairs and Human Resources departments deployed the full force of their networks to free Wrigley. I fully expected a march to be organized and t-shirts to appear at any minute. Thanks to this team, however, we receive pictures of Wrigley daily to verify his well-being.

We may have been able to spring Wrigley but it would have brought unwanted attention to the "special relationship" that the Animals Away team has with customs (not that it seems so special to us). This relationship allows you to skip quarantine (not exactly skipped by us) and get your dog in 24 hours (again, not us). We did not want another family waiting the way we have been waiting, so we decided to ride it out without any special intervention.

Our dog — without a country or passport or medical history form — is sorely missed by the gang here. We'll send photos when we have our happy reunion with Wrigley — keep him in your thoughts. There's a chance he has a new Chinese name by now and may no longer respond to English, but we'll deal with that if we have to!

Political Prisoner Freed . . .

Rumors are spreading like wild fire in the Shanghai, Pu Dong area that political prisoner, Wrigley, will be freed later this morning. His staunchest supporters maintained a low profile this morning, boarding buses for their schools in an effort to keep the media at bay. Meanwhile, Wrigley's Chief Counsel, Jack Fox, dodged cameras and refused to comment on the rumored release. Government officials could not be reached for comment.

After 2 weeks, Wrigley is home!

Political prisoner Wrigley free and home.

China Rocks; China Sucks

September 2011
Shanghai

I have noticed a direct relationship to the amount that I swear and Notre Dame football. China has helped clean up my bad habit.

The bad news is that I cannot watch Notre Dame football live; the good news is that I cannot watch Notre Dame football live. I checked this morning and was thoroughly disgusted. Jack's standing in the house is on thin ice (our current coach hails from Central Michigan University, Jack's alma mater, and if things don't improve, Jack will take the blame).

However, my swearing level is down to the 1988 football season low (that was the last time we won the National Championship) and I think there is a direct correlation. Sling Box be damned, I don't want to watch . . . I think it is better for everyone that we return to glory (once and for all) over these next 3 years, while we are in China. I will avoid a heart attack, my marriage may survive and my children can learn to swear from their friends when they get back to the States!

Now that I have that out of my system, here is your update:

The roller coaster goes up and; therefore, it must come down. This sums up the past 2 weeks for the kids and signals that everything is on track. Jack and I were feeling good last week after having dinner and hearing how Henry stopped two goals during recess soccer, Bella made three new friends and Jane's drama teacher was so cool that Jane decided to try out for the school play. Feeling good about ourselves and our ability to navigate the children's transition with such deft, we retired to the rooftop deck for a bottle of wine and some adult time.

The hangover arrived the following morning. The same three kids have no friends, school is too hard, there is too much homework, we'll never learn Chinese, no one talks to me or plays with me, the teachers hate me and on and on and on. Even the dog was unhappy and refused to go for the walk to the bus stop — China is just too darn loud.

And so the long walk to the bus stop began — without the dog. The would-be Defectors talked quietly amongst themselves as they walked ahead of the Warden and her husband. They certainly were plotting their escape.

Indeed, Jane already announced that she had "given China a chance" and "hated it" and was "demanding" to return to the States immediately. Surely, the other two were negotiating safe passage with her. We'd have to alert the Ayi (housekeeper) and Driver. A Shawshank escape was clearly under development.

Frankly, Jack and I wanted to head for the States ourselves and leave the three Defectors and the dog in Shanghai.

When the first two Defectors were loaded on their prison bus, we learned the truth from the third. "So, is school really that bad?" the Warden asked. "No, I kinda like it," the littlest Defector replied and rode off to school without a care.

%$#@!! So maybe Notre Dame football isn't the only thing that makes me swear!

In fairness, it is hard to make the transition from living in the States to China. School is a particularly difficult transition because the teaching styles are so different. In China, school is more demanding. You are expected to be responsible for yourself, your work, your extra-curricular activities. There is no spoon feeding here.

"Little Defectors"

We have issues with the uniforms. Our Ayi ("Alice") is very efficient. She does laundry every day. If you leave it out, it gets washed, ironed and put away whether it needs it or not. She irons my workout clothes. She does. Having your laundry done for you daily is great except that we never know exactly where Ayi puts our clothes away.

Each morning, the children hunt for school uniforms that could be anywhere — in the dryer, in their sister's drawer, in Mom's closet, in Henry's closet or with the dry cleaning. It's funny, after everyone's dressed and on the bus (and even when you are throwing clothes every which way in the morning). But it adds to the children's morning stress about school. Each morning, as we go through this ritual, it reminds them that they are not at home.

Still, it isn't all porridge and drudgery. Jane already spent a day with friends exploring a new mall. Henry is fielding requests for more play dates than we can schedule and is the neighborhood playtime leader. He and Bella have an organized gang and kids are at the front door every day. Bella has made loads of friends at school and seems to be settling in well.

Our informant network is better here than in the States. The Defectors are not loyal to each other. Having Henry at Jane's school is a real boon for the Warden. Henry reports that Jane does talk to other kids on the bus, does have friends and does smile at school — even during gym.

Bella is an even better informant. According to her latest report, Toby has asked Jane whether she is busy next weekend, and Toby is a BOY!! While no confirmation has been made of his national origin, we believe this young man to be an Aussie.

Jane tells me that this is not a date. He is a friend only. But, she asked me to make an appointment for a shampoo and blow dry on Saturday before her mani/pedi. She'll be done at noon and will spend the afternoon with Toby.

The smaller Defectors have proven useful and are rewarded often with chocolate croissants and extra rations of Nutella.

Two weeks in and things seemed pretty good. I had to work over the weekend in Tianjin. Jack picked me up at the airport and we headed to our favorite blues bar, The Cotton Club. It was a good night.

On Sunday, the girls got new haircuts, we went out for breakfast, finished homework, ate dumplings and gelato, watched Henry at soccer and had a great day.

Later that night, Henry "Skyped" with his best friend in the States for an hour and we all laughed as Jane went running up and down the three flights of stairs to the roof with her phone.

The on-again-off-again Internet and phone signals were interfering with Jane's texting obsession. Bella explained to us that Jane was going to the rooftop to check her messages and text her friends. Bella figured it was Toby but we never asked Jane. She was all smiles though. She'll have great legs after this is over!

So, feeling good about ourselves, we opened a bottle of wine and put the kids to bed and headed to the rooftop deck . . .

This morning, the hangover returned. China sucks. The Defectors are plotting again . . .

Oh Martha

September 2011
Shanghai

"I don't know" is the phrase we most often hear out of Jane's mouth. I don't know what I want to wear. I don't know what I want to eat. I don't know what I want to do. I don't know what's wrong. I don't know if I can do that. I don't know . . . I don't know . . . I don't know.

Well, there is one thing Jane does know, and it's that she has no talent. Just ask her.

She is the worst kid in school, she can't make friends and she has no natural ability to do anything. She is a 14-year-old girl on her way to oblivion. Worse, she has found oblivion and it is in Shanghai.

That is, until she met Mr. Bell, her drama teacher. I haven't met the man but when I do (this evening), I may kiss him. He told Jane on her second day of school that she was the kind of kid that really "ticked him off." Jane has "loads of talent" but won't show it to anyone. I love this man.

Mr. Bell coaxed Jane to get up on a chair in front of the drama class, told her to stand on one leg with her hands over her head and threw a box at her. Jane never flinched. He fell in love with her in that instant, and she with him. Thanks to this little drama exercise, Jane tried out for a part in *Arsenic & Old Lace* even though she didn't know if she could really do it.

Drama is serious business here. The International School has its own theatre. It is a very professional theatre — sound, lighting, professional sets — the whole nine yards. This place knows "art" and "craft." So, on Tuesday, Jane went to audition for a part — any part — in the play.

Mr. Bell had all of the actors read for the lead roles. Jane read for the part of Aunt Martha. Mr. Bell told her she did well, suggesting she return for another reading on Wednesday and to try and be "older." To be "old," Jane took one of her Mom's old lady sweaters, Henry's glasses and a pair of knee highs — worn slightly askew — and returned on Wednesday. Mr. Bell was polite but non-committal. There were many older girls trying out too; auditions are open for students from Year 7 to Year 14 (middle school and high school).

Jack and I are so proud of her. Jane is shy and it's hard for her to put herself out there but after the first step, she shines. Today we learned that Jane was cast as the understudy to Martha. We are over the moon! The high schooler cast as Martha has some "commitment issues" so Jane may take the stage as Martha for at least one performance. She will prepare as though she was the lead.

Mr. Bell called her out in class today and congratulated her on her audition, her ability to take direction and to return in character and avoid over-doing "old" by being ancient. Her lack of stage experience was a concern but her choir experience made clear that, while she is quiet, she understands projection on the stage. Jane claims she has no idea what Mr. Bell was talking about but we think she did.

We really are thrilled. It is the perfect way for Jane to get comfortable in this new genre, make friends and build confidence. She'll call you and underplay her excitement but she was beaming today. I really think this will help the transition.

Of course, when you ask Jane how things are at school she will be sure to tell you that they aren't going well. Oh, Martha!

Oh Martha II

September 2011
Chongqing, China

The theatre season is off to an exciting start.

The Shanghai production of *Arsenic & Old Lace* made a stunning cast change on Monday, replacing veteran actress Jenny in the lead role of Aunt Martha with a new talent imported from the States, Jane Fox.

The announcement came just one week into rehearsals.

It was a surprise to the entire cast, particularly Jane. Showing some real media savvy, Ms. Fox's only comment was that she hoped to be worthy of the director's confidence. Ms. Fox is a fresh faced, young talent who is, as yet, untested in such a major role.

Director David Bell said Ms. Fox has shown real dedication to the production and an understanding of the role. He said commitment to the role and the production drove the need for the change. Shanghai Theatre News will continue to watch this space.

The set for *Arsenic & Old Lace*

Congratulations, Ms. Fox! (If only I could have been there to hear the news directly from you!)

Hold the Water . . .

September 2011
Chongqing, China

We've all been there — you have to pee but you can't find a bathroom. Well, I'm here to tell you that you can find a bathroom and still not be able to pee. I don't mean the gas station bathroom is below your personal sanitary standards so you drive 5 more miles, I am talking about standing in the bathroom and wondering how you can get the job done!

China is a land of contradictions. A country that in some ways is stuck in time and in other ways is leaping ahead of the world's most advanced nations. The Chinese are selling their relics for pennies in order to replace them with particle board from IKEA. It has become such a problem that if you buy an antique in China, you have to be sure it is "younger" than 150 years old or you won't be able to take it out of the country. Truly beautiful pieces are given away every day and smuggled out. Entire historic neighborhoods are

"New China" growing up amongst "Old China"

leveled to make way for high-rise apartment buildings. It is a wonder to me — a sad wonder, really.

Along "The Bund" in Shanghai, the Chinese pack the public areas along the Haungpu River to admire the spectacular show when the buildings in Pudong light up each evening. The buildings on the Puxi side of the river also light up, but the Puxi side is "old Shanghai" so few care to gaze in that direction. "Old" is not good here. Even recycled content is a bad thing in China — recycled means "old."

With all the rush to embrace all that is new and modern, it came as quite a surprise to me to find that modern-day Western toilets had yet to reach commonplace status in China. I had meetings today in Chongqing at our new plant. The day started at 6:30 am with coffee, followed by tea and bottles of water during lengthy meetings. After many cups of tea, many bottles of water and several Coke-Lights, I had to pee.

Not surprisingly, none of the boys warned me. Among the 20-plus team members on this site visit, I was the lone girl. When I opened the bathroom stall and saw the hole staring back at me, I wanted to cry. Seriously, cry.

You see, I probably could have figured out a way to manage this little obstacle, even in my heels and wide-leg trousers, but I pulled my groin muscle a few days ago getting out of our "bus" in a skirt and heels. That's another story entirely, but let me just say that the world is not designed for girls.

A woman washes up in her backyard in the Puxi, Shanghai.

To master the task at hand, I needed a certain amount of leg strength and endurance and, frankly, it was simply beyond my capabilities at the time. I considered it, even tested the leg, but it just wasn't in the cards and I really didn't want to find myself on the floor or, worse, in the hole.

So, I left the ladies room and returned to the conference room with widescreen monitors, United Nations-style microphones, earpieces for simultaneous translation, computer hookups, Wi-Fi access, dual-projection capability and video conferencing and took my seat. I pushed the bottle of water aside and began counting the minutes until we headed to the airport. I could only hope that the airport has better facilities or I'd be waiting until I got on the plane. Who would have ever thought that the airplane bathroom would be my best option!

If you are wondering what I miss most from the States . . .

Big Bag O'Money . . .

September 2011
Shanghai

When 1.8 billion people decide to take a holiday, transportation becomes an issue. Jack and I were engaged in the great debate over where to go for Christmas. Ordinarily, we don't have these debates. We stay home.

We debate the Christmas menu, the number of presents to be placed under the tree, whether the *Christmas Story* and/or *It's a Wonderful Life* deserve a place in cinematic history, but we do not usually find ourselves debating the relative merits of Malaysia vs. Thailand vs. Australia vs. Bora Bora.

As surreal as it was to be comparing the beaches, the climates, the grueling flight patterns and the cultural opportunities of these various locations, we were indeed debating where to celebrate Christmas. When I mentioned this at the office, my colleagues looked at me with horror. Christmas was not my issue. My issue was Chinese New Year. Had I booked Chinese New Year?

"No, I have not." I hadn't really thought about it. Chinese New Year is in January. Surely, there was time.

"Time? Yes, there is time," I was told. "Space is the issue. There is no space."

When 1.8 billion people decide to take a holiday. . .

These people were surely exaggerating for my benefit. I waited a day — a full 24 hours — before calling my travel agent who told me I'd have to decide on the spot or run the risk of being stuck in China.

"Stuck?" I asked.

"Yes, stuck."

Here, stuck means actually stuck. No seats on the train. No seats on the bus. No seats on the plane. No Driver. No Ayi. Lots of Chinese piling out of Shanghai, which leaves it deserted and everything closes. Stuck.

So, on-the-spot decision making commenced this morning at 9. First we checked which flights were available. We had two choices. The better of the two was the 9 p.m. Friday flight out of Shanghai that arrives in Phuket, Thailand at 1 a.m. Saturday. (The return is much better — we leave at 2 a.m. and arrive at 7 a.m.)

Honey, we are going to Phuket, Thailand for Chinese New Year. We had a few options for resorts, all with special "holiday" rates . . . when 1.8 billion people decide to take a holiday, things get expensive.

With Thailand booked for January, we scrubbed it off the list for Christmas and decided to stop debating and just pick. It was an almost random decision. We are going to Malaysia for Christmas. Our travel agent was relieved and pleased. And, so the payment process began.

China is a cash society. You pay by cash. Stores have bill-counting machines like you see in banks. Cashiers check bills carefully to identify fakes. If you pay by credit card, there is an additional fee of 2 to 3% of the total bill. If you are paying with

Big Bag O'Money

an international credit card, the fee can be higher. Ordinarily, you pay with a bank transfer. But, sometimes, you have to pay cash to avoid any extra fees.

So, what is a girl to do?

Well, naturally, she puts on her best black stilettos, marches to the bank and demands 125,000 RMB in small bills, if you please. (RMB is Chinese currency, more formally called Renminbi or Yuan.) She places the wad of bills in what appears to be a lunch bag and walks back to her office.

What were you expecting?

Alice . . .

September 2011
Shanghai

You remember Alice from *The Brady Bunch*, don't you? She wore a blue starched uniform, lived with the Bradys, made their meals, cleaned their home, made their beds, did their laundry, cared for their dog (Tiger), solved most of their problems and, of course, was in love with Sam the Butcher. Well, Alice moved to Shanghai and she lives with us now.

Two things in the life of an Expat in Shanghai can make or break your experience — your Driver and your Ayi. We have Shanghai's best in both.

Mr. Cao drives a 9-seat Transit complete with a flat screen TV, screaming kids and Katy Perry blasting from the speakers. He navigates this beast all over Shanghai and appears oblivious to the chaos inside and outside the vehicle. He is a master.

Our Ayi is a wonder. Ayi roughly translates to Auntie in English and commonly refers to a woman who takes care of your home. But, in our house, Ayi really means "Alice" as in *The Brady*

Bunch. Ayi Zhan is our very own slice of Hollywood make-believe. She may not have the blue uniform but she is the glue that keeps our household functioning.

Our Shanghai ride . . .the Transit.

Imagine it: The dishwasher won't stop beeping, the oven won't turn on, the phone suddenly stops working, your satellite is out, you need to buy meat (and the butcher isn't Sam) or you want to pay your electric bill. Well, you think it's your electric bill, but you can't actually read it. Who do you call? How do you get these things done?

Well, if you are lucky enough to have Alice arrive at your home each morning, you don't have to do anything other than look utterly confused. Alice springs into action and everything is handled. We have an island in our kitchen, and the counter top was loose. Alice was unhappy with this situation as it presented a danger to the children. She had the counter fixed. Two days later, it was loose again.

Jack stepped in to take action and called the maintenance office. Alice watched from the kitchen doorway. Silly American man, she was thinking but she said nothing. Jack explained to the woman on the phone that "yes, someone had been to the house" but "no, it wasn't fixed." This went on for 10 minutes with Jack repeating the same phrases over and over. Utterly confused and exasperated, he looked at Alice, held the phone up and shrugged his shoulders.

Alice intervened. She grabbed the phone, spoke in a very loud and forceful tone, then handed the phone back to Jack and walked back to the kitchen without a word. Jack put the phone to his ear and heard the words "service on way." Sure enough, 10 minutes later Alice was yelling at the servicemen, marching them to our kitchen and standing over them while they fixed the counter again. It is very secure now.

Not long ago, Alice commented to our friend Lily (who speaks Chinese) that I did not own an iron or an ironing board. Thus, she was unable to iron the bed sheets. This was a major travesty because while it might be okay for me to sleep on wrinkled sheets, this would never suffice for "Sir." Lily, of course, told me about this conversation. I made a mental note, but I failed to move quickly enough for Alice.

Sir had apparently gone one night too many on wrinkled sheets. Alice took matters into her own hands, bought the iron and ironing board and brought them with her one morning to the house. Alice rides a scooter. There is no basket on this scooter. She arrived with

Ayi means "Auntie" or, for us, *Alice*

an iron, a large ironing board, a skillet, a large bag of dog food, 2 bags of groceries, a plant and my dry cleaning. Sir now sleeps on ironed sheets. His underwear is ironed too!

Clutter is always an issue when you have kids and it seems shoes are everywhere. In China, shoes stop at the door. Live here a bit and you'll understand why. Getting the kids to take their shoes off when they came in the house was a struggle — until Alice took over. Shoes come off and pile up at the front door.

We put an old dresser there to collect the shoes and Alice has now labeled a drawer for each of us. If Alice gets the kids to put their shoes in the drawers, I'm arranging a visa with immigration when we repatriate.

It wasn't long before Alice discovered that I was no Carol Brady and I was never going to get dinner on the table by 6 p.m. Truth is I have only seen Alice a handful of times. I get home very late and dinner is long since over. Alice decided she should start cooking. It took us about two weeks to figure out that she wanted to cook dinner. We needed our 9-year-old to interpret.

I was very nervous about this arrangement. I had been told that Alice was actually a very good cook, but our kids are picky and I didn't want her to be offended. Well, of course, my fears were misplaced. Her first meal was dumplings (two thumbs up all around), next sticky rice and chicken with veggies (two thumbs up all around), then beef with pea pods, carrots and the most amazing mushrooms you've ever had (two thumbs up all around) and this continues — now up to three times a week.

Last night, Alice made dinner again. It was like an episode of one of those Food Network challenge shows: Make dinner with only the ingredients in the pantry.

We are leaving for vacation, so the pickings are slim, as they say. We had ground beef, Coke-Light, eggs, flour, butter, milk and cucumbers. Naturally, we had crepes with beef and cucumbers. The beef was cooked in the Coke-Light with shredded cucumbers.

I wasn't there to see it but Jack and the kids swear that is how she made it. It was fantastic and tasted far more sophisticated than Coke-Light. She even left me some extra crepes and I broke out an extra ration of Nutella!

Typhoon Five . . .

October 2011
Ho Chi Minh City, Vietnam

This is a lesson that I should have learned years ago . . . when the signs all point to an impending storm, you really should pull in your sails and stay home.

October 1st is National Day and the start of a five-day holiday in China. It is a celebration of the "new" China, which began under Chairman Mao, 60-odd years ago. The kids had the full week off from school so we were heading out of town. A grand tour of Vietnam. I'd been planning the trip for months and was truly looking forward to some time away from work. So, you know where this story is headed . . .

On September 22nd, Jane raised the first red flag. Her knee was sore. Sore enough that she was limping and asking to stay home from school. We were certain that her knee hurt, but we also suspected that a certain amount of homesickness was worsening her condition. Not unusual at this stage in the transition. All the more reason to get out of town, we told ourselves. This trip was designed to build some excitement about living in Asia. And, true or not, I was steadfast in my belief that it was coming at the right time.

On September 26th, Jane upped the ante. She was no longer limping; she was barely moving. We made an appointment and took her in for a look-see. The doctor twisted the heck out of her knee and found nothing. So, he took an X-ray, which was designed to identify bone cancer. No cancer — whew.

Next stop, orthopedic surgeon.

While we waited for the orthopedic surgeon, the second red flag went up. Henry's homesickness elevated to a new level. He was tearful each morning and was missing his buddies. Jane was teary each morning, in pain and desperate to skip school. So, naturally, I drove them both to school and forced them to get out of the car each day. Yep, Mother of the Year — just ask my kids.

I was still telling myself that all we needed was a family vacation. So, when the weather reports said that Typhoon Nalgae was headed toward the Philippines and would likely continue on toward Vietnam, I had selective hearing or selective processing or selective stupidity. When the third red flag went up, I was looking in the other direction.

The orthopedic surgeon twisted, turned and tortured Jane's knee but, like the first doctor, found nothing. Yet, when Jane stood on it, she cried. Crutches were issued and she hobbled home. The initial red flag was getting bigger. The storm in the Philippines was getting bigger. My blind spot was getting bigger. I packed our suitcases. Jack scheduled Jane to see the University of California-Berkley educated traditional Chinese medicine man as a last resort. I packed a swimsuit.

Somehow, by October 1ˢᵗ, Jane was moving better. Henry was beginning to refer to Shanghai as home. And, our plane was at the gate and we arrived in Ho Chi Minh City without incident. It was too good to be true.

On October 2ⁿᵈ, the rain was torrential in Ho Chi Minh, Jane's knee was aching and Henry was running a fever, couldn't swallow and was, once again, in tears. Did I mention that Typhoon Nalgae had caused ruin in the Philippines and was now "just" a tropical

Lunch on the Mekong River, Vietnam

storm but was headed straight for our next destination — Danang, which had just weathered Typhoon Nesat.

On October 3rd, the rains continued, Henry's fever got worse and the girls looked like they were heading in the same direction as their brother. We canceled the rest of the trip, booked the earliest flight out and returned to China. By 2 p.m., the girls were back at the house, I was at the grocery store and Jack was on his way to the doctor with Henry.

All the signs were there. Typhoon Five was spinning. I didn't want to see it; I wanted to go on vacation. I thought some time away would make everyone feel better, ease the homesickness and make Shanghai start to feel more like home.

While Henry and his Dad were awaiting results of a strep test, I warmed up tomato soup, made grilled cheese sandwiches and baked chocolate chip cookies from scratch. The girls found a movie and sank into the couch.

When Henry arrived home, he smelled the cookies baking. "Mom," he said, "it is really starting to feel like home here."

I guess we just needed a little strep throat and some cookies.

Opening Day

October 2011
Shanghai

Well, it isn't really Opening Day. It isn't even opening day of the baseball playoffs. It is, in fact, pivotal Game 5 of the Divisional Championship Series between the dreaded New York Yankees and our beloved Detroit Tigers. The series is tied at two games apiece and we are playing in New York so, according to our son, all fans on deck!

As you may recall from my last post, we are on vacation, or rather "staycation" now. We came home because we had one child with strep (now 2) and a typhoon in our path. We should be sleeping in and lounging around doing almost nothing. Ordinarily, this would be the perfect mix for playoff baseball — late night games and lazy mornings. But, we are in China. So, the game is on at 8 in the morning.

According to Henry, the time of the game is irrelevant — *ALL* fans on deck. The kids even went to bed early so they would be ready to cheer their team all the way from Shanghai. Skype-dates were made with Nana and Papa and the cousins, so we could cheer with family.

The excitement about getting up at 7:45 on a morning that you could sleep until 10 baffled me. I mean you can get the score off the Internet and even watch the game in China at 4 in the afternoon, if you were so inclined. I rolled my eyes knowing that I would have to set the alarm and go room to room trying to get each little bundle out of their cocoon.

But, then, I tucked Henry into bed. "Mom," he smiled, "tomorrow is going to be so fun."

I went back downstairs and started picking up the mess. Somewhere between the dirty dishes and the DVDs, I started to think about my grandparents. My Grandmother Theresa loved baseball.

In fact, my Grandmother taught me to keep score when I was a little girl. If you went to her home during the season, you would find Grandma in her favorite chair, the game on the television set (with sound muted) and Ernie Harwell on the radio. (This is how Detroit Tigers fans watched the game when Ernie was on the radio.) She had her score sheet and her pencil. Grandpa was in charge of refilling the iced tea.

When I had children, my grandparents were in their 80s and nearing 90s but they both still watched the games, complained about the manager, offered advice to the batters and kept score. Jack and I would check the Tigers' schedule and plan a visit to their home during a game. And, Grandma would explain the game to Jane and Henry and try to teach them how to keep score. If you ask Henry about Great Grandma Theresa, he'll respond "Grandma Baseball."

All fans on deck.

Grandma died a few a years ago and Grandpa died the year after. My children had great grandparents for a large portion of their lives. They knew them, loved them and have memories of them that are unique to their experience of them. When I watch a Tigers game, I always think of my Mom's parents. In the fall, when the apples drop from the trees and pies are made, I think of my Dad's parents. "Grandma Pie" is how Jane always referred to Great Grandma Annie. Baseball and apple pie from people who immigrated to the States (or were just one-generation removed) . . . funny, really.

That did it. I knew I had to do more than just wake the kids up and put the game on the television set. So, I stole my Mom's Opening Day routine. When Dad couldn't get tickets from the postman (when I was a kid, I thought the postman carried baseball tickets with his

Playoff baseball in Shanghai . . . almost like Mom's.

letters and you could buy them on your porch!), my Mom got

us out of school early and put the game on the television and, of course, Ernie on the radio. She put down a picnic blanket and served up hot dogs with steamed buns, Better Made potato chips, candy and even some Faygo. Six small children on a blanket with red pop — the woman was crazy.

It is one of my fondest memories of childhood. I love Opening Day — at the ballpark or on a picnic blanket. My Mom made it wonderful. She watched and cheered with us and I thought it was heaven.

So, the menu for today's game: Breakfast pizza, pretzel bread rolls with cheese sauce, imported U.S. candy bars, chocolate milk and, for the 7th inning stretch, brownies with vanilla ice cream. I was up early to make the brownies but the smell got the kids moving and the excitement over the game was palpable as Auntie Minnie showed up on the Skype screen with Uncle Lyle, and then Nana and Papa.

Don Kelly hit a homerun, followed by Delmon Young. It is the 6th inning so I'll be going to cut the brownies soon. It's a great day in China to watch baseball. It's Opening Day — just like Mom used to make!

TAXI!

October 2011
Cologne, Germany

There comes a time in every woman's life when she looks in the mirror and wonders what in the hell happened. I don't care how fit or gorgeous or amazing or successful you are — it happens. You get up one morning, take a good long look and ask yourself: "Who is that person looking back at me?" If you happen to have a teenage daughter on that same morning, it can be even more depressing.

Moving to China ahead of my family afforded me an opportunity to tackle that person in the mirror without all the usual distractions of home, particularly the never-ending cookie jar of temptations that seems to be a centerpiece at every event we attend with our kids. And, work was so crazy during that time that I really had no opportunity to eat. I mean, one is not running to the vending machine in China — it isn't stocked with Snickers bars after all.

In those first three months, I dropped 30 pounds and several dress sizes, cut my hair drastically, went blonder than I have any right to be and took advantage of the duty free shop on every international flight I took — I am an expert on anti-wrinkle creams from Europe to Australia to Asia and back! To celebrate the loss of my decades-long baby-weight, I bought myself a stack of wrap dresses at the Puxi fabric market. Let's face it, you don't wear a wrap dress unless you've taken control of the middle!

And, then I flew to Germany and needed a taxi . . .

Cologne is hosting the International Food Festival for food professionals this week, so every taxi was in transit and I was stranded. The wonderful young woman at the hotel check-in desk made a call for me and said Jonathan — "limousine driver and concierge" — would be arriving at my door.

Jonathan is 27. He is spectacular. Spectacularly young. Spectacularly cute. Spectacularly German. Spectacularly flirty. He is the anti-wrinkle cream that I have been searching for these many, many months.

I may be a mid-40-something-year-old woman who has been off the market for more than 25 years, but I still know when someone is running their eyes over me and that, my friends, is spectacularly mood altering when done in the "not so obvious but no longer subtle" manner that only certain men can pull off.

I had not donned a wrap dress "in public" yet. I wore one once for Jack to a very dark restaurant where no one knew us. I got marvelous reviews from the hubby, but I had not yet dared to venture beyond the safety net of the husband and total strangers in completely darkened spaces.

Wrap dresses are easy to pack and I have four so I decided — with a great deal of encouragement from Jack — to take all of them to Cologne. I also took a safe pair of black pants and several cardigans, just in case I lost my nerve. I also took some completely impractical but oh-so-wonderful heels and the too-chic-for-words jewelry that my fashion conscious 14-year-old picked out for me at the "underground" market.

In my hotel room, I debated the safe black pants or the really cool wrap dress. I said "yes to the dress" and stepped in front of the dreaded full-length mirror. I ran through all the familiar reasons not to wear the dress to the office — it wasn't conservative enough, it made me look fat, it made me look old, it made me look like I was trying too hard, it was too young for me and on and on and on. But in the end, the darned thing was incredibly comfortable and I felt good in it. So, I silenced the inner critic and marched out the door.

The elevator ride down to the lobby was torture. I fussed with the dress, tried to steal a glance at myself in the chrome, and had to will myself not to stop the elevator, jump out and the take the next elevator headed up. Despite myself, I made it all the way to the lobby from the towering 4th floor!

The elevator doors opened — and just like in the movies — Jonathan was standing directly in front of the opening elevator doors and just a few feet away from me. He looked and then he lingered. It was unmistakable and it caught me completely off guard. I felt warm and I am certain I blushed. It was sublime.

Absolutely sublime. I mean, come on, this doesn't happen to me any more — heck, it never really happened to me before . . .

Moments later, I discovered this handsome young man was my chauffeur. Lucky me!

It really was too good to be true. He was charming. His accent was divine. He spoke enough English to allow for easy conversation, but his lack of confidence in his ability added to his charm and highlighted his youth. A single 20-minute car ride would simply not be enough. It was too intoxicating. I was completely enamored. I was having an awful month and this was far better than gelato with far fewer calories. I signed him up for the rest of the week on the spot.

So each morning this week, Jonathan whisked me to the office and every evening he carried me back to my hotel. He chats politely and, every now and again, I catch him watching me in his rear view mirror. He could be checking the traffic, but I convinced myself that he thinks I'm interesting — maybe even cute — and he is stealing a glance. He says it is "simply impossible" that I am the mother of a 14-year-old. This man knows how to get a tip!

On Monday, he also took me to a great little restaurant with wonderful food and very charming waiters. On Tuesday, he found me a great little pub. And, on Wednesday, he made reservations for me and two of my girlfriends who also were in town for business — an impromptu girls' night out.

My friends arrived and I had to share this little gem. Let's face it, I wanted to show him off. After all, where's the fun in keeping it all to myself? In conversation with them that morning, I mentioned that I had "hired" a driver for the week who would be picking us up that evening to drive us to dinner and wherever else we decided to go. "Your own personal driver . . . " My smile could not be contained and, with that, they were hooked.

At 6:30 p.m. — the appointed time for our chariot to arrive — we found ourselves locked in a meeting. I was clearly getting anxious, tapping my well-appointed toes, checking the time on my BlackBerry, fussing with the tie on my third wrap dress of the week and twitching in my seat like a school girl. Finally, things were wrapping up and I bolted for the door.

It was raining slightly and we had to walk to the gate to reach our carriage. I could not afford to have bad hair, so I took my paces briskly until I reached the covered walkway. I could see the slick, black BMW sedan waiting for us. I knew Jonathan would step out of the car to open the door the minute he saw me approach. I waited for my friends to catch up. I wanted them to get the full effect, and the rain only made it better. Very Hollywood!

Sure enough, as we approached the BMW, Jonathan's door opened and he stepped around the vehicle to open the rear door. There were three of us — someone would have to ride shot gun. I took one for the team. As Jonathan shut my door, I turned to the back seat . . .

"Oh my God. Where did you find him?" I smiled so hard it almost hurt. It was pure joy. They were smitten just like me.

It wasn't only that he was good looking. Lots of men are — well maybe not lots — but we've all seen good looking men. It was the ambience of the whole thing — the handsome young man, the beautiful performance car, the charm of this wonderful European city, all coupled with the knowledge that you have only after you've turned a certain age and endured a certain amount of de-construction.

Now, you know that these moments are rare and to be savored . . . with your best girlfriends, over bottles of soulful wine and luscious food. You are old enough to appreciate being appreciated — and smart enough to know it isn't real — most of it is in your head but that doesn't make it any less fun.

Taxi!

SLACKER!

November 2011
Shanghai

I slept in today. Until 5:40 am. Yes, that's sleeping in around here. I went to the gym before work and failed to arrive at my assigned work station until 8 a.m. And, I left the office tonight at 8:30 pm. I am a slacker. Truly.

When I left the office, more people than I could count were still on conference calls, in meetings and working at their computers. I have colleagues who stay until 10 or 11 at night. My boss installed a microwave and a fridge in his office and eats all his meals at the office. He is not a slacker. Me — I need my beauty sleep — I'm a slacker.

My slacker tendencies carry over into my personal life as well. My condition has even affected my husband — poor guy, he's a slacker too.

This week we had parent-teacher conferences. They were intense. We met with 14 teachers, one every 10 minutes. Each and every one of them was prepared. I felt guilty when Jack and I had no questions beyond "How are they adjusting?" Sometimes, even the teachers seemed disappointed in our lack of preparation, lack of critical inquiry and laissez faire attitude toward our children's education.

School is serious business in China. Kids go to school and then, after school, they go to school again to focus on math or science or reading or violin or something. Our kids go to school so Friday will come! We don't have them enrolled in extra school or extra anything.

China seems like enough extra for all of us sometimes but by Asian standards, we are a family of slackers. I think we spend more time debating which 10 movies to buy from the movie lady every Saturday than we do working on homework some nights.

Whether Mom pries your fingers from the Transit door or Dad force marches you to the bus stop, you are going to school.

Priorities.

School has been so intense that we had a solid week of having to pry the kids from the Transit and force them through the school gates — tears be damned. I was really feeling like a Tiger Mom — kids in tears, giving me the evil eye and occasionally calling me names as I pried their fingers one-by-one from the handle bar on the side of the Transit.

I remained focused all week and force-marched them to class. Of course, the next week I left for Germany and told Jack to let

Henry stay home from school to watch the Tigers and then the Lions on Monday Night Football.

Priorities.

The kids have clearly felt the pressure. Henry and Bella downloaded an app on their iPads to practice their multiplication tables. It awards them points for being both fast and accurate. It was perfect to get them ready to take their respective "minute" tests. Both of them were "behind" their Asian classmates in multiplication tables and wanted to "catch up."

Henry *after* school

Catch up?! Bella hadn't even started multiplication tables when we arrived in China. Were we really at risk of them going through life unable to multiply 4 by 6 and come up with 24? In truth, we haven't completely mastered tying shoes yet either (Velcro is the devil); so, maybe they won't learn to multiply but I wasn't really that worried. Every iPhone has a calculator — they'll survive!

At Jane's conference, it was suggested that we place Jane in the extended math program, which is akin to advanced placement math on steroids. We smiled politely and declined. Jane has never liked math. She has never been confident in her abilities in math. For the first time in her academic life, she is showing signs of believing in herself when it comes to math. Moving her into "extended math" does not appear to have any upside in the confidence department. At least not now. She's got plenty to handle already.

Her teacher was very polite. He got it. Her parents are slackers and they are raising slacker kids. Or, at least, they're trying to raise slacker kids . . .

On his own, Henry signed up to take his 7-8-9 multiplication test. Only kid to take it and pass. Well, his Asian classmates already took 10-11-12, but we aren't counting them . . .

Maybe I am the only slacker in the bunch.

Thanksgiving . . .

November 2011
Shanghai

On Monday night, Jack and I were watching Sunday Night Football. It was being replayed on the American Sports Network (ASN). There are very few commercial breaks when games are replayed on ASN. But when there are, they sometimes include commercials from the States.

This will sound odd but it is sort of a novelty to watch them because they are so rare. I know that sounds ridiculous. But, after 6 months of commercial-free sports, it really is a treat to see an American truck commercial. It feels like a touch of home.

On Monday night, a truck commercial came on and there was tinsel, snowflakes and people dressed in red and white Santa hats with some guy crooning ". . . it's the most wonderful time of the year . . . " in the background. Then it hit me. It's Christmas. Or, more accurately, it's the Christmas shopping season, which likely began in the States in October and is probably reaching a frenzied state today as shoppers prepare for Black Friday or abandon Thanksgiving entirely in favor of Black Thursday. Christmas.

It isn't like I hadn't realized that it was November. Though, to be honest, it doesn't seem like November. It isn't nearly cold enough for one thing. And, it certainly doesn't feel like Thanksgiving and the end of the college football season. I've watched exactly zero college football games this autumn. And, it can't be possible that Christmas is around the corner because I have not heard a single Christmas carol, unless you count the 30-second commercial.

But, in fact, today is Thanksgiving. However, in China, it's just Thursday, November 24th. There was no turkey for lunch today. And, there's no turkey for dinner either. I won't even get out the office in time to have dinner with the family tonight. No football game at noon or 4 p.m. No sleeping bags and coffee outside Shanghai's Super Brand Mall tonight. Just work, school and the usual evening routine. And, more work and school tomorrow.

I suspect that most of you would be thankful if the radio stations stopped playing 24 hours of Christmas carols. Or, at least, didn't start the round-the-clock carols until December 24th. I am sure that your eyes are sore from having to gaze at sparkling Christmas decorations since Halloween.

And as you fork out far too much money for that Christmas tree, you are probably wondering when things got so out of hand — when did Christmas become so commercial. I don't know the answer to that question but I am certain it was long before I was born.

Here's what I do know:

- I miss cooking that big bird and everything that goes with it.
- I miss Thanksgiving Day football and the parade.

- I miss making fun of my favorite neighbors and their Best Buy sleep out.
- I miss over-priced Christmas trees.
- I miss Christmas decorations — particularly ours.
- I miss 24 hours of Christmas carols — I really do.

Here's what I am thankful for:

- Having a resourceful husband who managed to "outsource" the turkey for Saturday.
- Having ASN so we can watch the Lions at 1 a.m. — yeah, really.
- Having the opportunity to slow down the "season."
- Having something and someone to miss.
- Having those dearest, nearest and realizing how great that really is.

You are in the midst of the craziest and most wonderful time of the year. Here, unless you are at Starbucks, it is simply November. To make it the most wonderful time of the year, you have to put in some effort. I found real vanilla the other day and cloves, which I could not find anywhere. I was so overjoyed you'd think I'd finally gotten that Big Wheel I'd wanted for Christmas all those years ago.

Sounds crazy to you, I know. I know. But, the best thing about China is that we are in China *and* it isn't just like home. Thanksgiving is an American tradition. We will have to make our own Thanksgiving.

And, like Thanksgiving, Christmas Day in China is a day like any other day. China is officially atheist and there isn't even a Santa Claus. So, December 25th is just another workday. Though I will not be working; I will be in Malaysia. We will make our own

Thanksgiving and we will make our own Christmas season. It isn't made for you on the radio, in the shopping malls and on television. There is something great about that, isn't there?

I am very thankful to have this opportunity to slow it all down — as our children start to move away from Mom and Dad a little bit. One teenager and two "tween" wannabes. It's a gift that I wasn't expecting and didn't realize I was getting until that truck commercial. It made us realize that if we wanted to

Turkey legs are good any day of the week.

have a Thanksgiving and a Christmas, we would have to supply the ingredients, which means we get to select them.

Still, I really do miss 24 hours of carols.

Hope you wake up to a great Thanksgiving and Go Lions!

The Smell of a Melt Down

December 2011
Shanghai

In the month since my last post, we:

1. Had coats made at the fabric market (and we look so pretty in them);

2. Ate real Chinese street food outside the fabric market (and lived);

3. Went to two school Christmas concerts (the concerts were more like a night at the theatre — so amazing and it was just kids);

4. Took final exams (and passed, even our Chinese finals);

5. Had our performance review at work (did not get fired but it was close);

6. Celebrated the Christmas Season with friends from Australia and England (and enjoyed the different traditions);

7. Lip-synced to Tina Turner's Proud Mary with drunk friends at the Christmas party to the giggles of 9 children (all of whom can now shake a tail feather like Tina);

8. Went to Malaysia and immediately felt like I had turned onto Elk Lake Road in Northern Michigan (the world just fell away and I was in paradise);

9. Walked with monkeys, stared at lemurs, marveled at eagles and were awed by the great horn bill (and marveled that we had brought the kids to this place that we never imagined we would see ourselves and one of us had never heard of); and . . .

I could write volumes about each of these experiences — and a better woman would have — but I am not that woman. You knew that when you started following this little stream of consciousness. Didn't you? Yes, you did. Item #10 explains why I haven't posted in more than a month.

10. Had our house tested 3 times for toxic levels of formaldehyde and other volatile organic compounds.

In our list of the Top 10 things we did this month, this is the one that pushed me over the edge.

Most expats in China will tell you that, after about 6 months in-country, they experience their "China moment." Almost anything can trigger it:

- Waiting 2 hours at China Mobile to get service for your kid's new phone.

- A complete and increasingly frustrating inability to communicate the simplest things.

- Missing your favorite food or the taste of a real Diet Coke not that Coke-Light stuff.

For me, it was setting up air quality monitors in our family room for the ***third*** time.

Just before Thanksgiving, or maybe just after Halloween — I can't recall any more — it started. A neighbor was sick. Her husband thought it was morning sickness but she insisted the smell in the house was making her ill. Eager to forestall her departure back to the States, her husband arranged for testing.

The results were downright scary. Formaldehyde was 2.5 times the "legal" China limit and more than 6 times the U.S. recommended limit. Of course, other toxins were found but the formaldehyde gets top billing. Why? Well, think back on those Katrina trailers and you'll understand why.

Of course, we considered the air pollution and the water and food safety issues before we agreed to move to China. And, if you saw our sea container and the amount of food we packed, you'd know that we took these issues seriously. We did not, however, anticipate that the house itself might be toxic. Or, if toxic, not approaching lethal levels or potentially carcinogenic.

People say that I have a short temper but I don't. Really, I don't. If I had a short temper, I would have blown up months ago at any one of the points along this path — pick one:

1. Neighbor moves to hotel because toxin levels are dangerous to his infant and pregnant wife;

2. Salt Mine refuses to do testing for the remaining families in complex;

3. Salt Mine agrees to do testing only after negotiating a contract with a "Western-credentialed" company;

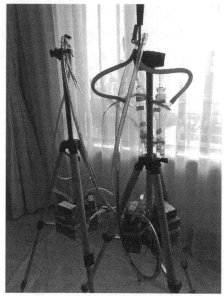

New decorations for the house . . .

4. Salt Mine's selected testing agency performs tests but the results are "too good to be true" and it appears testing company may have relationship with complex or was bribed;

5. Re-testing is scheduled with new company and equipment is flown to China from the States; tests are performed, with results promised before the Christmas holiday;

6. On Christmas Day, we receive an email advising that the test results may be within China's limits but quality checks mandate a third re-test; or,

7. After asking for the test results, we were told that Salt Mine does not have the results (see statement above where they talk about the results).

My temper isn't short. Signs that my temper is simmering are often not taken seriously or are somehow missed, but they are there. My temper is, however, explosive. Like a volcano, the little tremors might go unnoticed, but the big explosion is hard to miss.

It's like that scene in a movie when the kids are screaming or complaining, the husband thinks he's being helpful but isn't, and the room is spinning around you. Jane had been back in China for 36 hours and her China attitude was fully engaged, Jack was pleading for patience and I was spinning. And, then, I lost it.

Not sure if it was the equipment, the long faces, Jack's "be patient" attitude or all of it together, but I started to cry and I cried for two days. I also managed to yell at Jack and the kids for no good reason at all, slept on the couch, stopped eating and wore the same clothes both morning and night for two days. Oh, I was a real joy to be around.

Thankfully, I came to my senses around 5 this morning, brushed my teeth, crawled into bed next to Jack and apologized. This wasn't the way I wanted to end one year and start a new one.

And, if the schedule holds, in about 45 days, Jack and the kids are due for their China Moment. I expect the lack of Hershey Bars or the price of wine to be the triggers. If they cry for two days, refuse to bathe or change their clothes, those brand new air purifiers will be in high gear!

Ringing in the New Year

December 2011
Shanghai

The ball doesn't drop in People's Square like it does in Times Square. There are no revelers on the streets or parties in all the bars. Much like Christmas Eve, this is just another Saturday night in Shanghai. Preparations are underway for the *real* New

Year's celebration, which begins January 21st and continues for two weeks. The actual new lunar year begins on January 23rd.

2012 is the Year of the Dragon. The water dragon symbolizes an intelligent and laborious worker who never puts aside work though sometimes this leads him to excesses. The water dragon has enough courage to face challenges. If you are wondering, we have sheep, an ox, a snake and a horse in our home. No dragons. And, if you look each of those up, we are sure you'll be able to match each one of us to our year.

We made our resolutions: Make the school play, tackle Chinese, try new foods, etc. And, we picked our favorite moments of 2011: Our first home run, appearing in our first school play, going on a plane for the first time and visiting the rain forest in Malaysia. For Mom and Dad, the best was that all of these favorites happened either in China or because of China.

Not bad.

Part Two:
The Unravelling

Dear Mom . . .

January 2012
Shanghai to Detroit

Dear Mom,

I'm getting on a plane in the morning, destined for home. Leaving the kids, the dog and the husband in the Middle Kingdom and heading home. Business is the reason for my trip, but I'm coming to your place and it isn't to discuss the reinstatement of the dividend, the climb back to investment grade or the succession rumors. Our business is far more critical. So, you better get your paper and pencil ready because a shopping list is about to be dictated.

Avocado and cilantro

I haven't seen cilantro since June and avocados are nearly $15 for a sphere the size of an oblong golf ball. I am longing for the creamy texture of avocado, a hint of garlic, lime and the fresh bite of the cilantro with a salty, crispy chip and a shot of tequila. Taco night isn't the same without guacamole. Sadly, even sour cream is a rare luxury in China. Desperate for the fresh, made-to-order taste of chunky yet creamy guacamole — I'll even make it. Just please don't forget the cilantro. Parsley is a poor and, in my opinion, inferior substitute.

Strawberries

A strawberry — red, plump and juicy. No cream required. Just the berry, please. Berries — oh — berries, I miss you. A

Christmas without trifle. The fruits of the tropics are a wonder but, alas, a girl needs her berries. Yogurt, pound cake, champagne — and berries. I know it's January but cull those produce aisles and find me a berry, Mom.

And, of course, if there was any way to get them back for your grandchildren, we should do that too. But, hey, this is really all about me!

Ribs

A summer without ribs, potato salad and corn on the cob is a sad summer, indeed. I can get ribs here at the Australian butcher shop but it's not quite the same. And, my oven isn't big enough to cook ribs for the gang and we have no barbecue grill. Though that seems to be the next investment, just after the air purifiers. And, believe me, that nearly sparked a nuclear meltdown — air purifiers before a grill, what could we be thinking? The burger maniacs, also known as our children, sorely miss Jack's famous burgers.

The food in Shanghai is great. We can eat Indian, Malaysian, French, Italian, Korean, Moroccan and almost anything else you can imagine, but truly good, homemade favorites are much harder to find.

So, no need to book that fancy restaurant, Mom. I don't need to eat out and I don't want to go anywhere. If it isn't too much trouble, just get the gang together and fill that grocery

Dear Mom . . .

cart with the flavors of home. Turn on the football playoffs, chill the beer and bring on the nieces and nephews. Auntie Jen's suitcase is packed with presents and she'd kill for a Diet Coke and a Hershey Bar.

See you soon!

Love Jen

P.S. Henry wants you to pick up some beef jerky — honey barbecue, please.

AnnaBelle

December 2011 (written in January 2012)
Langkawi, Malaysia

We spent Christmas in Langkawi, Malaysia. One evening, we attended a cocktail party and ran into a great couple that we met on a rain forest walk earlier in the day. They were also an American expat family. They were living in Switzerland.

We did not meet their girls during the rain forest walk because the rain forest came to them the prior morning. It appeared in their hotel room in the form of six monkeys looking for $6 candy bars in the mini-bar.

And yes, I do mean monkeys and I do mean **6**. Before calling their parents, the girls took a photo on their iPhone and posted it to Facebook. Friends in the States probably knew about the mini-bar raid before the hotel

Leave your door open for me!

staff. The monkey warnings on the windows are real and are there for a purpose. Keep your lanai door locked or you will have uninvited guests.

During the rain forest walk, we had the usual expat exchange — what brought you to wherever you are living, how are you and the family adjusting, how is the international school and so on. In these conversations, I'm always amazed at how the usual gender biases come out — everyone assumes that Jack's career brought us to China. We play along.

Maybe "play" is a poor choice of words. It isn't like we do it intentionally. It is fairly uncommon to have the woman's career be *the* reason the family moves to China. There are women working in China for goodness sake, but there are less than five expat families at our company where the wife's career is *the* reason for the move and the husband is holding down the fort at home. And, the Salt Mine is seriously expat heavy in China at the moment.

Anyway, as the conversation moves from polite to more substantial questions, I always end up giving us away. I know nothing: School lunch (I presume Jack packs one; oh, the menu, no idea), athletics (I know there is a gym; oh, the International School league, no idea), the International Bachelorate Program (I know we have one but the pre-IB testing regime is beyond me) and on and on. I am the weak link and the jig is up.

Jack secretly enjoys this little charade because he can fake his way right through my job while I am lost in his. As our little yarn starts to unravel, he smirks watching me squirm under the intense pressure of questions about doctors, dentists, grocery shopping and, my Achilles heel, school.

I know the kids have been to doctors, but I don't even know the name of our international insurance company so how can I possibly be expected to know the international affiliation of the doctors' groups or hospitals, or have an opinion on Australian trained pediatricians compared to the English or American.

I don't even know the name of our kids' doctor in the States (I don't — the doctor kept changing and I gave up). Seriously, this is well beyond my capacity. Jack, however, knows all the answers and, worse, he knows that I have no idea.

He is, of course, reassuring as he rubs my back signaling correct answers and pokes my side for incorrect answers. He glances over now and again to smile at me and challenge me to try to top my personal best in keeping the discussion going "on all matters domestic." A knowing look tells me he has his doubts.

So, while Jack is deep in conversation with the husband about the policy and regulatory aspects of my job, as though it were his own, I see that Cheshire cat grin creep across his face as he listens to me try to maneuver questions about the Eastern vs. Western approach to math and the rigors of the IB and pre-IB programs. Finally, when pressed on which pre-IB program our oldest is in, I can only giggle. Jack wins. I lose.

Jack shifts his body slightly to face this lovely woman and I feel myself beaming at him as he explains the details of Jane's program and contrasts it to the programs at the British School and the "traditional" American program available at the two American international schools. His transition is seamless.

Truth be told, I have yet to figure out the proper pronunciation of the children's school. Is it "you" Chung or "yao" Chung. I have no idea.

As I listen to Jack and try to remember how to pronounce the name of the school, I feel him inch closer and wrap his arm around my waist. He's about to reveal that he is the "mom" in our clan and that the girl on his arm knows nothing about the school, the doctors, the shopping or anything else remotely connected to "all matters domestic." I don't even know how my dry cleaning gets done, he says — and I don't. He is entirely comfortable in his role and he knows how important it is to me and to our children. I find his utter confidence in this area astounding.

People are not as shocked as they once were when we tell them we are both lawyers but that Jack "gave up" his career to stay home and take care of the kids. But still, they're surprised. We get tons of questions about how we made the decision, what is it like for Jack

Sunset in Langkawi, Malaysia

and how have I adjusted? The last one is code for "how can you possibly turn over the responsibility of raising your children to this guy?" This couple, however, was non-judgmental. They toasted Jack and laughed with us.

I must have been four glasses of wine into this warm and fragrant evening. The sun was setting over the Andaman Sea and we were watching it melt away from our perch at tree level, tucked into the rain forest in an open-air cocktail lounge overlooking the white sand beach and blue lagoon. The kids were enjoying room service with the monkeys on the balcony and I was absolutely taken with the man at my side. I felt it was going to be a great night.

I can still hear the Black Eyed Peas in my head: "I got a feeling . . . that tonight's gonna be a good night . . . tonight's gonna be a good, good night . . ."

And then . . .

AnnaBelle II

January 2012
Beijing, China

I hear the words over and over and over again in my head. They have been reverberating in there for weeks. At first, they just seemed to be teasing me but, as the days passed and events conspired, the words began to haunt me. And, I haven't been able to stop thinking about Annabelle ever since that evening on the terrace in Langkawi.

"Annabelle," her mother called.

I turned to see a very pretty young woman looking over at us. This must be Annabelle. The girl with the monkeys crawling in her mini bar.

She really was a striking girl. She had long, wavy chestnut hair. I recall thinking that the humidity in Langkawi likely made it more wavy than when she was in Switzerland. I don't know why I remember that so well.

Her skin was fair and freckled from the sun and she had a great smile. She wore a long, print wrap skirt that emphasized her lean and long frame. She topped it off with a no frills navy tank. She had that girl next door appeal, but the minute she started to talk you knew she had plenty to offer. She was quite articulate, engaging and funny. I liked her immediately.

"I want you to meet Jennifer. She and her husband are both lawyers. They live in China . . . Jennifer is a successful businesswoman . . . you should really talk to her . . . find out what it takes . . . to be a successful businesswoman . . . a successful female lawyer . . . . "

Fergie and the Peas stopped singing in my head . . .

On my long list of insecurities, just after the one about not knowing how to properly pronounce the name of my children's school, is the question of whether I am successful and what that means exactly. I hate being asked "what it takes" to be anything because, the truth is, I have no idea what it takes.

I also hate that the question is always framed as what it takes to be a successful female "fill in the blank." Clearly, this assumes that what it takes for me as a woman is different from what it would take for Jack as a man. It reminds me that despite 50 years of feminism, we still have a long way to go. But, I digress.

Perception and reality are not aligned on the question of my "success status." At least, not in my head.

My job title makes people think I am more successful or higher ranking in the Salt Mine than I really am. That doesn't feel successful; it feels fraudulent. I've done well, but when I compare (as we all do) my responsibilities to the reality of my "status," well . . .

I got the title, the rank, the assignment only because I asked for it (some might say I created it and then asked for it, and they might be right). Lately, I've been wondering if I would even have been considered for the job if I hadn't gone after it on my own. Is that the mark of success? I am not sure.

With my already compromised feelings about whether I should even have this job, I had to battle the career storm troopers shortly after my arrival in Shanghai. These troopers operated by spreading rumors about me, my abilities (or lack thereof) and the means by which I was assigned to China.

I did what any self-respecting woman would do, of course, and put on my black stilettos, black pencil skirt and black button-down sweater to confront the dark forces. I find stilettos and pencil skirts to be helpful in many situations. I'm sure that's how the boys handle it when the troopers attack. Or, do they ever attack the boys in the same way they attack the girls? I'm guessing the answer to that question is "no."

Even if, standing there on the terrace in Langkawi, I could have made a case for being successful, it would have been destroyed just weeks later when I traveled to the States.

Finding your way in a large corporation, law firm or any institution with a tradition and history centered around most things male can be a bit tricky. Even today. To the surprise of some, it actually gets trickier the higher you manage to climb in the company. From a political perspective, I think this is true for both girls and boys. But, it is far trickier for us girls.

The higher you go, the fewer of us there are, and we know the spots are limited. We are, in some respects, still tokens. A critical mass of women in leadership in any company is rare. Without a critical mass, it is every woman for herself and that can be ugly.

In January, I learned just how ugly it can be when I traveled to the States for so-called global leadership meetings. My first meeting was with a white, male senior executive. I requested the meeting to review some outstanding items related to my position in China. He had a different idea.

He wanted to share some career advice with me. First, he explained the hierarchy of appropriate engagement. I was not to talk to his boss without clearing it with him. Funny thing — we have the same boss. The difference, he noted, is that he is two grade levels above me, which clearly makes me inferior. I had the distinct impression that my grade level was not the only thing that made me inferior in his eyes.

Secondly, he explained that while I was promoted to my current position — which included running the entire organization in Asia Pacific and Africa — the "real" leadership team might not agree that the experience was commensurate with the promotional grade level. The "real" leadership team in his mind included himself and the other white men who reported to our boss. Our boss was a white woman, but she was retiring in just days and an African-American man was assuming the global leadership role.

His advice felt more like a threat. When I recounted the conversation to others, including my father who is my non-company mentor and my female colleagues outside the Salt Mine, they all agreed. It was a threat.

At week's end, I got even more advice from a woman who I have respected for a number of years and who has been in the industry for nearly 40 years. Her opening remark was that despite her years in the industry and all of her accomplishments, she did not believe that things were going to change any time soon. "Women," she said, "will remain the exception in meeting rooms to boardrooms." And more specifically, I wasn't going to get any further if I insisted on differentiating myself. "Stop calling attention to your differences," she told me.

The cynic in me translated this to "diversity is okay as long as it doesn't make the boys uncomfortable." I'm sure that isn't exactly the point she was making but, whatever the point, the sound of it made my stomach turn. "Blend in," she told me.

After an entire generation of women had struggled to simply enter the work force, this woman who spent 40 years in the business and made it all the way to company officer was now telling me "it ain't gonna change, so don't rock the boat." Really?

Not rocking the boat seemed to include things that I just can't get my head around: don't call attention to yourself, don't be too smart, don't be too much of a girl, don't wear too much bling (aka your wedding ring), don't participate in or form an all-girl group. But don't try to be a man either. This really seemed to be a metaphor for don't be too confident, too assertive, too direct or you'll be labeled a bitch. For me, this seems to be the *very* reason to rock the boat.

Ironically, the constructive advice (I'm sure she believed all of this *was constructive)* made me ill and left me with an uncontrollable desire to cry and run from her office. Unfortunately, I did both.

If, after a generation, we are no further along, then we need to rethink the strategy. When I finished mentally counting all the 'ponytails' at the top of the house, I realized that there were fewer now than when I started at the Salt Mine.

Directionally, that just seems wrong. Don't you think?

This woman had the opportunity — not just for herself but for others — to change the status quo, to reach back and bring more women along. She hadn't. In fact, her entire leadership team was male. Although technically I counted among them by virtue of leading the Asia Pacific and Africa Salt Mine Organization, I was two grade levels below the boys and I hadn't made the "real" leadership team.

So, Annabelle, to answer your mother's question about "what it takes to be a successful businesswoman," I have to tell you honestly that I do not know.

So, you can follow some of the advice laid out above, or you can consider it (as I did) and decide to go your own way.

I will tell you what I have learned over the years:

- **You can't have it all.** If you have it all, then I have nothing. Leave some for the rest of us. And trying to have it all just sets you up to fail. Why do that? I know most people don't like hearing that but I think it's true.

- **You can have moments where you *feel* like you have it all, but they will be fleeting — and you will likely be on vacation.** So, if you really want it all, don't try to have it all at the same time.

- **You gotta pick.** You don't just pick once; you gotta keep on picking. By that I mean, you have to choose what is important to you and know that it will change over time. Evolve.

- **You better know who you are and be honest about it.** I can't stay home. I am no good there 24/7. Accept your strengths and your weaknesses and fill the gaps with someone wonderful.

- **Make time to love somebody and let them love you.** The journey is better with a buddy. But remember the point above — be honest about who you are. For instance, if Jack wasn't willing to be a full-time parent, do you think our move to China would have been possible? No, it wouldn't.

So, I don't share the views of some women on "how to make it." Hard headed as I am.

I do, however, agree with Madeleine Albright who said: "There is a special place in hell for women who do not help other women." As I look at where things are today, I wonder if we're doing enough for each other. I don't believe we are or have been for years. Somewhere along this journey, women became complacent.

I agree with Bobbie Barrett, who gave the following advice to Peggy Olson in "The New Girl" episode of AMC's *Mad Men:*" "You're never gonna get that corner office until you start treating Don as an equal. And no one will tell you this, but you can't be a man. Don't even try. Be a woman. Powerful business when done correctly."

Now, admittedly, this episode and Bobbie Barrett generated a lot of blogging. I am not suggesting that you behave as Don Draper, who is a philanderer of the highest order. Nor, does it mean sleep your way to the top. On the contrary, it means be you. You are worthy. You are good enough. You are equal to the task.

Be a woman. We are powerful.

So today, after watching *"Mad Men"* a few hundred times, I am not so haunted by Annabelle any more. I don't have to agree with what the women or men who came before me say is the right path for a woman trying to make her way up the ladder. There is no one right way. There is no recipe. If there were, we'd see a lot more women in leadership across all industries and businesses and in politics.

Since returning to China from the States, I've started wearing heels and skirts to work almost every day and I like it. I also decided to leave at 5 p.m. whenever I can; and, it turns out that I can more often than I thought.

No recipe . . .will her world be different?

I stopped taking meetings that interfere with our children's bedtime or our bedtime. I turn off my BlackBerry when I come home and I leave it off on the weekend. I am trying to redefine success on my terms and to leave behind the debate about what is or is not a "successful businesswoman." I also decided that I don't need anyone to approve of my choices — except me.

Of course, while I made these decisions, the struggle to implement them remains. Still . . .

". . . I got a feeling . . . tonight's gonna be a good night . . . tonight's gonna be a good, good night . . ."

My Very Funny Valentine

February 2012
Shanghai

Jack and I aren't the lovey-dovey type. We never bought each other flowers or wrote each other love songs. A big night out was a trip to the ice cream aisle at the grocery store for a pint or two to eat in front of the TV after the kids went to bed. Before the kids, I think a big night out was the same, except we didn't have to wait to eat the ice cream!

But, when you drag someone half way 'round the world for your job, you sorta "owe" them. Or, at least, you ought to try a bit harder. So, I told Jack that we'd have a late dinner after the kids were settled, and I told the kids we'd have a treat together as soon as I got home from the office. At least, that was the plan.

Execution of the plan was a little off.

I did get dressed up . . . black pencil skirt, great little sweater and some new peep toe heels that I know make my legs look longer and stronger than they really are. I spent a bit of time on the outfit and tried to get the "look" right. When I left the house, I wanted Jack to be looking forward to my return. I thought that went pretty well. He did walk me to the car!

I was planning to leave the office at 5 p.m., drop by the Australian butcher shop to pick up a couple steaks, get some wine and then stop at the ice cream store for a special cake and some ice cream for the kids. But, of course, I was delayed.

At 6 p.m., I was in the elevator and headed out to the car. Here, I don't drive myself. I have a Driver. It's a great thing, really. I'll miss it when we leave. So, as is my practice, I texted Mr. Cao to tell him I was on my way. Usually, he texts back "OK" to tell me that he is waiting at the door. This time he texted back "10 min." Odd, I thought, because he was expecting me at 5.

It was raining, causing drivers to pile up at the front door. Mr. Cao was forced to leave his parking spot and circle the building. As more people started leaving for the day, more drivers pulled up which led to a traffic snarl in front of the building thick enough to make Los Angeles traffic look like amateur hour.

It was so bad that Mr. Cao never actually made it back to the door — I made a run for the car instead. The Transit is a pretty large target so finding it was not a problem, but once I was in the vehicle, it took 20 more minutes to get out of the snarl and into actual traffic, which was even thicker.

I was late but I could still salvage this evening. I just had to execute the remaining elements of the plan. Get the steaks and wine and pick up some sweet treats for the kids.

"Today Valentine day, yes?" asked Mr. Cao. The Chinese do not celebrate Valentine's Day on February 14th. It is celebrated on the 7th day of the 7th lunar month. Usually in August. But, they know Westerners celebrate on February 14th, so flowers are twice as expensive as they are on the 13th or 15th. And the drivers all know it might be an evening out for "sir and madame" — which means overtime.

"Yes," I said smiling at Mr. Cao. "We go meat!"

"Ah, Jack," he responded.

"Meat" is the word we use to tell Mr. Cao that we want to go to Yasmine's, a steakhouse and Australian butcher shop. The steakhouse is on the first floor and the butcher shop is upstairs.

The rain wreaked havoc on the roads and traffic completely stalled. Sensing my growing frustration, Mr. Cao went "off road" in the Transit, weaving his way through streets that I'd never seen before. We crissed and crossed until Mr. Cao had us out of the traffic jam and on the road toward "meat."

I finished up a call as we pulled up in front of Yasmine's. It was 7 p.m. I got my credit card out of my wallet and — avoiding the puddles and dodging the rain drops — I sprinted inside. I shimmied past the line of customers waiting for a table and headed for the staircase. I made it up about four steps when I realized the stairway was dark and it wasn't meant to set a romantic atmosphere. It was just plain dark. My heart sank . . . the butcher shop was closed.

Okay. Maybe I can buy a couple of steaks from the steakhouse to take home. Easier said than done. I tried first to buy raw steaks but I was unable to communicate what I wanted. I could place a take away order, but I'd have to wait 30 minutes at least, which wasn't possible if I was going to get home in time for the kids. So, I decided on Plan B and headed out the door.

The rain came down. The wind kicked up. My toes were getting wet. And the street was empty. Something was not right. Where was Mr. Cao? I looked up and down the street but there was no sign of the Transit anywhere. Hmmm. Well, no worries, I'll call him.

It was really raining now and it seemed to be getting colder by the second. My pockets were completely empty — no phone, no cash, no umbrella and no idea how to get home. Hmm . . .

Well, nothing else to do but march myself back into Yasmine's and ask to use the phone, which should be pretty easy to communicate. I used the universal sign for phone. You know the one — you stick out your thumb and pinkie and put your hand to your ear. As it happens, that same sign (without the move to your ear) means "six" in China.

I was offered 6 RMB, a menu, a pencil, a set of chop stix, a fork, a towel, some napkins and a seat. I could not get a phone. The staff just looked at me and smiled. I could feel the tears wanting to make their way to my eyes but that really wasn't going to help. So, I pressed on. I started to accost the patrons. I visited four tables before a nice couple took pity on me. (I learned later that some thought I might be working a scam and trying to use their phone to place an international call.)

I know one phone number — Jack's cell phone. I don't know my phone number, our home number, Jane's number or even Mr. Cao's number. I dialed and held my breath. Would he answer a call from some random Chinese phone number? Yes, he did!

At 7:35 p.m., the unmistakable figure of the Transit appeared on the street. Mr. Cao leaped out to open my door and apologize. He thought I was meeting Jack for dinner at Yasmine's. Of course he did. I laughed and Mr. Cao looked at me like I was crazy, but he finally laughed too.

I was soaking wet but I was not giving up. Mr. Cao drove like a bat out of hell, which is really fun in a Transit. We headed for the Ole Market, which is a market with Western food frequented by expats and wealthy Chinese. I was wet, cold and late. I needed to make up time. So, the shoes came off.

In my bare feet, I ran through the market gathering my ingredients, threw down my credit card and then ran back through the complex to Cold Stone Creamery. I bought the last ice cream cake and a quart of ice cream, ran through the Kerry Hotel and back to the Transit. It was 7:55.

At 8 p.m. I had one last conference call with Europe and the States. We were supposed to be finishing our appetizers. Jack would get the kids to bed while I finished my last call of the day. But, I was late.

Just seconds before 8 p.m., I ran into the house. Mr. Cao carried my bags and gave Jack a look that in any language means "you are married to a crazy woman." Undaunted, I put the cake and ice cream on the table, kissed the kids and told them I was sorry. I left the dinner ingredients on the kitchen counter and raced upstairs to join my conference call. I spread my papers out on the bed, dialed in, and . . . fell asleep.

Thankfully, Jack and the kids have low expectations and a good sense of humor.

Three days later on Friday night, the Transit pulled up to the front door of the office with everyone inside. I was waiting right where I supposed to be at the time I was supposed to be there.

We went to Bella Mia in Puxi for great Roman-style pizza and some wonderful Italian wine. Afterward, we walked to Whisk, which has amazing chocolate desserts. We picked up five pieces of chocolate cake and five brownies.

We climbed back into the Transit and went home for game night, *"American Idol"* and dessert. It was better than I had planned for the Valentine's Day that got away.

Eye-candy in the Whisk window display

朋友 *("Peng You" or Friend)* . . .

February 2012
Shanghai

Today was another rainy day in Shanghai. The only thing different about today was that I took the day off from work and spent it with friends. Indeed, two of my best friends.

A couple of weeks ago, we had our first visitor. I was excited to welcome a visitor even if it was for only one night. Colleen was squeezing us in on her grand tour of China. She is here on business and enjoying the many splendors of China *in February*! She had just one night in Shanghai before heading home.

My excitement about seeing her was building, but when Friday night finally arrived, I was beat. As I often do, I was waffling. We planned to meet at 9 p.m. but after a couple of drinks at happy hour, I was fading. I really just wanted to go to bed. The hubby would not hear of it and kept me moving on the promise of one quick drink and then home to bed. Liar!

We met at Luma in Xintiandi. The bar was smokey (it is Shanghai) and crowded but as we stood at the entrance looking down the length of the bar toward the band, we saw her. Colleen is unmistakable and unforgettable. She was standing up, waving her arms wildly, smiling and calling after Jack. In that moment, I was so glad I had not gone home to bed.

And it only got better. I cannot describe the band; it can only be experienced. And to really enjoy it, you needed to go to high school in the '80s. It was a cover band of sorts. They took requests and banged them out one after another, complete with choreographed dance moves.

It was so bad and so funny that it was unbelievably wonderful. We drank too much, we sang too loud, we danced (well one of us danced) and made ridiculous requests that took us right back to high school, where we became friends all those years ago.

Sometime long past 2 a.m. we dropped our friend off at her hotel so she could 'nap' before catching a taxi to the airport at 5:45 a.m. As we all stumbled out of the Transit to say our goodbyes, our driver laughed and said "mei ban fa." Jack put his arm around Colleen and responded, "Wo men de peng you mei ban fa." (Loosely translated to "Our friend is unexplainable; she is what she is.") Ah, very true. It was a great night. It was high school all over again only so much better.

Only a few weeks before seeing Colleen, I was actually in the States. The trip was packed with business "stuff" and I had left Shanghai with things at home in a bit of a mess. I needed someone to listen and share a beer with me.

A good friend of mine from college was in a bit of transition herself — maybe we could swap stories over a pint. Just one problem — she was in Florida and I was in Michigan. I called her anyway.

Maya is that friend you have that your kids think is so much cooler than you. Our children have been watching Maya once a year at the end of the Super Bowl. They've been watching her 'live' or 'on tape' for years now.

Sometimes, they see Maya with the Lombardi Trophy, sometimes with a player, but always with a smile. My job does not take me to the Super Bowl or the Super Anything.

Maya will answer when I call even if I've neglected our friendship for years. And, at times, I have been neglectful. Still, if needed, I'd drop anything for her. As I was packing my suitcase to return to Shanghai, I called her. I just needed to let off some steam to someone I trusted. She didn't let me down. And, as it turned out, I was able to return the favor.

Getting back to today . . . my best friend — Jack — spent the day with me and helped me celebrate my Shanghai best friend's birthday. I love birthdays. I do. Celebrate life . . . it is so much better than the alternative. While sitting with Lily and Jack today, I was reminded of Colleen and Maya and how important friendship really is to a person.

Lily took me in when I arrived in Shanghai all those months ago. She kept me moving that first weekend, and the next 11 weeks while I awaited my family's arrival. I think, no actually I know, that I would have been lost without Lily. I was desperately lonely without Jack and no amount of Skyping could make up for it. Lily understood.

Lily showed me Shanghai and Bangkok. She spent Saturday afternoons with me. She helped me figure out where to buy shampoo, how to order food from Sherpas, how to make a dinner reservation with style. Together we decorated the children's bedrooms, shopped for treasures, drank good wine and ate good food.

It was a fast connection. Lily is something of a soul mate for me. I can comfortably be myself with her.

I was so happy during that birthday lunch to be with two of my dearest friends. My smile was genuine and deep as I reflected on how fortunate I've been in my life to have friends who are truly wonderful, generous and kind people. People who make me happy, just by being themselves, and allowing me the opportunity to dance to the rhythm of their unique and mysterious music.

朋友. . . "peng you". . . it means friend.

Father, Forgive Me

August 2012
Shanghai

Father, forgive me, it's been 6 months since my last post . . .

A psychiatrist recently told me that moving is among the top 5 most stressful life events. He added that moving to China was likely higher on the scale than other moves. Now, you might be wondering why I was talking to a psychiatrist but we'll hold that for the next blog. Suffice to say, when one moves to China with three kids, a large husband and a dog, someone's going to need a shrink sooner or later.

It has been stressful. I ain't gonna lie. As we've watched our children deal with the move in their own ways, it has caused me to re-evaluate the decision to come to China. The question I most often ask myself is *why* did I come to China? Did I come to China for my career or did I come to provide a once-in-a-lifetime opportunity for our family or was it both? When the kids are missing home, friends, ketchup — well, it feels like maybe I did this for me and not for us.

In those dark places, deep within, I am never sure why I did this . . . but I am glad we did. For better or worse . . . I am glad.

Father, forgive me, it's been 12 months since I last stepped into a church . . .

Faith is a struggle for me. Faith in God. Faith in others. Faith in myself. It has been 12 months or more since I personally stepped into a church for the purpose of praying. It isn't easy but it isn't impossible to go to church in China. This isn't about church, really, it's about having been away for 12 months and taking stock. Confession may be good for the soul, but it sure feels like shit.

I have to confess that this has been hard in almost every way imaginable. I confess that I have struggled to find any sense of balance between my family and my work. I confess that I have wanted to chuck it all and go home more often than I can count. I confess that I also absolutely love being in China and all of the experiences we have had over the course of this year. I confess I feel guilty about that too.

Father, forgive me . . .

Father, forgive me, I've had impure thoughts . . .

Not too long ago, I sent an email to a good friend saying that "when you find yourself on a rooftop deck, naked, sober and not having sex, you know something has gone terribly wrong." I was referring to an attempt to get a cell phone signal in the middle of the night to talk to our daughter who was in Russia and homesick. And yet, this image seems to capture most of our first year in China. Running naked across rooftops . . . with our hair on fire . . .

I would venture it isn't a stretch to imagine that I am not the only member of our gang to have had impure thoughts . . . and not just of the sexual variety. No, I bet they have been more of the "I'd like to kill her" variety. And, really, who can blame them? I've had the same thought, which leads to the next sin . . .

Gluttonous . . . prideful . . . envious . . . and without remorse . . .

Father, forgive me, for I have been gluttonous ... prideful ... envious ... and without remorse ...

Thailand, Vietnam, Malaysia, Russia, Germany, Austria, France, Great Britain . . . elephants, monkeys, exotic birds, sharks, sting rays, lemurs . . . food, wine, chocolate, theatre, music. . . and more, always more.

I have not only loved every hour, minute and second of these experiences, I have never been happier than to show our children the world and to experience their discovery of it with them. Yes, I am proud that we have been able to do it. And, I am envious of those who have been able to do more and do it better. But, I am not sorry.

We are closer than ever . . . partly out of necessity, partly out of shared experience and partly because we discovered that we can count on each other. It is true: *That which does not kill you, makes you stronger.* We are stronger as a family. We are, individually, also more fragile, if that makes sense. Our fragility, though, is in its own way a source of our strength. Accepting . . . loving . . .

Father, forgive me, for I will . . . do it all over again . . .

After 2 months traveling Europe and visiting family in the States, the gang returns to China in just five days. I am hopeful Year 2 will exceed the wonders of Year 1 and also be somewhat less stressful. This is my request for absolution for failing to post more regularly and for being selfish and dragging my poor family all over the world. But, as I haven't been to church in a year, it seems unlikely that I will be absolved of my sins or curtail them . . .

I anxiously await the gang's return and endeavor to see and do more than ever . . .

Where the Hell Have You Been?

August 2012
Shanghai

Spurned. That is the word that I would use to describe how I feel. Spurned. And, just like a good spurned woman, my wrath is far worse than the fury of hell. I believe it was Churchill who said that if you find yourself in hell, you best keep walking cause if you stop, it's gonna get hot. You outta be feeling the heat my friend, because you are in hell! You best keep walking.

While Wrigley did not *exactly say* those words, I certainly sensed a bit of "where the hell have you people been" in him when I returned to China a few weeks ago. He came to the door and ran directly to our Driver, Mr. Cao.

Worse, he would not come back into the house. He actually tried to get into the Transit. I half expected to see his suitcase sitting by the door just waiting to make this grand gesture: "I waited by the window for I don't know how long and now you come home and think you can waltz right in . . . Well, I'll show you," his tail smacking me on the leg as he made his way out the door.

This continued for the next 10 days. Every morning, I would get up and take Wrigley downstairs with me. Get him his food, fill the water bowl, let him out for his personal respite . . . I even let the dog eat cheese. Still, with his head held high and his tail whacking at me, he went to the front door and cried. The gentle hum of the Transit audible only to my four-legged friend, he was crying for Mr. Cao. He was not about to shed a tear for me.

Where have you been?

Feeling guilty about the weeks he had spent alone (with Mr. Cao walking him each day and, apparently, taking him for playdates with his own daughter), I attempted to soothe his bruised ego by offering a ride with me to the office. Head up, tail wagging, he lept into the Transit. This was good — I was making an effort to right the wrongs of summer and he was accepting of my apology.

Clearly, I misread the situation. Wrigley positioned himself between the driver and passenger seats. His head up and his tail smacking me in the face. I don't think this was an accident. Clearly, a ride and some cheese were not going to get me back in good graces with the Lord of the Manor. I needed back up. And, they arrived just in time!

While Wrigley may have been willing to play coy and hard to get with me, he is powerless in the presence of his one true love, Jack Fox. He heard the door open and my calling him, but he was not about to come downstairs from his perfectly air conditioned suite on the third floor, not for me. However, when he heard Bella, Henry and Jane, the not so subtle pound and patter of untamed claws on marble came swiftly.

With his tail wagging (or was it smacking) for his "siblings," he ran past their pleas and straight out the door. He stopped to greet Mr. Cao and looked just past him as if to say, "Our affair has meant more to me than you will ever know but I am powerless to resist his charms . . . ." and he was off. Jack was nearly tackled to the ground. The sight made even me uncomfortable. There really might be something to this "man's best friend thing."

But, as quickly as the reunion began, it ended. "Where the hell have you been?" he said as he backed away and moved closer to Mr. Cao. The game was back on . . . doggie treats were going to be needed and maybe even a new doggie bed!

Year 2

August 2012
Shanghai

I was hoping that Year 2 would be a bit less stressful than Year 1. But, come on, this is my life we are talking about – there was no chance that was going to happen. Things seemed to be off to a good start – the plane was early, the kids smiled upon arrival (sort of), I knew how to order $30 worth of pizza from Papa John's and had it *and* cupcakes awaiting their arrival. All good. Then came school orientation . . .

The difference between Moms and Dads goes far beyond anatomy. I know that I am generalizing a bit here, but indulge me. Fathers tend to be a bit laid back. Mothers are a bit more controlling. Mothers double check your backpack, constantly ask you if you brushed your teeth, packed your lunch and tied your shoes. Fathers expect their children to do all of these things and, frankly, no one is going to die if they forget to brush their teeth, pack their lunch or tie their shoes. This fundamental difference can be the undoing of a perfectly good happy hour.

It had been a long and horrible week, followed only by an even longer and more horrible week. So, on this particular Friday night, happy hour was not an indulgence, it was a survival mechanism. I wanted a beer and some french fries and I wanted them now – as in the moment that I pulled up in the driveway to pick up my beloved. Instead, I walked into a house with three children and only two uniform bags . . . hmmm.

Now, to be fair, absolutely everyone swears that Bella had that uniform bag in her possession from the moment they received the uniform to the moment she got in the Transit. Everyone. After a thorough scrubbing of the Transit, it was clear the bag was not there and that Bella had no uniform for school on Monday morning. Upon further review, it was also determined that Jane had a boy's gym "kit." In the immortal words of Winnie the Pooh: "Oh, bother!" (Looking back, I wished I had picked those words to express my . . . disappointment.) Either the Transit was the new Bermuda Triangle or we didn't have the uniform. Any guesses which?

A Summer Shandy was calling my name; no, screaming my name. And, the hollow spot in my stomach was aching – no food had I enjoyed in what seemed like a good 48 hours.

Seriously, didn't we check the bags when we received them to be sure we had the right uniform supplies? Didn't someone ask if everyone had their bags on the way to the car, getting in the car, while driving in the car, getting out of the car, walking into the house and, if not, didn't anyone notice that there were only two bags but three children?

No. This was not done because Mom did not go to orientation. I am not saying this is Dad's fault — I'm just saying no questions were asked . . . you may draw your own conclusions.

After some screaming (which was really more about being "late" to happy hour than the uniform), we decided that this was not the end of the world. If we needed to buy a new uniform . . . well, we'd buy it. Still, there were tears, car searching, room searching, closet emptying and all on a Friday night when things should have been calm. Especially this Friday, when school was looming around that dark corner known as Sunday night.

In the end, there were hugs all around and I still got my beer and fries. Jack took some ribbing and knew he'd be called out in the blog . . . so it goes. Year 2 is currently at DEFCON 2.

Postscript: Bella went to school in her brother's extra uniform and looked no different from the other girls — though the shorts were a bit big. Her uniform was turned in by a nice parent at the British International School (we had changed schools) and Jack received it while at new parent coffee on Monday.

He also made another friend . . . the Guy-Tai group is expanding. Somehow, he always ends up on top . . . figuratively speaking!

Wonder Woman

September 2012
Shanghai

People come and go in China. I don't mean that people are disappearing off the street. When you are an expat, colleagues and friends are transitory. They are on their way to some new place . . . the next assignment, the next country, home. Farewell parties are like retirement events . . . there is a lot of drinking, speeches, food and general frivolity. They are both a wonderful and sad reminder that your friends are world citizens.

A young woman is leaving this week. She is remarkably upbeat and truly talented. She is returning to Australia. It has been seven years since she was home. She spent four years in England and three in China. It's time. Time to go home. After the speeches were finished, I was making a bit of a sneaky exit. Jet lagged and just not "in the mood" for drunk world citizens, I wanted to go home.

I waved to the Aussie from across the room and she came over for one last hug. She stunned me when she thanked me and told me I was an inspiration to her and so many other young women in China. "Wonder Woman" she called me. And, now you know why I talk to psychiatrists — I practically stop them on the street!

There is just no such thing as Wonder Woman and, if there were, she would not be me. For one thing, I don't have the legs for the outfit. And, frankly, after three kids I don't have the boobs either! It just makes me so uncomfortable. And, yet, the Salt Mine has me standing in front of groups of young women in places like China, Australia and India (which is a constant, gnawing reminder that I am not young), to tell my career success story. I am fielding speaking requests from people and organizations that I don't even know. For "National Women's Day," I was featured in a Chinese magazine that depicted me as some icon of balance. Seriously?

I have got to be one of the most insecure people that I have ever met. I am truly committed to the idea that I am a total and utter failure and that any appearance of success is an apparition. I am, in fact, waiting for someone to discover the terrible fraud that I have committed. This discovery is imminent, I am certain of it. This has led to extreme anxiety. I don't sleep. I can't eat. I am a bit of a mess.

Still, I keep moving forward. I think it is stubbornness, to be honest. I refuse to be left behind. I refuse to defeat myself despite my best efforts to do exactly that; pull defeat out of victory. No, I'm not bipolar. I have Wonder Woman complex. In the words of Charles Barkley, I am not a role model. The problem is that people seem to think I am a role model.

If I am a role model, your daughters are in serious trouble and I apologize now to their poor husbands. I think Jack shaves his head to save himself the trouble of pulling out his hair.

China has been isolating for me in a professional sense.

I have lost my "circle" of women who have served as my sounding board, my support, my strength and my courage. Email and twice a year drinks just doesn't cut it.

I find myself in a position where I am constantly questioning my own judgment or maybe others are questioning it; and, I am second guessing myself. Either way, the revolving door is smacking me in the ass. And, my ass is sore.

Perception and reality can be so incredibly different. While I do not believe in Wonder Woman — she exists only in comic strips and re-runs — I am trying to embrace the idea that I have achieved some level of success.

The irony of it is that from the outside it appears that "I" achieved this success when the truth is that the guy with no hair is the real success. He is the one who made it all possible. But, the price of his success, is a perpetually perplexed wife. I am always asked to explain my "secret" to finding "balance" and having it "all." My polite answer is that I don't know what "balance" and "all" mean — it is different for everyone.

However, I should note that I did recently have it "all." It was in Paris — and I wasn't working!!

I really do wish someone would kill Wonder Woman . . .

BITCH

September 2012
Shanghai

The very best advice in the world is doled out at the hairdresser. Forget the Situation Room or the Boardroom or the Confessional. If you want good advice, make an appointment for color and a cut and start spilling the beans. Wisdom comes from behind the spinning chair.

Earlier this year, I recounted my lovely experience at the home office in the States when it was pointed out to me that I might be mistaken for a bitch if I wasn't more charming. Now, every time I'm told that I need to be more charming, I am, in fact, less charming. I hate being told to be more charming — really, I hate it.

So, having recounted this story to my wise and all-knowing hair therapist, I should not have been surprised when she placed a copy of Tabatha Coffey's book — *It's Really Not About the Hair* — in my hand and told me to read the introduction.

Really? Tabatha? As in Tabatha from Bravo's *"Tabatha's Salon Takeover"* and *"Shear Genius"*? This is the guru in whom all wisdom lies? Well, of course, silly. She does hair!

B.I.T.C.H.   Coffey takes the word back: **B**rave, **I**ntelligent, **T**enacious, **C**reative and **H**onest. Make it your own, she says. Love your inner B.I.T.C.H. I've said before that I am comfortable with my inner bitch and, truly, I am.

At this point in my life, I really find being labeled a bitch to be a compliment. I just didn't know that other women felt the same way. More importantly, I never realized that it isn't really a personality defect but rather a reference to my strengths – and how intimidating they can be, particularly when packaged in stilettos and a wrap dress.

Tabatha has a very interesting story. She was raised by her mother and transvestites who worked in her parents' strip clubs. Not your typical upbringing. She learned early to trust in herself and to accept being different because there was no ignoring that fact. She learned that being called a bitch doesn't define you unless you let it. And, if you are brave, intelligent, tenacious, creative and honest, you can redefine yourself using the very word others sling at you to cut you down.

I read the introduction and felt an instant soul mate. My hairdresser and I had the most interesting conversation that day during the three hours it takes to cover my ever-whitening hair. I left feeling better about myself than I have in quite a while. So, when all else has failed, remember: There is nothing that a good haircut can't solve. I like to add the stilettos and the wrap dress to my armor, but that's just me.

CHARM

September 2012
Bangkok, Thailand

This has really become something of a series at this point . . . my constant rant on "charm." As I've said before, some think I need to be a bit more charming. The suggestion seems a bit sexist to me and, frankly, makes me wonder what "activity" would make me more charming. But, my children might read this so I'll stop my speculation there.

Still, I've been thinking (obsessing) over this piece of advice now for months. The fact that it keeps coming up is really making me wonder if I am, in fact, suffering from a charm deficit . . . Jack is not allowed to comment . . .

To determine my charm quotient and its ranking in the "expected behaviors" of an employee at the Salt Mine, I decided to undertake a review of those behaviors. Yes, they are actually written down. Let's see:

- Know and have a passion for the business
- Demonstrate and build functional excellence
- Ensure process discipline
- Have a continuous improvement attitude and practice
- Believe in a skilled and motivated work force
- Include everyone: respect, listen to, help and appreciate others
- Build strong relationships; be a team player, develop ourselves and others
- Communicate clearly, concisely and candidly
- Show initiative, courage, integrity and good corporate citizenship

- Have a can-do, find-a-way attitude
- Emotional resilience
- Deal positively with our business realities
- Set high expectations and inspire others
- Make sound decisions using facts and data
- Hold ourselves and others responsible and accountable for delivering results.

Charm is not on that list. You might argue that "continuous improvement" or "build strong relationships" or even "appreciate others" qualifies, but then there is "courage" and "candid communication" and "hold ourselves and others responsible."

Let's be honest here, this is a long and comprehensive list. It borders on the ridiculous, really. We need not only a list but a card attached to our ID badges to remind us how to behave? Did no one go to kindergarten? Or, is the Salt Mine actually a cult?

Just for a moment, imagine the group sitting around a table coming up with this list of expected behaviors. Seriously, close your eyes and picture it. Not a very charming looking group of folks, is it?

Despite the thousands of man (and I do mean man) hours invested, the debate over each word, the eventual specificity of each and every sentence and the borderline neurotic need to fit all of the behaviors onto a card the size of my work badge, the five letters that comprise the word C-H-A-R-M did not make the cut. Charm, dare I say, is conspicuously absent.

So, as my Father would say: "Jennifer, consider the source!" And, he's right, as usual. There are lots of people that I work with whom I think need a real dose of reality let alone a semester or two at charm school. But, I don't tell them this; they are who they are, and I only need to work with them. We aren't dating.

And, there is the ironic fact that, if I were to suggest to any one of these individuals that they needed to be more charming, I would be . . . well, you can imagine where I would be!

Upon considering the source, the simple fact is that I don't find these men charming either. In fact, when I look at the list, I scratch my head. If you are commenting on my charm quotient, then I'm going to presume that I've met all the other prerequisites identified on the card, including exemplary job performance and the demonstration of the critical "leadership behaviors."

So, this charm attack, like calling me a bitch, is the last opportunity you have to take a swipe at me.

It feels a bit like being bullied. I think I've finally been able to put a word to the emotion, if you like. I feel like have been bullied lately and I don't like it any more than my 10-year-old would like it. The difference is I can stand up for myself.

So, here is the thing, charm is something I expect from my husband, not my boss or my colleagues. The Salt Mine can take their opinion of my charm and . . . well, you know.

Shanghai on a Shoestring . . .

September 2012
Shanghai

Stretching for the phone, which doubles as "our" alarm clock, I nearly fell out of bed. This is the usual routine and normally this routine forces me to get out of bed and head to the gym. But, on this Monday, I hit snooze, unplugged the phone from the wall, inched back into the crook of Jack's arm and laid the phone on his chest. This was *my* day off and while I am sure it would have been wonderful if I had gotten up and made pancakes for the kids and walked them to the bus stop, there was no way that

I was doing any of those things. Jack could make the pancakes, take them to the bus stop, feed the dog and bring me coffee — I mean he does it every other morning (except for bringing the coffee).

When the phone went off again, I rolled away from Jack (hard as it was) and clearly signaled that I was not getting up and he should get his butt in gear. I fell back asleep. It must have been an hour or two later when Jack reappeared in our bedroom.

Hmmm . . . if only I could think of something to do this morning . . . the kids away at school for the next 6 hours . . . the ever cloudy skies of Shanghai were keeping our room a subtle shade of grey . . . Jack all to myself . . . and me still in bed . . . yep, we should go for a run.

I know what you're thinking and believe me that is what I was thinking too but Jack had been telling me about this great lady who makes this great breakfast and, if I would get my "sorry arse" out of bed, we could log a few miles and end our run at her street cart and grab breakfast. "Come on, babe, you'll love it." I'll tell you what I'd love . . . well, I can't our kids might read this. And, is my ass really *that* sorry?

Unbelievably, I got out of bed and put on my running gear. After a little more than 2 miles, I could see the line of people standing outside what looked like a real estate office. "That's her," Jack said and, mercifully, slowed his pace. There were maybe six people waiting for their made-to-order breakfast. It smelled fantastic. Not surprisingly, the lovely cook greeted Jack warmly. A large Western man with blond facial hair and a shaved head is memorable here. He gets all the smiles — only Henry gets more, I think.

Breakfast consists of a very thin flat bread cooked over a large, circular hot plate — and I do mean hot. The dough is spread across the plate in a circular motion using what appears to be a large putty knife. Over the dough, she breaks an egg and washes it across the dough, adds scallions and chilies. She lifts the dough from the plate, folds it in thirds, adds a secret sauce and folds it again, then cuts it in half and puts it in a plastic bag. Breakfast to go. I added an extra egg to my Ji dan bing. The price for this delicious and surprisingly filling breakfast was 4 RMB. Less than $1 in the States.

早上好！ ("Zao sheng hao" means good morning)

This got me thinking — how cheaply can you eat in Shanghai?

While I have been in Shanghai longer than my family, I haven't seen nearly as much of it as the rest of the gang. I know where to get a great steak (Char), or a great roast chicken (Mr. & Mrs. Bund) or even some traditional Indian samosas (Marsala Art). Of course, dinner at any one of these places will cost us a couple hundred dollars, especially if we have wine (and we *are* having wine!). Believe it or not, a dozen cupcakes costs you $50 around here — they are good but $50?

So, while I have eaten well and expensively, I have not sampled the street cuisine or many of the Shanghai favorites to the same extent as Jack.

Back at the house, we showered and tried to decide what we should do next. I had a few ideas and Jack had several tempting suggestions. We still had at least 5 hours before the kids would be home. So, as you would expect, we got in the car and headed to Yu Yuan Garden. The food tour was on.

Xialongbao is a Chinese dumpling. The dumplings are usually filled with pork, chicken or mushrooms. The dough is pulled up around the filling and twisted into a "rose." The thing that makes these dumplings unique and ever so delicious, though, is the juice inside them. When you take your first bite, you have to be careful of the hot broth, which will burn your mouth but tastes so good.

Xialongbao is a traditional and delicious Chinese dumpling.

Xialongbao is available all over Shanghai and is a fairly inexpensive meal. We went to Yu Garden to get the dumplings from "the original" makers. This is a fairly famous spot to get xialongbao, so it's a bit more pricey. We spent 20 RMB or $3.50 for lunch.

Our Ayi was so aghast at the price we paid that she made us some later in the week so we wouldn't "waste our money." Secretly, I think this was Jack's original intent, as he had not been able to get her to make them earlier because she said the dough was hard to make . . . or I think that is what she said, who knows.

For dinner, we went for muslim noodles. These noodles are made fresh, right in front of you, in the tiniest little shop. The dough is stretched like taffy, pulled and plied and eventually stretched into submission, and cooked in a flash. You can have your noodles with beef, chicken, vegetables or even eggs. I had mine with cucumbers and egg. Jack ordered his with beef and peppers. The sauce is light, buttery and just slightly spicy. There are no forks at this little tiny spot and I have not quite mastered the

The little noodle shop around the corner

art of noodle eating with chopsticks . . . so . . . slurp!

This delicious and satisfying dinner cost 12 RMB for noodles with cucumber and egg or 13 RMB for noodles with beef and peppers — $2 per serving.

The total price for dining in Shanghai on this particular Monday: Less than $15 for *both* of us.

While I did enjoy the food tour, I do wish we'd taken a bit of time for some other indulgences . . . but you can't have it all!

Curing The Sunday Night Blues . . .

September 2012
Shanghai

I used to really dread Sunday night. The amount of dread tended to vary with how I felt about work at the time but, overall, I never really looked forward to Sunday night. My favorite part of the week was Friday at 8 p.m. — the cusp of the weekend. Then, I moved to China.

Sunday night in China is a complete revelation and one that I did not come to on my own. When I arrived in China, I was lucky enough to make a couple of good friends on my first weekend in town. Not only did these friends take care of me that first weekend but they introduced me to their cure for the Sunday night blues. It has been a revelation.

Now, I feel compelled to preface this with "I work very hard." My compulsion is no doubt related to my Catholicism. Admittedly, I am no longer a good Catholic or religious at all but some things stay with you – like guilt. I have a guilt complex to rival any devout Catholic and most good Jews too. I don't exactly feel guilty about my Sunday night addiction but, still, I feel like it should be justified. So, there it is: "I work hard." Yeah, I don't feel guilty at all.

Sunday night in Shanghai . . . always better at the Waldorf Astoria.

It takes effort to make this ritual happen and, yet, it is unthinkable that we would miss it.

Everything is timed down to the last possible minute — we get Henry home from football, dinner is on the table, backpacks are checked for school the next morning and shower reminders are issued to the younger set as we race out the door. Then Jack and I make the 40-minute drive to Puxi, which is on the other side of the river from where we live in Pu Dong. All of this would likely be a much greater hassle if we were doing the driving but we aren't. Mr. Cao picks us up at our door, drops us off and repeats.

We are dropped at the door. No parking hassle. We take the elevator up to 8th floor and as the doors open we hear: "Jennifer, welcome back." I love hearing this each week. I know my name is on the book and they are expecting us but, still, I love it. I do.

We sit down in the dimly lit reception area and are given the menu and a cup of tea. Everyone knows what our selection will be but perusing the menu is part of the ritual. These 10 minutes in the reception area are devoted to the ritual, drinking the green tea, scanning the menu and confirming our selection. Just as we finish our tea, the curtains open and we are greeted by our usual Sunday night hosts and led back to what has become our "usual" room.

The room is set up for two but, in all, there will be six of us. Because, on this occasion, we splurged and got the 4-hands massage. Yes, two pairs of hands working your body symmetrically. Please — there is no reason to ask the question — yes, two is better than one.

So, when you are watching your Sunday pre-game show, I'll be having quality time with my husband and two or four other women and I won't be the

The Long Bar, Waldorf Astoria in Shanghai

least bit jealous nor will I feel guilty . . . I will, however, feel all of the tension of last week and the week ahead melt away for a solid 90 minutes. And, when we are done, there will be tea and cookies or maybe that really good chocolate pudding! Or, maybe we'll make a stop at the Long Bar . . .

Monday is waiting, after all.

Business Travel . . . Asia Style

September 2012
Bangkok, Thailand

The life of a corporate leader is so glamorous. You jet about the world, stay at fancy hotels, eat at amazing restaurants and meet very interesting people. And, then there is my life.

You pay to upgrade yourself to business class because your flight leaves at 12:30 a.m., lands at 5:35 a.m. and you are going straight to the office for a full day of eye-drooping meetings, followed by the long and sometimes harrowing drive to the hotel (this is Southeast Asia and the first generation of drivers . . .) to find that you are staying at a mid-rate location that won't accept your corporate credit card. And this, my friends, is day one of an 8-day adventure.

It's rainy season. There is no humidity-resistant hair spray that can stand up to Thailand's rainy season. I dare Bed Head to prove me wrong! My flat iron is working overtime to keep the strands straight and in place but, really, what is the point? I look a mess and feel saturated (aka bloated beyond recognition).

I love Bangkok. The hotel I stay at here is actually pretty great. The rooms are really like small studios and there is a great breakfast and a wonderful bar with a great view. Of course, since I'm paying, the cocktails suddenly seem more expensive than necessary and I fail to ever get back in time for happy hour. The best thing, however, is that while in Bangkok I have the luxury of a Western toilet. Yes, for me, this is the new measure of luxury.

You may recall my trip to Chongqing and the issue of the "squat" toilet and my strained groin muscle. Well, as I made my way to my next location in Thailand, the luxury-level dropped a bit. Checking in at the lovely Holiday Inn on the beach was fine with the minor exception that my corporate card still wasn't working. But, the Thai people are wonderful. I've yet to find more hospitable people.

This location is interesting in many ways. The beach is lovely and if you are in need of female companionship you can certainly find it along the beach, along "walking street" or at any one of the many bars lining the street. And, if you like your female companionship in the form of a boy dressed as a woman or in the process of becoming a woman, you can find that too.

My room, of course, is on the beach side with a great view but it is also next to a very popular outdoor drinking establishment with a loud and not so good cover band that plays until 1 a.m.

My day is supposed to begin at 4:30 a.m. with a meeting with the "global team" but I sleep through it. Just not happening today . . . not on my dime, anyway. At 7 a.m. I am on my way to the plant with a driver who is definitely not afraid to drive on the wrong side of the road despite heavy oncoming traffic, which may be in the form of a bike, motor bike, car, or even a truck full of chicken. By the time I get to the plant, I need coffee just to calm me down.

Several cups later, the inevitable happens and I find that the Western toilets are not available at this location. I am pleased to say that I have mastered (sort of) this restroom arrangement.

My advice to those of you planning a trip to Southeast Asia — do your squats! I can't see my Mother doing this — no offense Mom!

I finally return to the hotel about 9 p.m. I am hungry and I have 30 minutes until my next call — North America is awake now. Room service is the only viable option (which will be on my dime).

At 10 p.m., I'm done for the day. Tomorrow, I move on to the next location. Vietnam, Northern China, India . . . who knows, but it won't be by private plane or involve 5-star hotels.

What To Wear To Lunch . . .

September 2012
Shanghai

I don't go out for lunch very often. Jack, on the other hand, manages to incorporate lunch into his Chinese language class homework. He's working on ordering lunch these days from his favorite street vendors in their native language. He's quite good actually.

Me? I still have lunch with people who speak my native language (chocolate). And the Chinese don't really like chocolate so much — a wonder, I know. So, when I was asked to represent the Salt Mine at an event that included lunch, I presumed there would be some great food and potentially some chocolate. I should really know better by now . . .

Lunch turned out to be a driving extravaganza. It took us 90 minutes to get to the lunch location. I know it is Shanghai, but jeez! Lunch itself was about 110 minutes if you don't include the "networking" that took about 20 minutes. And, the drive back was long enough that the party in the Transit had enough time to screen *Fast and Furious 5*, which is a movie I would not ordinarily watch but it was in the vehicle and we had PLENTY of time to kill.

Still, lunch also included getting to spend a bit of time with the Governor of the Great State of Michigan. It isn't every day that I have lunch with the Governor. (We already covered the fact that I rarely have lunch.) I am not entirely sure what I was expecting but I did think carefully about my wardrobe.

Governor. Republican. I'm thinking conservative, boring and sensible. Wrap dress seemed a bit too "casual" for the event. Pant suit seemed a bit

Michigan Governor Rick Snyder in Shanghai.

too Hillary Clinton (I like her, so watch it!) for this event. Black pencil skirt might send the wrong message — this is not an episode of "*Mad Men.*"

I settled on the conservative but sleeveless grey frock that my niece chose for me at Nordstrom when I was in town in January. Grey dress, black sweater and conservative jewelry seemed the right mix of style and substance. Of course, I did wear the red stilettos. I had to have a little fun.

Oh, and aside from the photograph that I insisted upon to prove to our children that I really did have lunch with the Governor, I had no other interaction with him. While my tablemates laughed at me, you know they wanted the same photo but didn't have the nerve (or the shoes) to ask. I wonder if my red shoes scared him?

Oh, I almost forgot, dessert was marble cheesecake! I guess the drive was worth it.

What's Your Soundtrack?

September 2012
Shanghai

The other morning we were huddled around Jack's computer going through every song we could think of on Spotify. Jane was looking for her soundtrack otherwise described by her teacher as "the song that reflects who you are; represents you in some way." Of course, this had to be explained in her drama class the next day, so it couldn't be too close to the truth. She is, after all, a secretive, mysterious and wonderful creature — a 14-year-old girl.

I loved this assignment.   I knew exactly the song I would pick for her because is it the song that I have sung to her at night since she was a baby: *"You Are My Sunshine"* (Elizabeth Mitchell).   She is indeed my sunshine even in her darkest moments — as I said, she's 14.   But to her mother, who struggled to bring her into this world more than she will ever understand, she is the sun, the moon and the stars.

Searching for her soundtrack . . .

Of course, when I suggested this song she rolled her eyes as only Jane can do. "Mom, this is the song that *I think* reflects me; **not** the song that *you think* reflects me." Such sarcasm at 8 a.m. on a Sunday morning. Okay, then how about the song that expresses my wishes for you . . . *"I Hope You Dance"* (Leeann Womack). More eye rolling.

We had a great time with Dad picking songs that made her laugh, like *"Popular"* from *Wicked*. "I'm not so sure that's meant as a compliment, Dad!" Well, then how about *"When You're an Addams"* or *"Full Disclosure"* from the Broadway musical, he retorted. "Dad!" You get the picture — we were having way too much fun and she just wanted to stop with the introspection — especially in front of us.

So, finally, Jack and I turned to U2 — a place from which all wisdom for our generation emanates — *"I Still Haven't Found What I'm Looking For."* Jane laughed but wasn't sure it was for her and so the tour through the musical library continued.

This got me thinking about my own soundtrack. I could certainly pick *"I Still Haven't Found What I'm Looking For"* (as I suspect many middle-aged — did I just write that — people would).

But, over time, there would be many different tunes. My father called me "Jenny the Jet" when I was a little girl. He took it from the Elton John song, *"Benny and the Jets."*

If this were my assignment, my soundtrack would include the following, along with a few others:

- *"Betrayed"* . . . Patrick O'Hearn
- *"Help Me Lord"* . . . Bonnie Raitt
- *"Wide Open Spaces"* . . . Dixie Chicks
- *"Strong Enough"* . . . Sheryl Crow

- *"XXX's and OOO's (American Girl)"* . . . Trisha Yearwood
- *"Home"* . . . Edward Sharpe & The Magnetic Zeros
- *"This Is Us"* . . . Emmylou Harris & Mark Knopfler
- *"Dark Side"* . . . Kelly Clarkston
- *"Not Ready to Make Nice"* . . . Dixie Chicks

I'll let you figure it out. But the phases or scenes of my so-called life are in there somewhere.

Of course, I have songs in mind for the other two "little" people who light up my life (and, no, Debbie Boone does not make the list). Henry will likely want to kill me if he reads this and then actually listens to "his" song, which is by the Dixie Chicks — I know that is rough on a boy: *"Godspeed."*

I am guessing you've not heard it. Look it up. Since the moment I heard it, it has reminded me of Henry. It is the last song on my iPod when I go running. I like to finish a run to that tune. It always makes me smile and cry at the same time. If you decide not to look it up, no worries, I plan to dance with him at his wedding to this song; you'll hear it then.

When it comes to the little lady of the house, it's not hard to pick, really: *"Just the Way You Are"* (Bruno Mars). She is perfect in every way to her mother. I even love those imperfections. Her tough upper lip and her heart of gold. Her "I can do that" attitude mixed with a "maybe you should hold my hand" reality.

I love my little marshmallow with the crusty outside and the gooey inside. I love her sense of humor, her smart sass and the fact that at 10 she still can't sleep without Pinky Bear. That Bear has been to the top of the Eiffel Tower and trekked the Great Wall.

And, Jack . . . well, he's in my list above but, of course, he had a request: *"American Bad Ass"* by Kid Rock. I'm afraid to even listen to it.

Truth is that when I hear the song *"Forever and Ever Amen"* by Randy Travis I think of us, of him. Not much I can say here except that I got lucky. Anyone who knows me, knows that I got lucky. I am hell to live with but I love Jack more than I love myself and he is the best partner a woman like me can have — and there are few men who are up to the task. Very few.

Thanks for being so darned persistent, babe!

Jane actually picked *"Drift Away"* by Uncle Kracker. Jack later used the same song as the soundtrack backing up a video of his photographs capturing our first year in China.

I would be remiss if I didn't tell you that Jane picked a song for her Dad. *"Sexy and I Know It"* by LMFAO — no shirt, no shoes and he still gets service. Jane has her father's sarcastic nature — obviously!

If I had to pick a single song for us today I might pick *"If I Need You"* by Emmylou Harris (Duets Album). China has been an experience we will all carry with us forever in our own ways. But, collectively, I believe we now know the answer to the question we all wonder about the people we love . . . will you really be there if I need you. We know. We know without hesitation the answer to that question.

Oh, and lest I forget, Dad who picked my first song . . . there is only one song for you: *"My Way"* by Frank Sinatra.

Okay there it is . . . hit iTunes or Spotify and take a listen.

姐妹 *(Sisters)*

September 2012
Shanghai

Sisters. I have a few of my own and, yes, I recall that we all wanted to throttle one another at some point in our lives. Sometimes, we may still want to do that but we have the good sense to yell at our husbands instead and leave them baffled as to what they may have done wrong.

My daughters are not yet married and so they take it out on each other. This makes me crazy. Now, of course, they love each other (or so they claim) but they are — at times — on each other's last nerve dancing the tango. It makes me crazy. Truly. Utterly. Crazy.

When I come home, I want peace and quiet. And, if I can't have peace then I at least want quiet. But, let's face it, we have three children, one large man and a dog living in fairly tight quarters. There will be no peace and certainly no quiet. Our oldest — who will turn 15 on October 15th — is a mysterious and monstrous creature known as the teenage girl. And, yes, Mom, I am sure she is exactly like me so your curse upon me has rained down in spades.

In China, the lovely ladies Fox share a bedroom. This room is ginormous. Not large, not extra-large but ginormous. Truly, it reminds me of the bedroom my Mother created for us at our cottage on Runyan Lake. It held 4 twin beds and 4 girls — all in one room. Unfortunately, despite the objective evidence, the room is "too cramped to share."

Jane locks herself in her bathroom and locks the door to the bedroom as well. Jane is double locked in and we are double locked out. Quite a statement. Bella is yelling at the top of her lungs while banging on the door. "It's my room too!" Jane never hears it because those ear buds are glued into her ears. This is not peace. This is not quiet. This is hell. And, despite Churchill's advice, I cannot keep walking.

For months now, I have been saying to the both of them: "I have never had my own room in my entire life — my entire life. In fact, at the very moment I was about to have my own room, your father showed up in Los Angeles, no job, no money and no place to stay. So, quit complaining. My first opportunity to have my own room will likely be my coffin."

Okay, a bit gruesome perhaps and a bit of a lie. I actually don't want a coffin, I want to be cremated and thrown into the Seine. But, geez, girls — get a grip.

Gripping is not an option as it turns out. Let's face it, no 15–year-old wants to hang out with a 10-year-old unless it involves $8 an hour. And so, it was up to me to solve this dilemma once and for all. Peace and quiet can be bought, I decided. And, I was going to buy it *today*.

I took the day off and hauled my sorry ass off to IKEA with an expert. Look, this is China not the States. You don't go to IKEA on a weekend and you don't go without an IKEA expert. On the weekend, you find the locals sleeping in beds, sitting in chairs, eating lunch in the kitchen showroom, putting their babies down for a nap in the cribs, and yes, even using the IKEA showroom bathrooms, which are not actually working bathrooms. This is China. They put up a sign and everything but . . . .

Clearly, I was not going to do this on my own. I can't find my way out of IKEA in the States, where the signs are written in English. No, I needed an expert and I went and got one. A Louisville woman, who always has a bourbon ready when the girls are making me crazy, is an IKEA expert. Yes, I took a Louisville

Slugger with me to IKEA. Not sure how the Swedes would feel about that but I did it anyway.

In 3 hours, we purchased:

- 1 sofa that has this very cool slide out part that makes the sofa a double bed
- 1 thin mattress to lay on the couch/bed
- 1 table on casters with storage
- 1 curtain rod to string across the "doorway"
- 1 curtain for the curtain rod
- 2 pillows
- 3 throw pillows
- 1 duvet cover with 2 pillow cases
- 1 duvet
- 1 blanket
- 1 large alarm clock
- 1 clip-on bedside reading lamp
- 2 plastic bathroom organizers
- Some napkins
- 2 boxes of plastic bags
- 2 red lanterns for the outside deck.

Okay, the last three items are unrelated to this story. We navigated our way through the maze that is IKEA and found the check out lane. Paid. And, then went to merchandise delivery.

Merchandise delivery took a bit of work. The table and couch were supposed to be delivered today. Then, they could not be delivered until tomorrow. Then, the table could not be delivered at all and I should get a taxi. We went round and round like this for a good 30 minutes while Sue searched for someone with some level of English proficiency. I note, I am in China — I should be making the effort but without Bella I can't order a fortune cookie.

Finally out of merchandise delivery, we made our way to the grocery area. Bought chocolate, cinnamon rolls, and beer — yes beer. Doesn't everyone buy Swedish beer at IKEA?

The IKEA delivery guys just left. The IKEA assembly guys come Thursday and by Thursday night I will have peace and quiet for just under $1,000. If I don't, you'll likely hear the sound where you live . . .

Sisters

Ayi, a China Handyman & Me

September 2012
Shanghai

I promised an update: I believe there will be peace in our time . . . in our little home . . . in this great big country called China.

In China, there is very little that you can't get done, have made or find . . . if you know where to go, who to ask and how to bargain. I mean, look at your label on your shirt, go ahead, I'll wait. (Humming a tune while you look.)

Exactly! This *is* China!

My good friend Lily returned from a long European vacation and found her home in need of some repair. I have been following the drama of the Chinese Handymen on Jack's Facebook account. It is classic China — much drama but it gets done.

Today, I had my own little adventure.

At 9:30 a.m., he arrived in blue coveralls, tool box in hand and his work order sticking out of his pocket. He came up the

that's Shanghai magazine cover proclaims "Ayi Can Do It!"

stairs to "the room" that would be a parent-free hang out zone by day and Bella's bedroom by night. This room has no door. It has open shelving dividing it from the "hallway" and the stairs to our room on the third floor and the stairs to the first floor living area. Critical to our success was finding a way to close off this area and create a private zone for Bella without closing off the room during the day.

My friend Louisville Slugger Sue had a great idea and, after two trips to IKEA — it's like Target, you can't go once and you can't go and not spend more than you ever intended — we had secured the supplies: 3 sets of curtains, a very long curtain rod, 4 wall hanger-whatchamacallits and an expandable shower curtain rod. These items — combined with the couch that turns into a double bed, pillows, throws, accessories and some re-arranging of pictures and the transfer of the ever growing paraphernalia that makes Jane crazy but screams Bella — were going to make a great "bedroom."

By 10 a.m., the couch was put together but facing the wrong direction. After several attempts at charades (you would think "turn the couch around to face the TV" would be universal but

By day, one way & . . .

apparently not), I called Ayi who immediately recognized the issue and sorted it. Next, the handyman assembled the table on casters and a glass top, under which I placed photos of family, friends, and awards from school. Check.

By 10:30 a.m., there was cardboard and plastic everywhere. The handyman was not originally contracted with IKEA to hang the curtain rod. The curtain rod was a second trip inspiration. But, as I said, this *is* China. A land where cash is still king and a little goes quite a long way (unless you are buying Cinnamon Toast Crunch), particularly in the service industry. Ayi and the handyman had a few words. There was an exchange. It got loud and then she turned to me and said, "si shi quai" — 40 RMB. This is less than $7. Deal!

Our walls are concrete and hanging anything is an ordeal. A real ordeal, which is why I knew Jack could not do this, and let's be honest here, he'd never have gotten the table put together. So, there we were, the handyman, Ayi and me staring at my ceiling and the little area of wall above the bookshelf where the curtain rod had to go. "Bu Hao!" the handyman exclaimed. (That means "No good!")

Hmmm. He drilled and again said "bu hao!" This was not going as planned. Ayi started pointing and yelling (which is normal in China — it is very loud here) and then pointing at me. I sat on the stairs and waited. At some point, I would hear "Jen-E-fer" and that was my cue. So, I sat and waited. It wasn't more than 10 minutes when I heard the signal and I got up from my perch, crawled over the mounds of cardboard and entered 'the room.'

. . . by night, another.

I have no idea what was said next. For 20 minutes there was loud talking, much gesticulating and a general commotion. Much of the Chinese discourse appeared to be directed at me and, as it became clear that I did not understand, the discourse got even louder.

The only words I understood were "bu hao," and that was getting through loud and clear. I pulled out the computer, called up Google Translate and tried to communicate with Ayi and the Handyman virtually but to no avail. Finally, Ayi made the call.

We really should have a red phone in our house. Because when all else fails, Ayi sends out the "Bat Signal" and dials my administrative assistant. It's like a hot line direct to the President of the United States. It cracks me up. The call is always taken — day or night — and someone is always apologizing to me because I don't speak or understand Chinese — seriously?

Jasmine and Ayi talked for a bit and then Jasmine talked with the Handyman. I sat on the stairs waiting for my cue. "Jen-E-fer!" And, the phone was in my hands. "Ni hao, Jasmine." Jasmine laughed. Yes, this is all I can say after nearly 18 months. To be honest, I have no earthly idea what the commotion was about. Jasmine said something about the children and safety but, in the end, none of it made sense to me.

I looked at the Handyman, went downstairs and grabbed a Coke Zero, a water bottle and bounded back up the stairs. He took the water. I handed him 50 RMB. He smiled. Up the ladder went the Handyman, up went the curtain rod, on went the curtains and 'the room' was done.

The Handyman used something to locate the right spots in the concrete to drill and then miraculously the safety concern went away and

The offending curtain rod.

the rod was secured to the wall. Ayi laughed. As he packed up, he asked if he could keep the pencil that I had given him and I nodded. I also handed him 100 RMB. He handed me his name card. I may need to hang something else, you never know!

At 11:45 a.m., I had the duvet cover on the duvet, the pillow cases on the pillows, the games in the table, the pillows and duvet put away in the cupboard, the knick-knacks placed and was sitting down to admire the room. Ayi cleared the mess of cardboard and plastic and came back upstairs, looked around and smiled at me "Ni hen hao!" (You very good.)

For $20, we pulled together a room that the kids will love and Bella will find suits her. Can't wait for her to get home and see it. Today, I agree — "wo hen hao" (Today, I am very good). In China, you can get it made, find it or have it done, you just have to play the game.

12 Hours

September 2012
Shanghai

You know that feeling you get in your gut when something just doesn't feel right? When I saw the heading of an email from my functional manager in the States today — "Mandatory Team Building Meeting" — I got that feeling. The awful, sinking feeling that tells you no good can come from this.

Let's pretend that you can build a team in a mandatory fashion just for the sake of argument. If you suspend disbelief for a moment, can you also pretend that you can build a team in 12 hours? If you can, you are a miracle worker and I would like to shake your hand.

Team building is the new corporate kumbaya. We bring it out whenever things aren't going the way we planned. We have a meeting, an offsite, a team building session. I will go on record right now and say that these events are useless and a waste of time, energy and productive spirit. No one wants to be there and whatever they agree to in that room, they will immediately disavow when they walk out. Team building is a flight of fancy.

Jaded? Perhaps. But 20 years into my career, I have yet to be involved in a constructive team building event. In fact, the last one I attended (in January of this year), resulted in me being scolded for not sharing enough personal information with the "team." The team being those who would like to destroy me and my career. To "help them understand me," I should give away personal information that could be used to manipulate me, discover my pressure points and insecurities. No, I don't think so. Not me. Not I. No way.

Now, months later, we were at it again. I suspected this had something to do with my continuing lack of charm. Still, I wasn't going. It might be mandatory but unless you are prepared to put me in a straight jacket and force me onto a plane, I will not be in attendance. Truth be told, I had plans. My plans involved our oldest daughter and being available to her. They also involved her birthday, which I was not missing again.

My first attempt to get out of it was to be honest and say that (1) I didn't think I could do what was being asked of me because I didn't trust any of the people in the room, and (2) even if I did trust them, I couldn't travel at this time because of a personal matter that required my attention. The response was quick. I got a phone call the next morning. The meeting was scheduled for Thursday afternoon and all day on Friday.

This, of course, meant that I could not fly back to China until Saturday. Leaving the States on Saturday means landing in

China on Sunday afternoon. I lose the weekend and miss our daughter's birthday. Not exactly convenient or courteous of the planners. But, then everyone else was already in the States.

I dug in my very pointed heels and said no. I have never said no before to any request related to my job. Never. I wasn't negotiating. I wasn't coming. Period. I needed to be home with my daughter. This simply wasn't good enough. I was pressed and pressed until, finally, I gave up and explained that there was a medical issue that needed to be dealt with and, as her mother, I wanted to be in China with her to support and help her. I offered a doctor's note when my manager complained that he would have to explain my absence to the others. Really?

Despite the obvious violation of the Family Medical Leave Act, I sent the doctor's note to human resources. My manager immediately responded that I "offered" the note -- ass covering at its best. I responded in kind that I offered it after it was made clear to me that I would not be excused without providing some excuse that could be offered to the rest of the leadership team. Not exactly charming, I know.

Someone actually expected me to spend close to 32 hours in a plane or waiting at the airport for the plane to attend a 12-hour team building meeting. Common sense would suggest that the 12-hour time difference between our locations and the travel would render me useless. Arrogant, in my opinion.

I have no doubt that this team building session grew out of some discussion among the "real" leadership team about me and my lack of cooperation or my poor attitude or my lack of charm. And, now, I wasn't coming. I also know that none of these men know anything about our organization, the work we actually do or how it gets done. Frankly, I am tired of educating them. I'm just plain tired. More importantly, my daughter needs me. And, this time, I am going to be there for her even if I have to take a 2-week leave of absence to do it. (I did!)

Most Powerful . . . Luv Mum

October 2012
Beijing, China

The October 8th issue of *Fortune* hit newsstands with this year's ranking of the 50 Most Powerful Women in Business. Did you see it? Did you hear about the controversy over the cover photo — a decision to be pictured thin and svelte vs. pictured as one appears today — pregnant? Hmm . . .

Just days later, I received an email from a good friend of mine at a Fortune 50 Company.

Her "Mum" had forwarded the email to her:

"Morning again.

I have just finished reading an editorial in a financial adviser's monthly mag and thought you may be interested in the following:

Dr. Terrance Fitzsimmons from the University of Queensland's Business School interviewed 31 female CEOs and 30 male CEOs. He concluded that, for women to become CEOs, they needed most, if not all, of the following:

1. *A dramatic/traumatic childhood event which interrupted family life*

2. *Growing up in a small-business family balancing the books, dealing with staffing, and developing self-resilience*

3. *Their own children were born either very early (when the woman was between 18 and 23) or in the woman's mid-late 30s*

4. *Full-time career path (because flexibility was the kiss of death as it was seen to be a lack of seriousness about career)*

5. *Grandparents were the carers for their children*

6. *Their husbands were supportive*

7. *Mentors were found quickly at work.*

In stark contrast, he found that males shared two traits:

1. *Their fathers were professionals*

2. *Their mothers stayed home*

And, very frequently they captained their school's football teams — thus developing goals, strategy, leadership and teamwork.

Thought you might be interested in his findings.

Love Mum"

[Source: "Navigating CEO Appointments: Do Australia's Top Male and Female CEOs Differ in How They Made It to the Top?" Doctoral thesis by Terrance William Fitzsimmons, University of Queensland, September 2011]

I recently found myself asking how much is enough? I actually asked myself aloud: "When will I have given enough to the Salt Mine? When will I be able to participate in the lives of my children?"

I have no burning desire to be the CEO but it appears that I have most, if not all, of the "necessary traits." It is those very traits that haunt me and make me wonder when enough really is enough and whether I am good enough.

Food for thought, as my friend's Mum put it . . . food for thought.

45 Minutes in Beijing

October 2012
Beijing, China

The following is written in the third person because, at this point in time, I often found myself sitting in the dark examining my life. On a few occasions, I captured those thoughts on paper as though I was looking at myself and my life from the outside.

She left her hotel at 6:15 that morning. It had already been a long week. Beijing is much harder for Westerners than Shanghai, and she was certainly having a harder time in Beijing than she ever did in Shanghai. The days were long and the nights seemed longer, particularly without her husband. She'd been going at this pace for months now and it was beginning to take its toll.

Like most days, she finally shut down her computer at 9:15 p.m. Everyone else had long ago left the office. She shut the lights off and headed for the elevator. She knew it would be tough to get a taxi; it had been difficult all week. But she had struck up a bit of a friendship with the building's doorman and he had taken pity on her. A smile can go a long way she had learned and when required, she could pull it out and make it work. Getting home at the end of a long day seemed worth the extra dose of "charm."

On Monday, she was able to get a taxi after waving down four or five and agreeing to pay 100 RMB for a trip that should cost 20 RMB at most. But tonight she was rushing out the door — if leaving at 9:15 p.m. can be called rushing. Her family had flown in that evening and checked into the suite she had arranged for them. She wanted to see them.

As she left the building, she smiled at the doorman and he escorted her out the door to the gathering of taxis at the side of the building. Not surprisingly, no taxi wanted the short trip to her hotel. Even with her inconsequential knowledge of Chinese, she knew they wouldn't take her because it "wasn't on *their* way home." This is a common excuse used to avoid unwanted fares in Beijing, particularly with Westerners.

But, she just wanted to go to the hotel and fall into bed with her husband. So she held up 200 RMB, smiled and waited. The doorman laughed and shouted something in Chinese that she didn't understand but made clear that this woman was willing to pay big for the 12-minute ride to the Park Plaza Hotel next to Tiananmen Square, where her children were jumping on the beds and her husband was checking whether the Club Level bar was still open.

Minutes later, she was in the back seat of a black sedan headed to her hotel. She leaned her head back and shut her eyes. It really had been a long week and she knew exactly how she wanted to unwind. He was just 12 minutes away. His warm, strong arms. Their soft little kisses and hugs. She missed them. "Travel sucks," she thought to herself. She needed a break. Or maybe she was just starting to break. She pushed the thought from her mind and replaced it with a vision of the man who makes her feel warm every time he turns the corner.

She was pulled violently from her reverie before she even realized that the car had stopped. The door suddenly swung open, an arm reached in and tore her bag from her arms, then her purse and, finally, wrestled her out of the car. There were people everywhere screaming in Chinese. "What the hell?!" she thought. The taxi driver had been yanked from the vehicle as well. Her head was spinning. Was this her hotel? What was happening?

As they opened her purse and grabbed her passport, her senses kicked in. These were undercover Chinese police officers and something was wrong, very wrong. They had her belongings, her computer, her passport and her. The taxi driver was being interrogated on the other side of the car. No one spoke a word of English.

Three of them kept screaming at her in Chinese. She called and waved frantically to the hotel concierge, to no avail. She clearly needed a translator. Was she being arrested? This was her hotel. If she could only move inside, she would feel more comfortable. She felt vulnerable in the open with these officers, which she now realized also included uniformed men. A crowd was gathering.

Desperately trying to get the concierge's attention but failing, she yelled into the lobby to the closest guest she could see and asked them to find the manager. "I'm a hotel guest." She was calm but nervous.

He was just 13 floors above her sitting comfortably in the suite she'd arranged for the children earlier that morning. She had a room — much smaller — but a nice room for them to share. She still had business to complete in Beijing while they would be touring. She just wanted them close.

After what seemed like hours but was surely only minutes, the hotel manager appeared. He seemed more concerned with the chaos in front of his building than helping her. But, then, Chinese police action in front of your establishment is not likely the image you want presented to your guests.

Still, she was a guest and she wanted some damn help. He wasn't getting the smile. He got the glare. The glare is universal too, and when he turned his attention to her he suddenly recognized her. She wasn't just any guest. She stayed there for a week almost every month and this time she also had booked a suite for her family. He took control and things began to calm down.

Another 30 minutes passed before she understood what had happened. The car she hired was not a legal taxi. She was not under arrest but she was a foreigner, which made the driver's crime worse or, more accurately, more expensive for him. The hotel manager translated the police documents for her, she signed them and retrieved her passport. She finally made her way up to her room on the 5th floor to drop off her bags. Then she hurried off to the 13th floor where her three children and husband were waiting.

"Mom, what took you so long . . . "

It was just 45 minutes in Beijing . . . unfortunately, it was my 45 minutes.

Tomorrow is another day . . .

If It's Forbidden

October 2012
Beijing, China

After the United Nations skirmish outside our hotel, Jack and I made our way to the bar for a few drinks. As we are nearing the mid-point of our China experience, I am nearing my college-level drinking experience or worse, Jack's college-level drinking experience. Frankly, I don't think it has anything to do with China. The source is surely North American, but that is another blog entirely.

The Forbidden City

In truth, Jack and the kids joined me in Beijing mid-week because I've been traveling and working so much that I only see them on Sunday night and then not again until Friday night. I almost never make dinner with the family during the week. When I do, it's only for a few minutes before I have to start doing conference calls. It's a very common expat experience but one that has consequences for all of us. So the big guy, in his infinite wisdom, said "screw it" and pulled the kids out of school a few days early and got on a plane to Beijing. Good man!

I arranged my day so I could work early and very late and do a few calls while still finding time to be with the kids and Jack. I was nearing complete exhaustion trying to be "wonder woman" but I wasn't going to miss out on this experience with them, even if it killed me — or turned me into a hard drinking woman — as the country song goes. And, let's face it, my life is sometimes just like those country songs. My dog won't even greet me at the door anymore!

After putting in a few hours of work while Jack and The Terrible Trio had breakfast in the "Club," we were finally off to Tiananmen Square with our lovely and line-skipping guide, Sunny. (Ah, yes, the line-skipping guide, I am never without one these days.) Because the national Mid-Autumn Festival holiday was upon us, the Square was in full dress uniform. All of Beijing was decked out in its "holiday best." Absolutely gorgeous.

Unlike most of my visits to Beijing, we had blue skies. Blue skies are so rare in Beijing that you could likely count the number of sunny days in a year on your fingers. It is seriously "foggy" in the words of the Chinese government (that's smog to you and me). The opportunity to see The Forbidden City in full color was really exciting. My last visit there was a 60-minute sprint through the 980-room complex, a race to find a cab back to the hotel and off to the airport, in December — *BRRR COLD!*

Our guide explained the different bridges that offered entry to The Forbidden City and that your rank in life determined which bridge you would take. The central bridge was reserved for the Emperor (much like today's Executive Elevator). Even the Emperor's wife had to use one of the outer bridges. (I won't comment.)

The Emperor's bridge entrance to The Forbidden City.

Each bridge further from the center denoted your lowering status. We took the center bridge and that is when I said, "I really can't believe we are here and walking where the Emperors walked . . . here in the Forbidden City." The slap came fast and furious: "Mom, if it's so forbidden, then why is it so easy to get in?" Jane dead panned.

Jane gets her sarcasm and smart ass attitude straight from her Dad. They are both reserved, quiet individuals, so you never see the verbal slap coming, which makes it even better. The two of them can really go at each other, it's hysterical. She smiled broadly, which is rare these days. Have I mentioned she's a soon-to-be 15-year-old mystery woman?

Allow me to digress for a moment. One of my favorite areas of The Forbidden City is the building of rooms for the "retired concubines." No leftovers for the next Emperor, and no one outside the City wants a "used concubine" either. What's an Emperor to do? Build a retirement center, of course. When I picture all the "retired" concubines running around The Forbidden City, I just can't help but smile. I am sure Jack would have been trying to climb the wall!

After making our pilgrimage to one of Beijing's best-known sites — The Temple of Heaven — Jane suggested we ask for a refund. "This is false advertising. This isn't a temple, it's a platform." Technically, she may be right. There is no actual building; instead, it is a very high "platform." I did not ask for a refund.

We had a great time in Beijing. We walked ancient streets, climbed to the top of the "Drum Tower" that was used to tell time in ancient China, visited the Summer Palace and learned the history of the Dragon Lady. "Mom, I didn't know you lived here." She is quick.

After two days of Beijing, we headed 65 miles outside the City into the villages surrounding

The Temple of Heaven . . . platform.

the Ming Dynasty Era of the Great Wall. The kids traded in their hotel suite for the "Barracks." Jane got out of the car, looked around the "barracks" and remarked, "I told you, I don't like nature."

Yep, the next couple of days should be fun . . . so glad I am not missing this!

Banging Our Heads On The Wall . . .

October 2012
Outside Beijing, China

The following is written in the third person because, at this point in time, I often found myself sitting in the dark examining my life. On a few occasions, I captured those thoughts on paper as though I was looking at myself and my life from the outside.

The cold was just outside the blanket. It was cold, dark and cold. It was also dark, cold and dark. All bundled together in one bed, they looked so peaceful, it seemed almost cruel to wake them. Although she was nearly gleeful at the thought of it, she wouldn't wake them yet. She wanted just a few more minutes to herself, clinging to the darkness and the cold — it was becoming her blanket. She felt it to her bones and it was oddly comforting.

The sleeping quarters were dubbed the "Barracks" by our host, William Lindesay. He is a Great Wall historian and an archaeologist. He described the barracks accommodations as "basic" and, by any definition, they

Bedtime in the "barracks."

were. Each room was equipped with a table to place your pack upon, a platform bed (think concrete covered in a thin "mattress"), a blanket and a pillow. No sink. No toilet. No shower.

There was a communal sink that accommodated up to five at one time. The toilets weren't exactly outhouses but they were outside. And if you wanted a shower, there was a basin you could fill up and a wash cloth left on your bed. Perfect.

The single platform bed held three to five people, so she and her husband snuggled with the three children until they were warm and nearly asleep. Magic, she thought. The food was authentic and prepared by local village people who helped at the barracks. It was perfect, honest and simple, which was everything her life was not at that moment.

The Barracks were intentionally basic. This was merely the launching point for the real attraction — The Great Wall. And, not the restored and repaved Wall that most Beijing visitors see, but The Wall as it exists centuries after being abandoned. The Wall is wild and untamed and visitors must prepare to sacrifice a little bit to conquer just a small slice of it. That sacrifice began with a 4 a.m. wake up call and 20 minutes to get ready.

She stepped outside her room and breathed deeply, filling her lungs and her soul with the cold air and dark night. She could sense a change in herself but couldn't place it yet.

It felt a bit like camp all over again. Camp was more than 30 years ago. Had it really been that long since she'd gone on a serious hike? Where did the time go?

By rights, at 4 a.m. she should have been exhausted. But she was inexplicably invigorated. She couldn't wait to get started.

As they began the walk, William explained that if everyone in the six surrounding villages was home that early morning, the inhabitants numbered 600 people. With the five interlopers, tally up to 605. In a country with more than 1.3 billion people, this was pretty isolated.   She looked again at the black early morning sky, speckled with stars so white and bright that she could imagine navigators of long ago finding their way home by the stars alone.

"Could I find my way home?" she wondered aloud to no one in particular. "What is home?" she thought as they walked through the village — not where, but what.

With the Mid-Autumn Festival moon full and bright, they didn't need their torches (aka flashlights) as they made their way through the small village. It was quiet, and they walked with reverence. They turned on their torches as they approached the hillside and the woods to help guide their footsteps over rocks, tree roots and wet leaves. She'd given up her belief in a "higher power" years earlier but these were the kind of moments that always made her wonder. The tranquil beauty of the dawn. The majesty of the mountains. She was a sunrise girl; she liked the sunrise because at sunrise anything was still possible. She wondered if she still believed even that . . .

The hike was rigorous.   Steep, unstable rock challenging every step. Narrow pathways through thick brush and woods forcing you back as you moved forward. Ledges with such steep drops she wondered if it was too much for the children, especially Bella at only 10. But, never did she consider abandoning the hike. Never.

She knew they could do it and she felt she had to do it. This wasn't about hiking The Great Wall of China anymore, this was about clearing her head, leaving it all behind and focusing on a task that had nothing to do with her career but everything to do with who she was or maybe still could be.

The sunrise seemed to lift the darkness in her head. The world was falling away — the world of deadlines, expectations, and unfulfilled promise — and she could feel herself breathe again.

It took more than an hour to reach the jumping on point of The Wall. Her husband went first and helped each of the children move up and onto The Wall. Expectation filled her as she climbed up and took his hand. He smiled at her and said, "It's worth it." What he really meant was "you're worth it." He hated heights and, yet, here he was climbing thousands of meters in the dark on steep and unsteady slopes because she told him she thought it would "help."

Sunrise along the Great Wall of China.

Time stood still as the pink and orange hued sky revealed the waking villages below them. Smoke rose slowly from burning stoves. The air was so clear and bright that the buildings of Beijing were visible in the distance paled amidst the amazing landscape in the foreground.

As she looked out over the vista, she felt it slowly creep away. The haze in her head and the darkness in her soul were drifting away. She hugged her girls and even her son allowed her one public hug on the mountain. Then she found him, waiting for her as he always has. He smiled and put his arm around her. "This helps?" he quipped.

She'd been banging her head against a wall for years, or so it seemed. Maybe she just needed to trek a wall instead of bang her head on one to remember why she had done all of this.

She knew it wouldn't last; it couldn't last. It was, however, a wonderful reminder that she still existed inside somewhere. A reminder that she was, in fact, "worth it."

Maybe middle age in the Middle Kingdom was exactly what she needed.

Another Year Older & Deeper In Debt

October 2012
Shanghai

One morning I got up and went to work and when I came home my baby had turned 15. Sound familiar?

For me, that morning was *this* morning. My "sunshine" is 15. Fifteen. That's a 1 with a 5 after it. She is a high school freshman, which you can easily miss here in China because of the way the International School is set up. Jane is on the same campus as the primary students but in a different building.

She gets on the same bus as her younger brother and sister. She wears a uniform that looks a bit like Harry Potter fashion — yes, there is a tie. But there is no "homecoming." She attends the British International School and I don't think cricket renders itself to floats, homecoming queens or dances. But, I could be wrong.

Shopping for a 15-year-old girl is never easy. It could be a bit more interesting here, however, because you can take her to the fabric market and have a coat, dress or a great pair of jeans made to order. Maybe go to the "underground market" and let her buy a pair of 'Chanel' sunglasses and an 'Hermes' bag. Or, we could go to the pearl market and get a bracelet to match her necklace. But, we aren't doing any of those things.

Fact is, we have no gift for her today. Instead, we're letting her skip school and we are spending the day with her. Fortunately, she still wants to spend time with us (or, at least, we think she still does). I have no idea what we'll do together. It might be a walk in Century Park and taking pictures with Dad. It might be hanging out at her favorite coffee shop (she doesn't drink coffee, she hangs out). It might be going to see the "movie lady" and then watching movies all day. Or, it could be nothing more than wearing our PJs all day. I really have no idea. The point is we'll be doing whatever it is together.

Happy Birthday, Jane!

Like any parent, I want the world and more for my children. But for me, the "more" is actually less. Yes, I want them to see the world but I want them to enjoy it; not conquer it. There is a big difference.

Jane is a third of my age today. She's lived a third of the life that I have lived but in some ways she has lived so much more, so much better and so much richer a life than me. In the year since she turned 14, Jane has been to Thailand, Vietnam, Malaysia, Russia, Germany, France, Austria, England and, of course, China. In a few months, she will go to Hawaii. She'll follow that this summer with a few weeks in Italy. And, if we can swing it, there will be a trip to Cambodia and the Philippines in there too. Not bad for 15.

Jane performed in leading roles in two wonderful stage productions this past year, learned to speak just enough Chinese to order pizza over the phone and made friends from around the world. She also learned the importance of being resilient. She is a teenage girl, which is never easy, but when your Mother drags you out of your comfort zone, away from your friends and family and forces you to move to China, well, it's a bit harder. There is good stuff too but when you're 15, the good stuff doesn't stick like the bad stuff. It's just the way it is.

This past year has been hard on her as it is on most teenage expats. (Frankly, it's hard on everyone.) It has been hard to watch her struggle and harder still to find the means to help her. At this age, you can't kiss the boo boo and make it all better. Some things can't be "fixed" but they can be "shared." Jane knew this long before I did.

Moving to China is huge. You just can't overstate it. Yes, the culture is different. The language is a barrier. The food can be challenging. All of this is true, but it is the little things that push you over the edge — things like ice. There is no ice maker in our fridge and no ice trays or even room for ice trays in our freezer. If you want ice, you have it delivered. Otherwise, you go without ice. And, if your favorite thing to drink is ice cold water — well you get the picture.

Silly? Maybe it is silly in a world where ice drops out of the door whenever you want it, but not in a world where you are dealing with a strange and mystifying world culture, a different and unique school culture and a language you can't decipher whether it is written or spoken. And, just to rub salt in the wound, you can't even call your best friend when you need her because she is sleeping when you are awake. This is when the silly becomes the earth shattering and perspective is hard to find, at least at 15.

So, it might seem like we should have a wrapped box with a really terrific present inside for her. But, we don't. Time. We are giving her time. And, not just today. In order to give her (and her brother and sister) "more," I will be doing less. Because, as it turns out, less is more. And sharing the experience is more important than fixing it.

Perspective.

I still wonder if coming to China was the right choice for our little clan of five. I don't exactly regret the decision. It's more like a debt. I won't know for years if the gamble paid off or if I still owe. As Jane turns a year older, I feel a bit deeper in debt — to her, to all of them and even to myself. Time is both a cruel master and the purest and most generous of all gifts.

Passion

October 2012
Shanghai

Prior to my leave of absence, my human resources professional asked me what is it that I like to do; what makes me want to get up in the morning and come to the office? Well, at this moment, it is the fear of not being able to put food on the table that makes me get out of bed and show up at my assigned work station. But, when asked: What do I like to do? What do I want to be when I grow up? What am I passionate about? Well, the answer (sadly) is that I have no idea.

As it turns out, I am not alone (I asked around). Interestingly, though, I found that more women than men gave me the "I don't know" answer and most of those women didn't feel very fulfilled in what they were doing. I wasn't talking to the cleaning staff, here. I was asking really high-powered women who — like me — have children and are married and are carrying all or most of the bread-winning load. They get up and go to work because that is what they have been doing every day for the last 10, 15 or 20 years. I imagine some of the men might secretly be feeling the same thing.

Looking a little closer to home, though, there is plenty of passion and a few people who know exactly what they like to do. Jack loves wine. He writes a great blog, attends wine tastings, hosts wine tastings and — even in Shanghai — has surrounded himself with oenophiles.

If that wasn't enough, and apparently it's not, he has taken up photography too. This has incidental benefits to the rest of us, though at times we find it annoying when he is standing in the same spot on the beach seemingly forever photographing a snail coming out of its

Tyrrell's vineyard in the Hunter Valley, Australia.

shell — yes, imagine how quickly that happens! Of course, we love to complain about it but we love the results even more. He takes a photography class and managed to buy a camera that must have a college degree — it was *that* expensive.

And, now, he is even taking intensive Chinese language courses. Seriously, did you really think my husband was a Renaissance Man? Well, don't let the beer, football and t-shirt wardrobe fool you. He is.

Jane has always had passion for the theatre. We first took her to New York for her 8th birthday and we saw three Broadway shows that year. In the years following, it grew to five shows in three days! She has gone back almost every year and, because we were in Shanghai for her last birthday, we hit London on the way home for the summer. She has taken drama seriously now for a couple of years. She writes, helps direct, acts and even sings. She's currently playing the role of the sarcastic principal in *Grease*. How fitting.

Lyceum Theatre, London

Henry is a typical boy who loves all sports and plays many. He also has a passion for the theatre and is quite a good writer. He was in a play last year and will be in the primary school's play this spring - stay tuned! And, Bella swims. My little Olympian in the making.

Me? I work. I like wine. I like photography. I like the theatre. I like sports, especially football and baseball. I like these things, but am I passionate about them the way my family is passionate about them? Henry and Jack are up at 4 a.m.

Henry is an American boy in China who plays rugby for a British School.

watching the Tigers and I sleep until at least 5 and then fall asleep again.

I love tasting wine with Jack but when I travel on business, I call him when they hand me the wine list. I actually called him from the table in Sao Paulo, Brazil once. Why? I have no idea what kind of wine I like, but Jack does. Love that about him!

I do love to cook, or I did. I can't remember the last time I really cooked and, let's face it, the oven we have in China is not exactly reliable. Cooking here is more of a frustration than a passion. I loved to travel before I started trekking the globe for business and it became a pain in the ass. I like to read but I'm too tired most nights to read anything, even a magazine. I have many excuses and having a passion means no excuses or it isn't a passion.

I've been thinking about this question — What makes you want to get out of bed and come to work in the morning? It is a good question. That is what I need to be doing — something that makes me want to get out of bed. Now, if I could just figure out what that is . . .

Bella chases Olympic dreams.

快車道 ... 慢車道 *(Fast Lane ... Slow Lane)*

October 2012
Shanghai

You hit middle age and you look back and wonder about the road you didn't take, the opportunities you squandered, the time you spent unwisely. I suppose some may look back and find the road, the opportunities and the time spent worthy. I look back and wonder, question and find a bit of regret.   This is not to say that I am unhappy with my life. I am, actually, quite lucky.

I am married to a man who loves me despite my many attempts to make that difficult over the years. He has been my touchstone for more than 25 years. Through the wonder of science, we have three amazing children. They are miracles of science and determination but they are also wondrous, brilliant and bewildering creatures of some other worldly portal that I cannot fathom. I have enjoyed a successful career (for a woman) though it has come at a cost. And, this is where the questions of middle age arise. So while we have been in the Middle Kingdom, I have been dealing with middle age . . .

Most mornings (I can't say every morning) I go to the gym and run, bike, swim or lift. Several years ago, I did a few triathlons and I've rediscovered my love of the pool. The running not so much — the half marathon was enough to make clear to me that running was not

Fast Lane

something I enjoyed. I endure it but don't enjoy it. I like the pool. I like to be surrounded by water, the silence of the swim, the focus required to keep from drowning and the smooth and rhythmic nature of it appeals to me. I've always been a water girl. Swim or ski — swim every time.

Usually, I enter the pool while it is still dark outside. The pool is 5 floors up and surrounded by windows. The darkness melts away slowly as I swim. Both the literal darkness and the figurative darkness. My head clears in those 50 minutes. Focus on the stroke, don't let the mind wander. Focus.

On this particular morning, however, I was not rushing around. I was not racing to get into one of the lanes, I was actually taking my time. And, because of that I noticed something. Was it new or had it been there for weeks already? I had no idea. But it stopped me in my tracks.

It is funny how things can suddenly pop up and completely resonate with you, with where you are at that moment in life and the decisions you are trying to make, even if you don't really know it at the time. The signs above the two swim lanes sum it up: Fast Lane or Slow Lane.

I know the Fast Lane. I've lived there for years. Early morning workouts, followed by 12- or 14-hour days, rushing home in the hopes of not missing bedtime, and after tucking the last one in for the night getting on the phone for conference calls and finally falling into bed long past a reasonable bedtime.

The Slow Lane is less familiar to me. Structure and purpose. A sense of purpose, a raison d'être. Can the slow lane provide that or is the slow lane code for "also ran" or "quitter" or "not good enough?" I never picked the "flexible schedule" option because I feared that it would be seen as a lack of commitment. Instead, I purchased extra vacation - at a premium price - but a far more discrete means of trying to "have it all."

Fact is, I am frustrated. The Fast Lane has been and continues to be frustrating and the faster you go the faster they expect you to go until you just can't (or maybe won't) go anymore. And that is where I find myself today. I can't keep going or, more accurately, I don't want to.

When, I wonder, will I have given enough to the behemoth?   When will my commitment be evident? When will all of the hard work and late nights be rewarded? When I am dead at my desk?

Slow Lane

No. They'll just call the Ayi to take the body away and replace it with a new one.

If the Fast Lane is so frustrating, then why am I in it? Is it ambition? Is ambition bad? Is it for money? Is money bad? Is it for recognition? Is recognition bad? Why do I expect a different result? I've been banging away like this for years and getting exactly nowhere. Well, I got to China so not exactly nowhere but you know what I mean. From my chair, the ceiling is still made of glass and the glass is bullet proof.

And, are there only two choices? Fast and slow? The road to "company officer" or the road to "also ran." Are there no choices in between? What about valued contributor, respected expert and colleague? Did the road really fork in only two directions?

While I don't know the answer to the question, my suspicions are that you are binned in one of two boxes; and, once binned, you are boxed.

On that particular morning, I picked the Slow Lane . . . but since that morning, I have opted to swim in neither lane. You see, there are only two roped swim lanes at the pool but you can swim outside the lap lanes where there is no label. I don't like the choices or maybe I can't decide. I don't know, really. But, each morning when I approach the pool, I smile and take a moment to consider where I will swim.

What Comes Next?

October 2012
Shanghai

The first week of October is a national holiday in China. Most expats leave the country during this holiday week and travel. We stayed home.

The week before, I was in Beijing for business and Jack and the kids met me there. We saw some sights in Beijing and took a hike on The Great Wall.

October really is the best time of year in China. The weather is warm, sunny and slightly breezy. The wind helps keep the air moving and there is more blue sky than at almost any other time in the year. So, why not enjoy it?

And, we did.

We sat on our rooftop deck and watched fireworks from Century Park. We walked the Bund, had dinner at Mr. & Mrs. Bund one evening and watched fireworks over the river. We played pick-up sticks at Bistro Burger in Puxi and watched people pass by on the street. We went to a friend's house for dinner and watched fireworks from Century Park (again). We watched movies late into the evening, slept late, walked the dog and did nothing at all.

Just before this holiday, I began a two-week leave of absence from work. The pace in China is grueling and the toll on me and the family had reached a critical point. I return to the office soon.

What comes next, I wonder?

I finally have a parent identification card for our children's school. I know, it's almost November of Year 2. Still, I went and got one while I was on leave. I used it too.

I went to Bella's swim practice, picked Jane up from play rehearsal, took cupcakes to school for a teacher's birthday at Bella's request, watched football practice and even met a teacher.

The "ah ha" moment, however, was when I received a text message from one of our children that made my heart break. I never would have gotten that text if I hadn't taken time off because (1) our child would not have wanted to "bother me" at work, (2) if our child had texted me, chances are that I would have seen it too late to be useful, and (3) if I had seen it, I am not sure that I would have left the office. More likely, I would have called Jack. This time, I went and sat on the cold concrete step outside the school auditorium for three hours just so our child knew I was there — no need to talk — I was just "available." Truly and completely available.

Brenda Barnes was #10 on *Fortune's* 50 Most Powerful Women in Business list in 2009. In May 2010, she suffered a stroke, fell off the list and resigned from her job as CEO of Sara Lee. Not long after, her daughter, who had recently graduated from the University of Notre Dame with a good job, decided to leave her job and help her mother recover from her stroke. I read this story in this year's edition of *Fortune's* 50 Most Powerful Women in Business. What struck me was that in 1997, Brenda Barnes quit her job as CEO of Pepsi-Cola North America to spend more time with her children because they needed her. Now, she needed them and they were doing the very same thing for her.

When I read this article I was on the plane from Beijing, and I wondered if my children would do that for me? I wondered if I had given them any reason to. That was the moment I stopped feeling guilty for asking for the two-week leave of absence, and committed myself to really thinking about what is important to me. I still have no answer to the question of what makes me want to get up each morning and go to work? I think I may have burnt out. Or, at least, stalled.

I am worried that I won't be able to turn it off when I go back to the office. Will I fail to honor the very boundaries that I am complaining others will not honor? We teach people how to treat us. I have rarely said "no." When asked to take on an assignment, handle a meeting, prepare a presentation, speak at an event or fly around the world for a 12-hour meeting, I have done it. Until just a few weeks ago when, for the first time, I refused to get on a plane — I said "no." We teach people how to treat us. I want to be treated differently, and I want to treat my family better.

I did this with the help of a therapist. I am not embarrassed to say it — my life is complicated and at times overwhelming. Do you really think it is easy to be a "senior" woman in a Fortune 10 Company? Do you think it is easy to be part of a team trying to build a business in Asia Pacific and Africa? Do you think moving your family to China for your career doesn't come with some complications? Do you believe that I have no demons haunting me at night? No, you don't because you have your own complications, your own challenges and your own secrets and demons. We all do.

When I said no, the reaction was swift and deafening. It reaffirmed what I already knew. I was the dependable cog in the wheel. "No" was not in my repertoire. Pile it on and she will get it done. Someone once wrote in my "360 review" that I have an amazing capacity for work. What this person was saying is that I am a workaholic, a mule. I am a fool. In some ways, I feel taken advantage of but I let it happen. I am responsible because I allowed it. We teach people how to treat us.

I am trying to use this break as a means of altering expectations. How? I don't have that figured out yet. My first goal is to have dinner three times a week (not including Saturday and Sunday) with my children and husband. Can you believe that I had to make that a goal? Pathetic, truly.

So, what comes next? Only time will tell . . .

The Expat Amble . . .

October 2012
Shanghai

On one of my last mornings off before returning to the office from my "leave," I met the "guy-tais" (trailing spouses of working women — a rare breed in China) for coffee. It was a real eye-opener!

Jack and I walked our children to the bus stop, kissed the girls and I pretended that I had never seen Henry before in my life. I mean, how uncool to have your mother walk you to the bus stop and try to kiss you, especially when you are a full grown man of 11.

"Come on, woman, what are you thinking?" was the look he gave me from under his baseball cap. "Seriously!"

The bus is not your typical yellow school bus. This is the Tour Group Bus. Plush seats, seat belts, nice windows with curtains in case the sun is too strong. There may even be video for all I know. This is not the bus in which I rode to school. There's a bus Ayi who checks them on board, assures they are secured and confirms the afternoon return plan — are they coming home on the 3:30 bus or the 4:15 extra-curricular activity bus? Very organized.

We stand there for a few minutes and I start to feel antsy. Why are we standing here? They are on the bus. The chances that they stage some sort of bus coup seem remote. Can't we go for coffee now? I am literally tapping my foot at this point. Jack is smirking at me. He knows that in my head I am ticking off the list:

Task #1: Kids on bus. Check.

Task #2: Walk to Baker & Spice. Delayed.

Task #3: Order coffee. On standby due to delay of Task #2.

Task #4: Chat with friends. See above.

Task #5: Check email. See above.

And so on . . .

Jack is not in this mode at all. He is in no hurry. There is no reason to rush. "I usually wait until the bus leaves but I can see that is hard for you, so we can walk now," he says to me almost mockingly. Whatever, I think to myself.

A few minutes later I realize that I am standing at the corner and Jack is not standing next to me. No, he is a good block behind me. We are going to miss the light. Get a move on. What is taking him so long? I am literally going crazy but I am being very cool about it. Not!

"Come on!" I say just loudly enough. And he keeps plodding along. Nothing gets under his skin. He just moves at his own pace, which happens to be the pace of a freakin' glacier. Finally, after a near ice-age, we arrive at Baker & Spice (it takes all of 6 minutes). I secure the table, enough seats for the group (5), and send Jack off to place our order. I even ask him to place the others' orders so we won't have to wait. He shakes his head. He won't be placing any other orders, I can just tell.

After a millennium (maybe 8 minutes), the others arrive. First is Nigel, followed about 2 minutes later by Sue and Scott. Just as I am about to ask what took them so long, Sue asks Nigel how he beat them. Nigel's response "I power walked." Before I can say a word, Jack says he'd love to see that and Nigel says it wasn't hard, "just a bit quicker than the usual expat amble."

"Expat amble?" I ask. Everyone laughs.

After the kids are on the bus, there isn't any reason to rush around anymore. So, the expats amble through their day. Or rather, the trailing-spouse expats take their time walking to coffee, take even longer drinking their coffee, and sit and talk for a bit. You get the picture. They have 'a lot' to do but they aren't in a hurry to do it. They'll get to it, eventually.

Expat cooking classs with Nigel, Ayis & Georgia.

Some of the pressing issues for these expats:

- Talking to the staff (telling their Ayi what they need done that day from laundry to dinner)
- Making tee times for golf
- Scheduling the next wine tasting event
- Struggling through a Pilate's class or, at least, considering the possibility of struggling through a Pilate's class
- Going for a massage — foot massage, full-body massage, stone massage (decisions, decisions)
- Going to Chinese class, doing Chinese homework, going for more coffee or a beer to practice Chinese or — my personal favorite — going on a field trip to a restaurant to practice ordering food in Chinese
- Going to photography class, doing photography homework, planning an outing to do more photography homework
- Taking the kids to football, baseball, soccer, cricket or swim practice where there always seems to be a bar nearby
- Thinking about doing any of the above
- Napping due to the exhaustion caused by thinking about doing any of the above.

It can be so overwhelming for these poor fellows and Sue — the honorary guy-tai. Nigel even sets his alarm for 2:45 p.m. each day. He is worried he might nap through school pick-up time. Pressure.

This explains why Jack isn't planning our vacations, doing any of the research on Cambodia, Vietnam or anywhere else. He is far too busy already with his guy-tai duties.

Truth be told, none of this is possible without him or Nigel or Sue or the other "trailing spouses" who make "home" run. It is a bit easier here for them in Shanghai because they have help: their Ayi, their driver and incredible delivery services. I am jealous. They are enjoying the expat experience far more than me.

Jack and his "crew" are still ambling their way through Shanghai and other parts of China but soon they will be

Golf, anyone?

strutting. As I understand it, there is a hierarchy in the tai-tai (wives) and guy-tai world. And, you move from the expat amble to the expat strut once you've been in China for a year or so.

The strutters are superior to the amblers, or so I am told. I had no idea that the life of a guy-tai was so hierarchical, politically charged and stressful. Just hearing about it made me want to take a nap.

Competitive Fires

November 2012
Shanghai

I want to sleep until I'm not tired anymore. That isn't my line. I think it belongs to Kid Rock. The sentiment, however, is mine. Tired. I am tired.

Thing is, I really can't sleep. Haven't been able to sleep for months now. I even have pills to help me sleep, which they did for the first few weeks, but then time passed and I went back to not sleeping. So, the alarm *doesn't* go off but I still get out of bed.

It's an odd feeling to be truly tired and yet have an urgent need to do something — all at the same time. I think this might have something to do with why I feel like I am going crazy. To silence the competing needs, I get into the water — the pool, actually. I swim. Swimming makes me tired, physically tired. My arms, my legs, my core — all of me. It also focuses my mind in a way that forces it to shut out all the extraneous crap. In the muted blue, cool liquid, it all falls away. It is just me and the water. Clarity. Silence. Peace.

But, you knew it couldn't last . . . this is my life we're investigating in this blog after all. My peace and tranquility were interrupted by a man with a whistle.

A woman was swimming in the "fast lane." He was pacing alongside with a whistle and a stopwatch. An actual whistle. He was actually blowing a whistle. It was loud. Very loud, in fact. It wasn't even

The pull of competition.

6 a.m. My muted blue, cool liquid was whistling. As I walked from the shower to the pool, the whistle taunted me.

There it was — right there in front me. My first test.

I stepped into the shower and let the warm water rush over me. I put on my swim cap, walked to the "slow lane," and jumped into the pool. Goggles in place. I splashed the water over me and then started. I have a routine. Actually, I have several versions of the routine. Still, it is a routine and as I submerged myself into the water, I said aloud to myself, "Just do your swim."

I swim several laps at a very even and relaxing pace to warm up. This is where the world starts to fall away. Slowly, I catch the water in my hand and pull it back to move myself forward. Kicking at a moderate, even pace. I even count 1-2-3-4-5-6. Repeat.

When I begin to feel the water — actually feel it, the texture and weight of it — I'm ready to increase the work. I might grab a kick board and kick for several laps, working just my legs at a quicker pace until they feel a bit like Jello. Next, I move to the pull buoy and it's all arms. I may or may not add paddles or web gloves to work my shoulders and arms harder. Each morning depends on the night before, the day ahead, the demons to be exorcised.

I break down the stroke into bits. Focus on the bits. Fingertips dancing across the water as I lift my arm into the air, keeping the elbow high through the stroke. I count the strokes on each lap, finding the rhythm, clearing my head so there is nothing but the stroke, the water, the catch and the pull. Consistency. Pace. Rhythm.

It isn't until I've been through almost 40 minutes of breaking down and rebuilding the stroke that I am ready to actually *swim*. My muscles tired, the stroke requires more focus and discipline. And with the stroke put back together, I begin to glide through the water. Easy and smooth at first. Peacefully.

But on this morning, there was a woman next to me in the "fast lane." She was easily 15 years younger than me. Her workout followed a similar pattern. Her "coach" was pressing her to go harder, to keep moving, to push herself as hard as she could and he used his whistle to move her along. I tried to push it out of my head and focus on my routine.

"Just do your swim." I said it over and over in my head but as I came out of the flip turn I caught sight of her. She was just ahead of me. She was increasing her pace.

The whistle blew.

I can catch her. Just do your swim. I can catch her. Just do your swim.

Each of my workouts ends with laps that increase in speed until I can't swim any farther. I swim to the point of exhaustion — even if exhaustion strikes in the middle of the lane. I stop. I slow my pace, change my stroke and cool down. I stop.

But at the turn, I heard the whistle. I moved to the left side of the lane and felt the surge of adrenaline. I can do maybe 200 meters before I start to falter. I picked up the pace. I was making up ground. At the

Chinese fighting cricket: ready for battle.

next turn, I came off the wall with more force than I expected — she was mine. She had age on her side. She had a coach on her side. She had time and distance on her side. But I was not going to let her win. No freakin' way.

I overtook her at the wall and, when we came to the next turn, her coach blew his whistle. I kept going until I was exhausted. Finished my cool down and left the pool. She was still in the water when I hit the shower.

I returned to work last week with the goal of pacing myself and focusing more on our family. Seems I haven't quite figured out how to ignore the pull of competition in whatever form it may take. Pace. Balance. Call it what you want, I haven't figured it out.

It will be a challenge to keep to my pace in the slow lane when the fast lane is still moving . . . well, fast.

Are You Ready . . . For Some Football

November 2012
Shanghai

Football, futbol or footy . . . to be ready in China you had better plan ahead because you can't just play a pick-up game. No, you gotta plan it.

Henry plays American football at the Shanghai Rugby Club, where they also play futbol — aka soccer, Aussie Rules, footy or Australian Rules football. Call it what you will — it all involves a ball and your feet. They share the playing fields with baseball, cricket and rugby teams, so you have to plan ahead.

A dedicated group of Dads organizes leagues, runs practices, forms teams, teaches skills, schedules fields, orders uniforms, and arranges for an expat to buy replacement mouth guards when on a trip to the States. Shoulder pads, baseball gloves, batting helmets all have to be purchased over the summer and lugged back to Shanghai along with cleats, bats, hockey sticks, pucks and even Girl Scout badges.

On Sunday, after we've finished watching college football, we all get in the 'bus' and head to the Shanghai Rugby Club for some American-style football. The "stadium" is first class with a bar on the sideline complete with all the usual concessions — hot dogs, burgers, chicken tenders and even ice cream. We get two games — the Senior Dragons and the Junior Dragons. It feels a bit like college ball given the tailgate atmosphere and all the college sweatshirts walking around.

We had an "away" game a couple weeks ago at one of the local American International Schools and our sideline concession was there — grill and all. Our Dragon lost that week but he didn't seem to care — he loved playing. Last week his team tied. Equally happy.

I love football. I love baseball. I really love watching our son play. The effort it takes to organize these sporting opportunities for the children is tremendous. The Dads are coaches, teachers and referees. They move the chains, pop shoulders back into place, and pull jammed fingers out of their jam. From 12 until 4, it's Sunday afternoon in America — right here in Shanghai.

For the first time in the league's history, a game is scheduled to be played under the lights. I will be in Thailand, but on Friday night, November 2nd, it will be Friday Night Lights Football in Shanghai. I hate to miss it but that is also part of my experience as an expat in China. You miss a few things now and again.

I am going to miss this one, but I'll catch him next Sunday . . .

Are you ready for some football?

TMI . . . Times 50

November 2012
Bangkok, Thailand

Living in China, I don't know which song is at the top of the American music charts, or which book everyone is talking about. I don't even know who made the cast for this season's "*Dancing with the Stars.*" I could know this last one but, frankly, I don't really care. I am at a point in my life where I simply don't recognize the people on TV or in the movies anymore, unless it's Matt Damon or George Clooney.

Still, I'm not completely out of touch. So, last spring, while at our son's baseball game, my curiosity was peeked when I kept hearing the other Moms talk about some guy named Grey. You know exactly where this is going, don't you?! Of course, this is me, so you can expect we don't get there easily.

Christian Grey. For a good two weeks, I thought he was an expat living in Shanghai. I did. Thankfully, I didn't ask around about him — can you just imagine? "Excuse me, but do you know this Christian Grey fellow? I'm dying to meet him." Yes, as if I wasn't already a complete embarrassment to my children, this would certainly have done the trick, so to speak.

It took about a month — yes, I have a job, so it took about a month - to figure out that Christian Grey was a character in a book titled *Fifty Shades of Grey*. The mothers at baseball couldn't stop talking about this book. Since there isn't a Borders store around the corner (heck, I'm not sure there's a Borders around your corner any more), I had Jack download it to the Kindle. Yep, I asked my husband to download *Fifty Shades of Grey* to our daughter's Kindle.

I had no idea what the book was about, but I was getting on a plane to Thailand and I wanted something to read that wasn't work related. "Sure you do," was the coy response from my husband of 20 years. I looked at him not quite understanding the remark . . .

"I struggle to keep up with him because my wits have been thoroughly and royally scattered all over the floor and walls of elevator three in the Heathman Hotel."— E.L. James, *Fifty Shades of Grey*

I didn't know about Elevator Three when I asked Jack to download the book, I really didn't. He gave me the Kindle a few hours later and told me the book was under "ZZZZ" — it was hidden. "Why is it hidden?" I asked. He smiled. Oh, this was clearly too much fun for him. "You don't want your daughter to read this book, nor do you want her to know *that you are reading it.*" It was dripping now — his sarcasm was so thick it bordered on arrogance. I had no idea what was so damn funny.

"Whatever," I said.

Somewhere over the wilds of China on the way to Bangkok, I got it. I felt flush. Who was sitting next to me? Did he know what I was reading or, worse, what I was thinking?

I looked around business class, expecting the fasten seat belt sign to be illuminated saying "Yep, she's reading *Fifty Shades of Grey!*" Fortunately, when reading a book on a Kindle no one can see the jacket cover.

I got it now. I asked my husband to download my porn *and hide it* on our daughter's Kindle. Seriously. I was at once mortified and simultaneously desperate for a connection to Google. I needed a dictionary of sorts.

"There's a very fine line between pleasure and pain. They are two sides of the same coin, one not existing without the other." — E.L. James, *Fifty Shades of Grey*

I really didn't need Mr. Grey to explain to me the fine line between pleasure and pain. I did, however, need a phone line so I could call my husband and ask him if "fisting" was really what I thought it was . . . He couldn't stop laughing either. Look, I gave birth three times — and I'm just saying that those heads were, well, the size of fists — at least the size of my husband's fist!

So, there I was in Thailand. Not just anywhere in Thailand either but in Pattaya. "Walking Street," *the* place where you can find and have anything and almost anyone you desire.

Opportunity rarely knocks twice and, at this point in my life, what did I have to lose? I took my daughter's Kindle, my Google definitions and hit the Street. After all, if I needed instruction, I could certainly get it here. And, if I just wanted some toys, I could get those too. Mostly, I was curious.

I'm not going to tell you the details of my shopping list, or whether or not I purchased everything on that list, or whether it was just a fun way to kill some time. But I will tell you that $300 can go a long way and, if you've had a couple of cocktails, you can really have a good time shopping. And, why is that such a big deal, really? It was, in fact, a helluva lot of fun and an incredibly judgment-free experience.

Back in China, the conversation up on the roof with my girlfriends from somewhat less puritanical European and Oceania countries has become much more interesting after *Fifty Shades* and a few bottles of wine. At 45 and with 20 years of marriage under my belt, a little adventure isn't such a bad thing.

After all, when I arrived in China I dropped 30 pounds, cut my hair, bought a stable of wrap dresses and decided to always wear 4-inch heels to the office. Do you think I did that just for me? Or, for someone at the office? No, I did it for the man who waits for me to come home at night . . . he likes my shoes.

Along with that $300 that I may or may not have spent in Thailand, that self-transformation is one of the best things I ever did for *me*. I'm not just the bread winner, the mother, the lawyer, the director, the travel agent, the cog in the wheel of commerce. I am — still — a woman. A woman who wants to feel desirable and be desired.

There is nothing anti-feminist about that. Nothing is that simple. I am as complicated as the next creature. I don't want to be taken for granted, and I don't want to take my partner for granted either. I didn't re-make myself just for me. There are perks for both of us.

Fifty Shades didn't turn me into something new or different. Truth be told, I never finished the book. I couldn't get past the red room of pain. Hey, if that's your thing fine, but I have a thing about women being portrayed in such a submissive and dismissive way. Giving up control isn't a sign of weakness, but kneeling down with your head bowed awaiting your Master is just more than *this woman* can stomach. Still, those few chapters provided a needed distraction and the impetus to think differently about things I already thought about . . .

I remade myself long before I ever heard of Christian Grey. I did it on my own, on my own terms. As it turns out — like most women — I already knew what I wanted in and out of the bedroom.

"Oh . . . a lot of one and some of the other." — E.L. James, *Fifty Shades of Grey*

Anonymous Perspectives

November 2012
Melbourne, Australia

Most things do depend on your perspective. A picture taken from a particular vantage point can make it appear that angels are bowing to commerce, for example. And this might suggest that commerce has taken over even the purest of intentions, minds and souls.

When you work for a large conglomerate, you can often feel like you are nothing more than a cog in the wheel or you might think you are a rock star. It depends on your perspective.

To help with this issue of perspective, most large companies today use a tool known as the "360-Degree Feedback Process." It is a process by which the people to whom you report, those who report to you and others with whom you work provide anonymous feedback on your job performance. It is meant to be constructive. But, like most things, this too, depends on your perspective.

I never really liked this process at the Salt Mine because it comes too close to performance reviews. Part of the process requires that you self-nominate your raters. People tend to nominate people from whom

Angels of Ljuiazui bowing to commerce.

they expect overwhelmingly positive comments to bolster their own performance review. And, frankly, the anonymous option is crap in my opinion; it's gutless. People love to hide behind anonymity.

I have long suspected that I have been working with a bully. From the moment I met this guy, I have had a bad feeling about him. Admittedly, I find it very hard to work with him. I truly do. We've even had a conversation about it and, of course, we agreed "to start over." So, in the spirit intended by the 360-Degree process, I nominated him as one of my reviewers.

Given our track record, I didn't expect a glowing review. But I hoped for a modicum of professionalism in response to the olive branch I had extended. Nope. He's a bully and he put it in writing:

"You are lacking in both emotional resilience and professional maturity. You have created a work environment characterized by poor morale, fear, anxiety, and uncertainty. Your team is not empowered to make decisions. I never know what to expect from interactions with you. Sometimes you are rational and other times you are emotional, negative, and irrational. Your first priority in everything you do is to put yourself above all else including [the Salt Mine]. You speak negatively about others and don't realize how quickly this gets back to them. You are on your best behavior with Senior Executives and poor with everyone else.

You are unable to accept even the smallest amount of feedback for improvement. You attack the person providing the feedback and do not seem capable of self reflection.

You look to others to act rather than taking ownership of issues."

My Dad would tell me that he's jealous, intimidated and threatened by me. He would say that I am smart, beautiful and have more ability in my little finger than most people do in their entire body. Of course he would, he is my Dad! His perspective is skewed.

Still, when you read something as venomous as that, you begin to wonder if this is really worth it. You wonder if bowing to the power and seduction of commerce — like the angels — is worth the price you pay. You wonder if the glass shards that tear at your soul as you try to crack the ceiling are really worth the pain. What's on the other side? This guy? Seriously — this is the guy you let into the club? This is the kind of leadership that is valued?

And then . . .

You come home and find your oldest daughter back from a week in southern China with her classmates. Jane's trip was designed to bond the kids, show them a beautiful area of China and challenge them physically with hiking, rafting and biking. Something like "Outward Bound."

As it turns out, Jane enjoyed all the activities but the most rewarding part of her experience happened at a remote village where children invited them to play and even share a meal. Unable to really communicate with words, Jane still made friends.

She simply lit up when she told the story of how the girls were playing one of those clapping, singing "my mother had a whatever" games. Jane didn't know what they were saying in Chinese, but she knew the game and played it. She was a hit — as she would be — she is magic, after all.

It changes your perspective. The bully — to quote Taylor Swift — is never gonna be anything other than mean. Me, I get to be the Mother of Jane (and Henry and Bella). And, according to the rest

Commerce soars on the wings of an angel.

of my 360-Degree Report, I am also a pretty good person to work with and I'm good at what I do. More importantly, according to the woman who stopped by my office today, I am an inspiration to her and many other local Chinese women. That ain't bad.

So, while one vantage point makes it appear that even the angels have sold out; a different vantage point can make it appear that commerce is flying on the wing of an angel, perhaps even guided by her. For me, it is a means to an end . . . and listening to Jane talk about the children in the village makes it worth it. For today, anyway.

Merry Merry . . . Very Very

November 2012
Shanghai

In Shanghai, every "Western" restaurant is offering you a chance for a traditional American Thanksgiving and even a traditional Christmas Feast at top dollar. It will be nice, I am sure, but I have to work on Turkey Day and the kids go to school (British International School). The Brits don't seem all that excited about our American Thanksgiving for some reason.

We will celebrate Thanksgiving on the Saturday after Turkey Day. We will gather around the table with friends from Louisville. The meal will come from our Australian butcher — yes, an Aussie will prepare our turkey and deliver it to our door. Our friend "Louisville Slugger Sue" and I will make the "supporting" dishes but it won't exactly be like Thanksgiving in the States.

I know that my Mother is shaking her head as she reads this — her grandchildren are having a half-baked Thanksgiving. But hey, it is the best I can do. I will be in Taiwan the week of Thanksgiving, arriving in Shanghai on Friday.

Saturday morning, I'm squeezing in a final crown fitting for a root canal that I had to have this week. I should be done in time to get the side dishes prepared because we have to eat before Sue needs to leave for the Girl Scout sleepover. And on Sunday, well, I hit the skies again. India for a week and then straight to Australia. I return on December 10th.

I really don't want to do Thanksgiving at some restaurant or hotel. The only picture that comes to mind is from the classic Christmas movie: *A Christmas Story*. Yep, that one. You remember the scene at the end of the movie — just after they cut the duck's head off, the waiters come out to sing Christmas carols . . . "fa ra ra." I know this is culturally insensitive but that is what is rolling around in my head. I can't help it.

So, as you sit around complaining that Christmas decorations were out at Halloween, I envy you. If it were not for Spotify, we would not have any Christmas music at all. I didn't pack ornaments, Christmas music, nothing. (Never claimed I was mother of the year . . .) I really miss those Christmas classics like *Grandma Got Run Over By A Reindeer* and *Dominick the Donkey* . . . seems crazy, I know. Where is Andy Williams when you need him?

To ease our pain, at 3:30 p.m. Shanghai time on the 10th day of the 11th month, we did the unthinkable . . . we put up our Christmas tree. I am using the term loosely . . . the "Christmas tree" was purchased at IKEA. Henry is taller than this tree. We only had enough blinking lights for half of it and the lights play some nutty Chinese song. The star on top leans to the left and makes the tree look like it could topple

Bella decorates our little Shanghai Christmas tree.

over. It is not exactly a Charlie Brown Tree. It's more like a Charlie Brown Tree that had too much eggnog or watched too much Rachel Maddow on MSNBC. Yes, my tree leans to the left . . . just like me. I LOVE IT! I *LOVE* IT! I ***LOVE*** IT!!

I love it because our children dance around that tree like it was some enormous Blue Spruce.

Back in the States, my favorite family tradition is the Saturday after Thanksgiving. On Friday, we'd have two trees delivered to the house. They bring the smell of evergreen and pine and Christmas into the house. They usually arrive late in the evening from our former nanny's Christmas tree farm. Jessica, who now has two of her own, visits with the kids while we drag in the trees.

That Saturday afternoon I untangle the lights to go on the "main" tree. This is the family tree. I make dinner and cookies and we have hot chocolate and start the process of dressing the tree. It takes hours.

From the time they were in the womb, the children's grandparents have been purchasing unique and personal Christmas ornaments for them. The kids also collect them as we or they travel. Each ornament is marked with the year and their initials. We open these one by one by one.

The kids squeal in delight when some of their favorites appear — Batman, the taxi from New York, the music box. Each ornament is a story, a memory that comes to life as the owner recounts the story while placing the ornament on the tree. We even have ornaments that Jack and I made as children (because our Mothers were, and still are, Mothers of the Year!).

It is hours of pure joy for me. There is nothing I love more — it is Christmas. The Saturday after Thanksgiving is one of my favorite, and possibly my single most favorite, day of the year. The people I love most in the world sharing their lives with each other.

It is bliss. And, it will not last much longer. Jane is 15. We have not done it in 2 years . . . remember, I failed to pack the ornaments. But, I digress . . .

As the ornaments are unpacked, we are all waiting for the "first" one. The "ornament that started it all" as Henry would say. It's the ring box disguised as a Christmas ornament that held my engagement ring all those years ago in Chicago. Our basement studio apartment; we thought it was heaven on earth. Jack hung it on our Christmas tree that we bought the day before . . . a tradition born.

So, I beg your indulgence as we revel in putting up a Christmas tree on November 10th, playing all the Christmas music we can get our hands on, and starting our Secret Santa shopping before you've even ordered your Turkey Day pies. It had to be done.

We actually miss 24-hour non-stop Christmas music, we miss all those old Christmas specials like *The Year Without A Santa Claus* and *Miracle on 34th Street,* we miss the Christmas lights and the smell of nutmeg and peppermint sticks. Of course, at this time of year, we miss our family and friends most of all.

In 37 days, on the 17th day of the 12th month, we will travel more than 5,000 miles. It will take us three flights totaling more than 15 hours and almost as long in lay overs to get to the President's home

Left leaning Christmas tree. . . just like me.

state of Hawaii, but it will be worth every minute.

This year we get to spend Christmas with family. Thanks Uncle John, Megan, Sarah and Nana and Papa — you are our gifts. Because living in Shanghai has taught us to appreciate each other and you so much more than we ever did before.

And while we are busy appreciating you, could you please pick up some old Bing Crosby music and a copy of the *Polar Express* and put it in your luggage for us . . . thanks.

Votes for Women

November 2012
Shanghai

> It was we, the people; not we, the white male citizens;
> nor yet we, the male citizens; but we, the whole people,
> who formed the Union . . . Men, their rights and nothing more;
> women, their rights and nothing less.
>
> ~ *Susan B. Anthony*

Now that the election is finally over both in the States and in China, I have been thinking about all that rhetoric and how it shapes people and perspectives. How the things said and done today will shape the future and how we will view our world, other nations and even individuals.

How do I explain the phrase "legitimate rape" to my daughters and my son? What makes a person, not to mention one of our nation's congressional members, put those two words together — legitimate and rape?

How do we value people in our society? There are many ways to answer that question but in terms of a fiscal society, we tend to assign value based upon their pay. One's income, in many places in the world, determines their place in society, their access to education, access to health care, access to legal representation — it can, in fact, determine their level of civil and even human rights.

And, how do women do in this category? You might be surprised to hear that we aren't doing as well as men. The glass ceiling is firmly in place in many countries, even my home country. Why is that important? Because it means we are not equal. And, those who are not equal have no standing in the debate. Those who are not equal can be easily dismissed. Those who are not equal are, quite simply, *worth less.*

When women are paid less — just because they are women — the implication is that they are worth less. *This is why closing the gender pay gap is among the most important fronts in our fight for equality in the workplace and beyond.*

But we can't fix what we can't see. . . . With few exceptions, pay gaps remain entrenched — for now.

1) *In the United States, the gender pay gap remained unchanged in 2011. Women earned 77 cents, on average, for every dollar earned by men — a number that has barely budged for years.*

2) *The six jobs with the deepest gap in pay between women and men in the United States are all within the financial sector: insurance agents, managers, clerks, securities sales agents, personal advisers, and other financial specialists.*

3) *The gender pay gap hits women of color particularly hard. In 2011, the earnings of African American women were $33,501 — 69.5 percent of all men's earnings — while Latinas' earnings were $29,020, or 60.2 percent of all men's earnings.*

4) *Looking globally, the gender pay gap remained relatively unchanged in this past decade in 26 countries.*

5) *China and India have particularly steep pay gaps. Women in China earn 69 percent of what Chinese men earn, while Indian women earn 66 percent as much as Indian men.*

[Source: *"Take 5: Pay Gap,"* Catalyst blog by Illene H. Lang, Oct. 10, 2012]

Like many Americans, I have smirked at the sex trade in some parts of Thailand, like "Walking Street" in Pattaya. But I was naive. I didn't understand the plight of these women, or at least I didn't fully appreciate the horror of their situation. They take incredible risks on a daily and nightly basis. I should not have been so glib.

I don't know how many of those women — girls, actually — are there under duress or will find themselves in a situation where they will be taken by force to some other location in Southeast Asia or even the States. Does that seem impossible to you? It shouldn't. It happens. It happens all around you. You just aren't looking, so you don't see it.

The Protection Project, based at Johns Hopkins University in Baltimore, Maryland, has documented the rising trends in the sex slave trade.

- More than 15,000 women are trafficked into the United States every year, many of them young girls from Mexico.
- Asian women are sold to brothels in North America for $16,000 each.
- Almost 200,000 girls from Nepal, many of them under the age of 14, are working as sex slaves in India.
- An estimated 10,000 women from the former Soviet Union have been forced into prostitution in Israel.

- Some 60,000 Thai children have been sold into prostitution.

- As many as 10,000 children aged between 6 and 14 are virtually enslaved in brothels in Sri Lanka.

- Some 20,000 women and children from Burma have been forced into prostitution in Thailand.

I spend time in Thailand and India and I've been to Malaysia, Vietnam and Cambodia. I have seen girls walking the streets day and night and find it hard to look directly at them. It is hard to look them in the eye because I don't want to pass judgment but I also don't feel comfortable. I wonder if the girl walking arm-in-arm with a man old enough to be her grandfather is safe. And then, I heard some of the campaign rhetoric from back in the States.

It scares me to think that my daughters are growing up in a world where women are still "less than" in the eyes of many. Particularly, in the eyes of "the majority." It disturbs me to know that women and children are being trafficked across the very continent on which I am living. That the young girls sitting in the back of the plane, who don't quite seem to belong, might be headed into danger. I wonder about the unsolved crimes in Vietnam and Cambodia involving 20-something women that the police ignore with a simple "they were out drinking" . . . as though that conveys some sort of "legitimacy" to the crime perpetrated against them . . . murder.

Not long ago, a video made it onto the China-version of You Tube showing the forced abortion of a fetus at 7-months gestation. Why? Because this mother already had one child. The government forced the abortion because she had violated the one-child law. Later, after serious political pressure, the government apologized. But they could not bring her child back to life. And, no one considered sterilizing the father. I cannot wrap my head around the way China controls the reproductive rights of its citizenry.

In my own country, people attempt to impose their religious or personal beliefs on my rights. It is nothing less, in my opinion, than an attempt to limit my civil and human rights. Interestingly, this debate usually is centered around my ability to pro-create, which is inextricably linked to my gender.

I personally am both pro-choice and pro-life. I believe I should have the right to make decisions about my body and my life without interference from politicians, dictators, interest groups, celebrities or anyone else for that matter. And, I believe that life is worth protecting. Life and the decisions that come with it are complex. I am complex. I have had experiences that I would never wish on my worst enemy and fought my way back to life when I truly believed there was no reason to continue it. I was wrong.

It is important that we take some time and reflect on the 24-hour news cycle. It is important to reflect on what's being said about women and how it affects our daughters, our nieces, our mothers, wives and sisters. It is important to look at children and remember that they are human beings deserving of the same human dignities that the taller humans expect.

It is important because someone — *often a man and a woman* — raised those tall human beings who tried to categorize rape as legitimate, who purchased a woman for a day, a week or a lifetime, who enslaved a child. Children are living in a time that is as dangerous as any time has ever been. Our children have the luxury of growing up in a nuclear family with loving extended family members. We are trying to raise them to be enlightened and aware and to understand that they are, in fact, among the lucky few in this world with freedom. Unfortunately, the most recent campaign season makes me wonder if the degrees of freedom enjoyed by our daughters will (continue to) be less than those of their brothers? And why that cycle continues to perpetuate itself?

No school for these Cambodian girls. They are lucky to be selling trinkets and not themselves.

House Points: A Tale of Two Williams

November 2012
Shanghai

When we returned to China for our second year, the children wanted to change schools. We switched from a more traditional Asian school to the British International School, which requires students to wear uniforms complete with ties and scarves. It seems almost Hogwartian — they even have houses. As you might imagine, house points are awarded and deducted based upon performance, behaviors, etc. This week, our little man, received 5 house points for his project on explorers.

I realize that every mother's son is the finest boy ever to walk the earth, but in this case it is true. He is sweet, charming and in every way more than I deserve or could have ever hoped for in a son. He is like his father, which means he will certainly be a fine man.

Several weeks ago, we went to Beijing and met an archaeologist and Great Wall of China historian named William Lindesay. He took us on an amazing trek along the "wild wall." William came to China in the early 1980s and set out to see the entire Great Wall, which is actually several walls built over many Dynasties using an assortment of materials, depending on the Dynasty and location of the wall. During his quest, William was arrested, his film confiscated and deported several times but he never gave up and, eventually, he finished his journey and chronicled it in a book.

You may have heard of William Lindesay or have seen him in a *National Geographic* documentary about the Great Wall of China. He is a very interesting and accomplished man. But to Henry he was simply a good story teller. Indeed, he was a *very* good story teller.

For Henry's school project, the children were asked to prepare a presentation about a great explorer. Many children chose Christopher Columbus or Marco Polo. Henry chose William Geil. Never heard of him? Most people haven't.

During that grand adventure with William Lindesay, we learned that he was not the first person to trek the full distance of the "stone dragon." William had only recently learned about William Geil, a man who travelled from Doylestown, Pennsylvania to China in 1908 and went the distance of the Great Wall.

Henry chose this forgotten American explorer as the subject of his project. He used the stories he learned from William

Lindesay, the pictures taken by his father on the trip and the second book published by William Lindesay, *The Great Wall Revisited: From the Jade Gate to Old Dragon's Head.*

William Geil and his Chinese hosts.
Photograph courtesy of Doylestown Historical Society

The book was a real inspiration for Henry. In it, William Lindesay retraces William Geil's journey and photographs the same locations showing how one of China's, if not the world's, greatest treasures has deteriorated over time. Henry found it fascinating.

His presentation consisted of five slides including some bullet points, pictures and the You Tube video of our trip to the Wall. It was a very personal presentation about two Williams who inspired

Henry and me on the Great Wall.

Henry to think of himself as an explorer on a journey. That's worth 5 house points and the undying admiration of his Mother.

Taiwan, India, Australia . . . Home

November 2012
Taipei, Taiwan

For the next three weeks, I will be literally on the road. I got up at 5 and was headed for the airport by 6:30 this morning. After some flight difficulties, I arrived in Taiwan around 11 a.m. Not bad for travel in Asia. No one is forcing this grueling schedule on me but me. It simply needed to be done.

I needed to meet the team in Taiwan. A full 18 months into the job, I should meet the team. And there it is — the vastness of the job. Asia Pacific and Africa. Teams and individuals scattered in places like Bangkok and Rayong, Thailand; Taipei, Taiwan; Chennai, India; Melbourne, Australia; Jo'berg, South Africa; not to mention Indonesia, the Philippines, Japan, Korea, and on and on. At some point, you want to connect with people beyond the conference call, the PicTel and email. It is the *right* thing to do.

You want to personally thank people for their contributions and share their successes with them. You want to demonstrate that you care about them and their work. A leader shows up. Sometimes, that is all it takes — showing up. I am always surprised at how many leaders fail to show up. Hard to cast a shadow if you are never there.

My trip started today. Bella cried last night. Not so long ago, at parent-teacher conferences, I learned that I am often the subject of "circle time" in Year 5C (4th grade to us Americans). During circle time, Bella talks about her Mom traveling and how it makes her feel. This is good, I know. It apparently is therapeutic for the whole class as other children are inspired to share as well, but I appear to be the worst offender. Still, I hugged her and told her to keep on sharing if it helps.

If sharing helps, then let me share with you that this is beginning to suck in a major way. I am never home, I rarely see the kids and I am feeling less and less appreciated at the Salt Mine by the second. I missed the kids by 10 minutes tonight because my last call ran past 8:30 and they were already in bed when I phoned. Even Jack was too tired to talk. Sharing this lets me vent but I hardly feel better. I feel numb.

I'll have hours upon hours in airplanes and airports to think things over, which is what you do at the end of the year. And, then, a special treat — a nice long holiday to reconnect with those I love and feel better. But before that happens . . .

It's Taiwan this week, then India and straight on to Australia. I'll keep you posted. It's sure to be a real adventure.

Bull Durham . . . Shanghai Style

November 2012
Taipei, Taiwan

I spent the better part of the day meeting with government officials in Taiwan trying to explain our sustainability strategy, our commitment to reducing our carbon footprint and doing our share to stabilize the environment. You know, the usual cocktail conversation. After deflecting the questions about our specific product introduction plans about a hundred times, it was finally time to leave. I must have done pretty well because I left with gifts . . . not the kind of gifts that win you elections or get you sent to prison but the kind of gifts that you can take home and your kids will think are cool, like key chains, baseball caps and tiny pretty boxes to hold rings or other small jewelry.

After the government meetings, it was back to the humdrum of trying to get the product certified in time for sale (not happening) and figuring out whether we actually can meet the new regulations in — pick one: India, Taiwan, China, Thailand — without destroying the current cycle plan. And, of course, working out the budget . . . which basically means figuring out how to continue to do more and more with less and less and less.

I called home at 6 tonight so that I wouldn't miss the kids . . . again. It turns out all the drama is happening there.

The swim team coach is unimpressed with some of the swimmers' efforts and cuts are imminent. This has struck terror in the heart of our youngest. Auditions for the primary school play were today and our son was asked to read for the two lead roles, one being a monkey. Don't ask because I don't know, but I'm thinking he's a lock. And the senior member of the "little people gang" is fretting over how to let someone down without hurting their feelings. In the immortal words of Crash Davis: "We're dealing with a lot of shit."

So my advice to Jack is:

1. Get a live chicken and cut the head off,
2. Send the director cup cakes, and
3. Buy some candlesticks . . .

I find that most dramatic situations in life can be solved by going back to *Bull Durham*:

[*Larry jogs out to the mound to break up a players' conference*]

Larry: Excuse me, but what the hell's going on out here?

Crash Davis: Well, Nuke's scared because his eyelids are jammed and his old man's here. We need a live . . . is it a live rooster?

[*Jose nods*]

Crash Davis: We need a live rooster to take the curse off Jose's glove and nobody seems to know what to get Millie or Jimmy for their wedding present.

[*to the players*]

Crash Davis: Is that about right?

[*the players nod*]

Crash Davis: We're dealing with a lot of shit.

Larry: Okay, well, uh . . . candlesticks always make a nice gift, and uh, maybe you could find out where she's registered and maybe a place-setting or maybe a silverware pattern. Okay, let's get two! Go get 'em.

[Source: *Bull Durham*, 1988, written by Ron Shelton]

Jack, I think you should at least be able to get a live chicken without too much trouble! There is one running around the front of our yard. Good luck, Babe!

Not Feeling It

November 2012
Bangkok, Thailand

It is Wednesday night. The night before Thanksgiving, which at one time was as good as Christmas Eve. It was "bar" night — what old people like me now refer to as Amateur Night. Still, it beats being in my hotel room, on a global conference call that will last until 10:30 p.m.

Earlier, I read my husband's Thanksgiving blog on thewinemonologues.com, which is terrific and I made a quick call home to find them all eating pizza. It's what you do the night before Thanksgiving when you have kids and are going to be preparing a giant meal the next morning. I had room service. Not great. So, I guess I'm not feeling as thankful as I should be on the eve of Turkey Day.

I feel bad about that, actually. I feel bad about not feeling very thankful. As I listen to this conference call and the ineptness of the people trying to run this meeting at 8 p.m. my time, I am feeling less and less thankful and starting to feel less guilty about it too. I'm such a Thanksgiving Scrooge this year! But, seriously, I am not in a thankful mood.

Don't get me wrong. I am grateful for many things, including my husband, our children, my family and my friends. I am grateful to have a job and I am grateful that my job has given our children (and us) the opportunity to see the world. I have much to be thankful for and I know that I am very fortunate. I guess I'm just in a place where I am finding it hard to get into the spirit, so to speak. While I'm sure this hotel room in Taiwan has something to do with that, I am not entirely sure it's the only thing turning me into such a Scrooge.

It is not that I am not thankful; I am. I just don't *feel* thankful. I feel something else and I am not entirely sure what it is.

So, what is the purpose of writing this at all? I am writing it to acknowledge it and to acknowledge that there are likely others entering this holiday period not quite feeling it either. In fact, it could be making them feel worse, even though that might seem to defy logic.

I've had a hard year professionally, and personally it's been a bit of a roller coaster. Some years are like that, I guess. I am, at the very least, glad that I have survived this year (so far) and I am truly grateful for the people who have supported me — most notably my husband.

Thanksgiving with "Louisville Slugger Sue" & our families . . . on a Sunday.

So, as you sit down to your turkey and stuffing and watch your football, be on the lookout for the person who seems to be hanging back a bit or forcing that smile. Reach out . . . they might not be feeling it.

Love you Jack, Jane, Henry and Bella!

Meditation

November 2012
Chennai, India

I have been in India now for several days. My location is congested and wildly exotic in terms of smells, sights and sounds. I love it. I know most people would find it overwhelming and some might characterize it in even more unflattering words, but I love it.

I love the chaos of the traffic, the mix of the buses transporting their passengers to work, school or wherever their final destination might be. I love the sight of the school children in their bright maroon and blue uniforms. The girls' hair twisted tightly in braids and adorned with flowers. Women riding sidesaddle on motor bikes in colorful Saris, holding babies as their husbands speed along the road darting between cars, buses, motorbikes, bicycles, people and cows.

I have not had much time for myself. I have been in meetings nearly every minute of every day. But, on the drive each morning and evening, I gaze out the window at the world before me. Barefoot children running after their parents, men in traditional dress, colorfully dressed women with deeply dark skin shimmering in the dwindling sunlight. Everyone seemingly purposeful. Everyone seemingly content.

I am certain that their lives — like all of our lives — contain challenges. Some may be more desperate than others but, for the most part, the view from my car window shows productive people living productive lives.

A monk in Cambodia at Angkor Wat.

As we drive, we pass a number of Temples and I am surprised by the number of men I see gathering early in the morning to start their day with prayer, reflection or meditation. I am equally humbled on the return trip when the line outside the Temple seems to stretch even further. I don't pray anymore. I haven't for years. I never found it gratifying in any way. That isn't to say that others don't find it gratifying, peaceful or meaningful. But I do not.

I have, however, found that silence and a long look out the window is calming. In that silence I hear something — something calling to me — I don't know what it is yet. But, I sense it. I just need to be quiet and listen.

The Parent Trap . . .

November 2012
Chennai, India

The parent trap is like the mob mentality — just because every other parent is doing something, you feel like you should be doing it too. It is one of the reasons that I am really glad to be in Shanghai right now. Not, that you don't have some of that parent mob mentality as an expat in China, but you have less of it than you do in the States, especially if you avoid the obvious traps for it.

Our son never played soccer. And, at the ripe old age of 10, he never would have been able to take up the sport in the States. Hell, if you haven't started by the time you are 4, you are too old to even consider it. He played for one spring in Shanghai. He loved it and he knows enough about the game and has enough skill to play on the playground. Perfect.

This year at age 11, he took up American football — at home, he would be on a waiting list to play. He may try hockey (though I hope not) but there is no way he could play hockey in the States at 12. By 12, you are either headed to the minors or you are a "has been" or otherwise "washed up," "burnt out" or "over-the-hill."

And, what is it with every girl getting their hair streaked for "graduation" from primary school? I don't actually care about the hair streaking or coloring, it's the "everybody is doing it thing." It almost feels like peer pressure for Mom; you have to make your daughter an appointment for highlights or she won't be cool or fit in or be 'normal.' I don't get it. Did the kid even want them? Did anybody ask?

Over the summer, our son was talking to his older cousins about "stuff" and I overheard him say that he can get an earring and dye his hair blue because his Mom doesn't care about that stuff. He explained that she cares about sex and drugs. Frankly I care more about *unprotected* sex and drugs, but he's 11. So, for now we'll leave it at sex and drugs. Rock and roll is fine.

Then, today, I saw the following on Facebook and thought: EXACTLY! Jada Pinkett Smith posted a response to criticism leveled against her for allowing her daughter, Willow, to cut her hair off and dye what remained pink.

"A letter to a friend...This subject is old but I have never answered it in its entirety. And even with this post it will remain incomplete. The question why I would LET Willow cut her hair.

First the LET must be challenged. This is a world where women, girls are constantly reminded that they don't belong to themselves; that their bodies are not their own, nor their power or self determination. I made a promise to endow my little girl with the power to always know that her body, spirit and her mind are HER domain.

Willow cut her hair because her beauty, her value, her worth is not measured by the length of her hair. It's also a statement that claims that even little girls have the RIGHT to own themselves and should not be a slave to even their mother's deepest insecurities, hopes and desires. Even little girls should not be a slave to the preconceived ideas of what a culture believes a little girl should be."

Just a week ago, our oldest daughter called me in Taiwan with a problem — how to let a guy down. She worried that he would take the news badly, would say mean things about her, would make her feel uncomfortable and she felt like "maybe" she should just agree to be his "girlfriend" for a short time even though she had absolutely no interest in this guy. I nearly lost my mind but I counted to 10 instead.

I gave her some advice on what to say, how to say it and where to say it. It isn't about him. She just isn't in that place yet — she likes being friends but she isn't into the boyfriend-girlfriend thing right now. And, that is fine. I also told her no boy, no man has any right to her and she doesn't have to say "yes" to something just because he asked. And, frankly, one day she may be asking and hearing "no."

The point is: She decides and she alone. No one should cast their expectations onto her and she should not accept them. She can choose what is and is not right for her. Provided she lives her life within the bounds of decency — without malicious intent to harm others — her decisions are not up for debate, discussion or derision. She doesn't have to be a role model either. She should be who she is and that person can and should evolve over time as she accumulates experience, knowledge and wisdom.

I applaud Jada. The earlier our daughters understand that they are in control of their minds, bodies and spirits the better. If cutting all your hair off and dying it pink helps you understand that, so be it. You decide what is right for you and you alone.

Learning to be comfortable in your own skin is a hard lesson. Owning your own skin can be even harder. And, there will be plenty of people trying to knock you down along the way . . . don't let 'em!

Do Not Board

December 2012
Melbourne, Australia

It is 8:30 a.m. in Chennai, India. It is hot but not unbearable. Arriving at the airport, I am surprised by the changes since my last visit. There seems to be a bit more organization than the last time I was here but still, it is not what we are accustomed to in the States. Trust me!

I am fortunate. I am flying in business class, which means I can bypass the long check-in line. I do, however, have to pass through several layers of security to enter the check-in area.

Armed guards are stationed outside the airport. They screen your luggage for the first time before you enter the building. Almost immediately upon entering, they screen it a second time. It is screened a third time after it is checked or, for carry-on luggage, as you pass through the security check-point.

I hand my passport and my visa for Australia to the woman behind the counter. A little boy next to me tells his Daddy, "She is going to Australia too" . . . and we begin to chat. He is very cute and not older than 4. But, after 15 minutes I am wondering what is taking so long and turn my attention to the woman behind the counter.

"Could your name be in the computer a different way?" she asks me. "Um . . . maybe my last name is first. The way it appears in my passport," I respond. Ten more minutes pass . . . she makes a phone call and security arrives. "Miss, can you please come with us?" It isn't really a question.

I find myself and my luggage in a very small room with a woman wearing plastic gloves, two security guards with guns and the nice gentleman who invited me to "please come with us." Oh, boy! When they put my name in the computer, a "warning" popped up telling them not to issue a boarding pass to me. I am on the "Do Not Board list." What does that mean — is that like "no fly"?

It suddenly seems very warm, and the questions begin:

- Have you ever been denied entry into Australia?
- Ever been denied entry into any country?
- What was the purpose of your visit to India?
- Where did you stay? (Man leaves the room to confirm my stay . . .)
- Where have you been in the last 6 months?
- Have you recently been in Africa, the Middle East, the Caribbean? (What is the connection there, I wonder?)
- Have you been hospitalized?
- When was the last time you visited a doctor?
- Do you have your immunization records with you? (Yes!)
- Are you on any medication? What kind? May we see it?
- Are you traveling alone?
- May we open your luggage? (Again, not really a question.)

This went on for about 20 minutes. My luggage was searched. A word of advice: buy the packing cubes because when security decides they need to rifle through your suitcase, it is nice to have your undies in one spot.

After a lot of discussion, they decide do what every corporation in America does with a non-performer: Pass them on to someone else. So, I was given a boarding pass to Kuala Lumpur, Malaysia. Once there, I would be their problem. But, my underwear was going all the way to Melbourne. Don't ask because I don't know either.

I have traveled a lot and had various odd experiences but this was certainly a first. I decided immediately to just go with the flow. If worse came to worse, I would go back to China — assuming I could get on a plane. It wasn't the fault of the people interviewing me; they were doing their job. Some other idiot was responsible, or maybe this was just the best practical joke ever played on me.

Uncertain of what might come next, I went to the "lounge" and ordered a vodka. No orange juice just vodka. I could get to Malaysia. If I got stuck there, it wouldn't be the worst thing that ever happened to me.

Upon arrival in Malaysia, I went directly to the transfer desk. One look at this woman's face and I knew. "Do Not Board?" I asked. "Yes, Miss." Security arrived a few minutes later.

Security took me to a room and we went through the same questions again. I have to say everyone was very nice and they were as stupefied as me about why I was on the "Do Not Board" list. My visa was checked and I had all the paperwork (don't call me over-prepared anymore — you never know!).

Eventually, they gave me a boarding pass to Australia (passing me along) and escorted me to the gate. I arrived in Australia and used my express pass to make my way to the immigration counter. First in line. I was out of the airport in 40 minutes. This is record time in Australia. No issues, no questions, no rooms. I was feeling relieved. Of course, when I arrived at the hotel, my corporate credit card was declined and I was now paying for this trip with my own dime.

Yes, I am living the dream . . . at least I wasn't strip searched.

The Last Glass . . .

December 2012
Yarra Valley, Australia

Getting to Oz (Australia) was a bit unusual but worth the effort. After Friday's meetings, I met a friend for dinner in a great little Melbourne neighborhood where she is looking for a house. It was lovely.

Traveling for three weeks straight is difficult. You're away from your family and, although you spend time with colleagues, the cultural differences in Taiwan and India make it more difficult to socialize. While my Team is amazing, it is also predominantly male. I think I can count the number of women on one hand. Something I am working on but this also makes it a bit awkward.

Being in Oz, however, allowed me to catch up with a friend who repatriated to Australia from Shanghai months ago. A chance to unwind, catch up on her search for her first home, rediscover her hometown with her and just be.

We ate dinner at Don Vincenzo's sidewalk restaurant, which reminded me of eating at a favorite spot in our old Chicago neighborhood — Wrigleyville. We sat outside, had a bottle of wine, shared some amazing calamari salad, mushroom bruschetta and margarita pizza. It is summer in Australia and sitting outside immediately unburdens you. Aussies are wonderful people.

The next morning, Sarah saw her "dream house" and then came to pick me up. She really had found "the one." Nothing makes you forget your own troubles quicker than seeing joy in someone else's life, particularly when you are genuinely happy for them. The pictures of the place are fantastic. I hope she gets it, so I can crash there soon. We headed to Yarra Valley with reason to celebrate. Not that we needed one, but always nice to have an excuse, a justification, a reason.

The Yarra Valley is truly breathtaking. We visited several vineyards and drove through the Valley just absorbing the beauty. I thought about Jack often — wine tasting and beautiful surroundings are a wine-loving photographer's dream.

As we stood at the tasting bar, ate our lunch in the vineyard and drove through the valley, I felt the bit of emptiness that I always do when I am away from him. There really is no one else with whom I want to spend my time. A bit of guilt always seeps into these wonderful experiences simply because I so often find myself experiencing them alone, without him.

On this day though, I had Sarah and it was a "girls" day. So, we could buy bread, cheese and figs, and eat them with gluttony. No reason to pretend you don't want them, or that the cheese isn't amazingly creamy and the figs sweet and tender. We tore the bread apart, used it to scoop up the creamy, soft cheese and sugared figs. No need for a knife.

When you're with your girlfriends, you can let your hair down in a way that is different than with others. At least you can if you have truly wonderful and worthy women as friends. While I have few truly close friends, those that I do have are truly amazing women in their own right. These are women with whom I can share my deepest insecurities and my greatest joys and know that they will be empathetic, joyful and, most importantly, non-judgmental.

We had an amazing lunch and a great tour at Chandon and then made our way to a number of other fantastic wineries in the Yarra Valley, including Sticks, Bianchet, De Bortoli and Yering Station to name a few.

Lunch at Chandon in the Yarra Valley, Australia.

When we arrived back in Melbourne, we had our gluttonous meal and, because it was "just us girls" in our PJs, we opened two bottles of wine and called room service for nothing more than a bucket of ice and, of course, some french fries.

We slept late Sunday, very late. We headed to the waterfront in search of breakfast. It was 12:30 p.m. We walked up and down the waterfront restaurant district in search of pancakes, only to be turned away time and again. To our dismay the restaurants were serving lunch, not breakfast. Finally, deciding to pick our spot based on the best view, we sat down for lunch at the Bear Brass. To our absolute surprise and delight, we were able to get breakfast. Ahh . . .

Indulgence being the theme of the weekend, I had lemon curd and rhubarb French toast. Yes, it was mouth-wateringly good. It is a breakfast that I will always remember, and you can bet when I am in Melbourne again I will return to the Bear Brass.

After breakfast, we headed to the market outside the Melbourne Art Center. I cannot tell you what I purchased, but it was a successful shopping trip. You'll know more after Santa makes his visit.

From there, we walked across the river and back into the city. Melbourne has great lanes or alleys. Graffiti artists decorate the alley ways with amazing artwork that changes frequently. There also are magnificent alley ways with shops and restaurants. Not surprisingly, we stopped for some mid-day champagne and lemon tart.

You can walk almost everywhere in this city. There are intriguing places to visit, unique shops and endless food choices. It is a foodies dream, so I was absolutely in heaven and unrestrained in my expression of gratitude. On weekends, the outdoor markets overflow with abundance. Melbourne is one of the world's great cities.

While the weather says summer (we are down under), the decorations say Christmas. The city is fully decked out. I do miss Christmas decorations when I'm in China, and the decorations here are so authentically Christmas that it feels as though I've stepped back in time.

The large department store here, Myer, has "Christmas windows" that harken to a time gone by. They are so amazing that children are lined up waiting for their turn to see the displays. The wreaths are hung, the garland is draped and silver and red sparkle along the pedestrian shopping area. Even some of the trolleys are dressed for the holiday. I almost expect the train conductor to visit me tonight and take me on the Polar Express.

Australia's Sydney Harbor Bridge at night . . . my last stop before returning to Shanghai.

But, every escape has its end, so I am having the last glass of Cabernet Sauvignon, the last bite of cheese with fig and crusty bread . . . for tomorrow is Monday and I must return to reality. Lucky for me, I will spend next weekend in Sydney with Sarah before returning home to Shanghai . . . and then there will be just 7 days until our Christmas holiday in Hawaii.

The last glass. On Sunday night.

Here's to you Sarah for a brilliant weekend. And, of course, to you Jack, for giving me this little gift of extra time away on my own, amidst the longest work "road trip" of the year.

Sydney Harbor at night.

Leadership, Courage & Charisma . . .

December 2012
Melbourne, Australia

They aren't the same thing. There are people who are able to lead, have courage and be charismatic. But it is not the norm, at least, not in my experience. I also find that charisma is often mistaken for leadership and too often courage is mistaken for anything but leadership, most notably insubordination.

For women, this presents an interesting dilemma. If you are courageous — if you are willing to have the courage of your convictions, to offer the dissenting point of view (rather than simply agree and complain outside the room later), you are often characterized as not being a "team player." Being charismatic can be a double-edged sword — you might be called a flirt or worse behind your back, or, if your charisma takes the form of more assertive behavior, you are pushy and aggressive.

Recent experience has made me think that the dominant male culture wants "its women" submissive. You can advance in your career if you are "charming" and "submissive" to the opinions of the men around you. In other words, if you (appear to) adopt their convictions, you may be viewed as a leader. And, it helps if you aren't charismatic enough to outshine them.

Not long ago, Catalyst published a report entitled "Calling All White Men." Catalyst asked whether training could make a difference in cultures dominated by white men and make them more inclusive? The results are interesting.

The study focused on employees of the global engineering company Rockwell Automation. The study supports Catalyst's belief in the importance of engaging men as champions of gender diversity. Catalyst concluded that training can produce a measurable shift in workplace attitudes and behavior that can begin to create an environment where women and minorities can advance in management and in leadership.

Key findings of the study include:

- **An increase in workplace civility and decline in gossip (e.g., snide remarks and behind-the-back comments).** In some workgroups, participants' colleagues rated the incidence of workplace gossip as much as 39 percent lower after the labs, signaling improved communication and respect.

- **Managers were more likely to acknowledge that inequities exist.** After the labs, there was a 17 percent increase in how much managers agreed that white men have greater advantages than women and racial/ethnic minorities.

- **Managers improved on five key behaviors for inclusion.** From seeking out varied perspectives to becoming more direct in addressing emotionally charged matters, managers improved on critical skills for leading in today's diverse marketplace.

- **Having cross-racial friendships mattered.** Managers without many prior cross-racial relationships changed the most after the labs when it came to thinking critically about different social groups—a 40 percent increase in ratings vs. a 9 percent increase for those with more of these prior relationships.

- **Those who cared the least about exhibiting prejudice changed the most.** After the labs, managers who initially were the least concerned about appearing prejudiced registered the most significant change in taking personal responsibility for being inclusive, as evidenced by a 15 percent increase in ratings.

In conclusion, Catalyst said:

"Companies can see a major shift in inclusive behavior when white men acknowledge inequalities and accept that while they didn't cause the problem, it's their responsibility as leaders to be part of the solution," said Ilene H. Lang, President & CEO of Catalyst. "We can't rely only on women and minorities to advocate for culture change. The results are much more powerful when white men, who are most often in leadership positions, are also role models."

[Source: Catalyst, "Calling All White Men," July 2012]

I am biased, of course. Because recently, it was suggested, in fairly strong and direct terms, that I need to do more to "rebuild" relationships with certain white male colleagues. I find the choice of the word "rebuild" of particular interest.

First, these relationships did not previously exist. These individuals assumed their current positions after I was assigned to my position in China. Second, all of these men outrank me, which would suggest that the behavior of building a relationship with me should fall more to them — as the leaders. Third, I don't seem to have relationship issues with my cross-cultural team (as evidenced by objective scores on corporate measuring devices) or with my cross-cultural management in Asia Pacific.

It appears this issue exists with the all-male, and predominantly white male, leaders in North America. It is hard to be certain because no one has given me any real details about the so-called relationship issue. But, what has been made clear is that it is up to me to fix the problem.

According to the Catalyst study, it might be more productive if the male leadership attended training and acted more like role models. Like Lang said, expecting me to the lead the change is pointless.

Catalyst recently launched MARC, Men Advocating Real Change, an online learning community for professionals committed to achieving gender equality in the workplace. I found one posting both enlightening and frighteningly disturbing. It is an unedited compilation of men's messages to their daughters. [Source: MARC, *"Messages to Daughters,"* Nov. 21, 2012.]

- *Speak your mind, but do so with dignity and grace. A pretty face is soured by ugly words.*
- *Women have been abused fighting for equal rights and justice. Do not become complacent by thinking they*

can not be taken away from you. They can and will . . .
never allow any of these rights to be taken away.

- *Women must take the responsibility and ownership*
  for change. There are not enough men of character
  standing up on behalf of women. Women must continue
  to tear down institutional systems that discriminate
  against women in all ways.

- *Don't take any crap off anyone. We teach people how to*
  treat us. If someone is pushing you around, push back.

- *Jealousy is a terrible thing. If there is nothing bad to*
  say about you-people will make things up. You have to
  rise above it. Over time people will figure out rumors
  are not true.

- *Be a nice b**** ('scuse my language but you know what*
  I mean).

While I believe the intention of the messages are to encourage women, several (and I did not include all of them) seem to suggest that women still need to take the lead in effecting change. This is the opposite of the findings from the Catalyst study. Further, gender stereotypes are evident. Even when attempting to encourage, the messages continue to be mixed: "A pretty face is soured by ugly words." Really?

Recently, the appointment of Yahoo CEO Marissa Mayer drew a lot of attention. MARC asked Marie C. Wilson, founder and president emerita of The White House Project, why this appointment received so much press. "Only recently," Wilson said, "have we begun to understand that we need a critical mass (usually considered one third of the members of any group) for women and other 'outsiders' to be seen as unexceptional." [Source: *"The Only Woman in The Room: On the Perils of Being a Token,"* MARC's Ask a Woman blog, Oct. 2, 2012]

In other words, women will remain the exception in positions of power and; thus, continue to be overly scrutinized compared to their white male counterparts. Indeed, the messages some men would give to their daughters suggest that we are a long way from eliminating gender bias in our society. When asked to send a message to one's daughter, one respondent admonished his real or imagined daughter to be a "nice bitch." Successful women still are characterized as bitches – nice or not.

High Heels, Pills & Booze

December 2012
Melbourne, Australia

Disclaimer: I know I have been writing that you shouldn't let others bring you down and you should ignore the "haters." But, hey, I'm human. Sometimes, things can get dark. I've debated publishing this but in the end, I decided I would because it is — in fact — part of the China experience for me. And, sometimes, it really sucks! However, while I wrote this more than a month ago, please know that I am now on holiday with my family in a wonderful and special location where I will have the opportunity to re-orient my perspective. Three-plus weeks with those I love . . . the greatest gift and the toughest task master remains time . . .

Ever wonder what trying to stay alive looks like? From the darkness, the light can be hard to find. Searching for it can be exhausting. Each day a struggle to get up and move. Getting up, even though you can't find the reason, pretending your way through your day, your week, your life.

Teetering. Teetering on my high heels, I go to the office each day wondering what new and ever increasingly ridiculous game will greet me. For me, staying alive has been both a literal and figurative struggle. No one likes the smart girl. At least, not until you need her as your Secretary of State.

The other morning, I woke at 6:15 and checked my phone to be sure that my 7 a.m. call was still scheduled. Having worked until nearly 10:30 the night before, I was tired. Friday mornings are tough for me — I hate the 7 a.m. Friday call. I do it from home because one too many times I've gotten to the office to find out it was canceled, while I was sleeping. Yes, it is a call with North America. And, yes, they cancel it while I am asleep. This is low-level crap — annoying but not worth fussing over. You just check your phone and do the call from home.

This particular Friday, however, I checked my phone to find out that my 1:1 would be attended not just by me and my boss but by a human resources representative. No idea why. Well, maybe a little bit of an idea . . . nobody likes the smart girl. Two anxiety pills. One-half glass of beer.

Teetering. The call lasted 30 minutes and was annoying and, in some ways, belittling. When you have the courage to be the dissenting voice, I guess you should not expect people to appreciate it. No one wants to hear that the Emperor has no clothes. While that is my take on the meeting, I was told it was about "relationship building." Interestingly, the relationships that need building are very specific and seem to be directly related to my perspective on the Emperor and his clothes.

Ultimately, I was told to be nice, which is not my strong suit. I do not suffer fools well; I never have and I don't think that is going to change any time soon. In my opinion — oh, you knew I had one — some people spend a lot of time talking but very little time doing, very little time helping and even less time being constructive. I am just not in the mood for "nice" right now.

Finish the beer.

So, lately, the Sunday night blues have started arriving on Saturday afternoon. The demons have returned in the dark hours of the morning. The cold calm has settled in once again. It is there in the corner, waiting for the opportunity to overtake me and my high heels.

This phone call really knocked me back. It made me angry. I found it incredibly sexist and parochial. I've been listening to human resources in the States tell me to be "more charming" for months — yes, the vision you have in your head right now is exactly the vision in mine when I hear that — "servicing" the man.

Ironically, it is a *woman* telling me this. How exactly have we made so much progress in this region if I can't work well with others? Something is off. I know all too well that it is easier to cast stones than build bridges. And, if things aren't going well from a broader perspective, then a scapegoat must be found. I feel a bit like the goat right now.

I stopped wearing pants to the office in January after I was told to stop calling attention to my differences. I love Hillary and her pant suits but, really, my "differences" are less noticeable in a pant suit? I don't know if a pant suit is the answer but when you tell me I can't or shouldn't do something, then I am going to do it. So, the dresses and heels re-entered my wardrobe and they were intended as a statement . . . yes, that statement. Further, they were a shield, a barrier against all the crap.

Suddenly, the high heels, the wrap dress, the pills and the booze are no longer sufficient to tame the darkness. I realize how awful that sounds but, really, the suggestion that I needed to charm my way up the corporate ladder — actually, just to stay on the corporate ladder — was and is depressing, demoralizing and demeaning.

When the reasons suddenly become illusions and you are moving by sheer force of will fortified by pills and martinis . . . well, you are struggling. Am I struggling to stay alive? Maybe. It is the structure, the repetition, the familiarity of the routine that keeps me moving now. Numb. I feel numb. Progress was halted by circumstances that I don't control and that are playing themselves out thousands of miles away from me but are, in fact, impacting me. Impacting me irrationally.

No one is causing that to happen except me. I control my reaction. I am overwhelmingly disappointed and really struggling to understand why, in 2012, it is still necessary to stereotype women — my tone is too aggressive so I should be more charming. Jack, however, is confident and assertive. He is driven for results and I am a bitch. Why do I care?

There are people struggling to stay alive in circumstances of poverty, war and violence. There are people who appear to have everything struggling to find a reason to get out of bed. It seems crazy. It is self-indulgent. But, it is real.

The demon in the corner lives in my head. It has lived there in one form or another for 30 years and I've kept it at bay with more or less success over the years. I've found it creeping back in over these past months making me angry at first, then sad and finally full of self-doubt and worse. Now, the cold calm is back.

Decision time.

It's That Time of Year Again . . . And I Don't Mean Christmas

December 2012
Shanghai

There is no getting around it. My performance review is scheduled for this week and, if you've been following along, I am not expecting it to be a thing of beauty. I expect to be told that I have met, if not exceeded, my objectives but issues will be raised about "how" I met them.

Was I sufficiently charming and submissive to the powers that be? Or did I stand up for myself, hold myself and others accountable and drive for results with a passion for excellence? Well, if I did the latter I am a bitch (which has already been keenly established); and, if I did the former, I may be well liked but then I didn't do my job.

And, there it is. The conundrum. I gave several performance reviews myself while I was on my 3-week tour. Indeed, I have not been home in 2 weeks and I am writing this from the airport lounge on Sunday.

The one I struggled with the most was for a young woman who, like me, has a strong and determined personality. She is smart and ambitious. She works extremely long hours and believes that delivering on her objectives, putting in her time and taking challenges head-on will help her get ahead. It won't.

Some of the feedback from others about her sounds like the recent feedback I received on myself. She is too strong willed. She is too opinionated. She doesn't listen well. The thing is, I have observed her and she does listen well. But, when she speaks, you don't like what she has to say or how she says it because she isn't afraid to be the dissenting view in the room and she delivers her message with confidence. She isn't afraid to say the Emperor has no clothes. What do I tell this young, bright, ambitious woman? Do I tell her the truth?

Yes. The truth is that at this point in your career — at this level of management — you will often be the only woman in the room. You will have to make a choice about who you are and what you want to be. That choice may not come for years but it will come sooner or later. And, the choice is simple, really — unbearably simple.

Do you want to change who you are to meet someone else's expectation of a woman and how a woman should behave? Or do you want to be true to yourself? If you choose the former, you may well continue to move forward. If the latter, chances are slim, very slim, that you will continue up the ladder but you may, ultimately, be happier being you than being the woman someone else thinks you should be. Simple. Heart-breakingly simple.

In her blog for *The Nation*, Jessica Valenti commented on Sheryl Sandberg's book and her own experience of trying to be "liked." The tongue-in-cheek title of her blog — *"She Who Dies With The Most 'Likes' Wins?"* — resonated with me, which is why I read it in the first place.

Valenti notes that when she started blogging in 2004, she responded to every comment regardless of how nasty. She believed she could win over these comment-critics if she was polite. Indeed, she believed she could "charm" these critics with her professionalism. She was wrong.

Valenti writes that:

"When Facebook COO [Chief Operating Officer] Sheryl Sandberg gave a TED talk in 2010, one of the issues she talked about—and later expounded on in her 2011 commencement speech at Barnard—was likability. 'Success and likability are positively correlated for men and negatively correlated for women,' she said. This isn't news to feminists, so what I can't figure out is why — despite deep knowledge of this pervasive double standard — so many women still insist on being likable, often to their own detriment.

For me, it was wasting countless hours arguing with people on the Internet — giving equal time to thoughtful and asinine commenters — because I thought somehow it would show me to be fair and open-minded. It pains me to think of what I could have achieved if I had that time back.

Women's likability is something feminists use as proof of inequity — he's a boss, she's a bitch—but not something we've put on par with standard feminist fare like reproductive rights or pay inequality. Because there's no policy you can create to make people like successful women. There's no legislation to fight for or against, or even a cultural campaign that would make a dent in such a long standing double standard. Besides, being likable seems like such a small thing compared to larger injustices — why *would* we spend a lot of time thinking about it?

But the implications of likability are long-lasting and serious. Women adjust their behavior to be likable and as a result have less power in the world. And this desire to be liked and accepted goes beyond the boardroom — it's an issue that comes up for women in their personal lives as well, especially as they become more opinionated and outspoken."

[Source: *"She Who Dies with the Most 'Likes' Wins,"*
Nov. 29, 2012.]

I am grateful that I came across Ms. Valenti's blog. It validates my own feelings or maybe it confirms my sixth sense of what is coming this week in my performance review. I know that there are men in North America who do not like me because I have had the courage to make decisions, hire and fire team members, streamline processes and eliminate redundancies. In short, these men don't like me because I did what they could not do — lead.

So, I'll know by mid-week whether I did my job or made friends. If I failed to make friends with the men in North America, then I did my job. And, the irony is that if I did my job, then I will be rated poorly against my male counterparts. It makes me feel like I can't win. I can only lose. Why would I want to continue in this vain? I don't know but I do want to finish the work that I came to China to do.

December 12th

2012
Shanghai

I had an appointment at 8:30 a.m. so I requested to do the 7 a.m. conference call from home, but I was told that I had to go into the office for the meeting. Clearly, this was a sign. Why did I need to be in the office when my functional manager was located in the States and my operational manager was on vacation in Thailand? Gamesmanship. Yes, my performance review was at 7 a.m.

I was forewarned yesterday that this meeting would be "tough" by my human resources representative in Shanghai. At worst, I thought, I'll be given a rating of "low achiever" and perhaps be put on some sort of performance enhancement plan. But I seriously underestimated the vengeance of the majority.

My performance review is a condundrum. It is internally inconsistent. It leaves one wondering if anyone in the legal department looked it over and, if they did, why they are still employed. I failed to meet any of my objectives – not one. And, yet I was rated an achiever. This may say more about the Salt Mine than me. I failed to meet my objectives because I failed to be charming. Yes, charm is my undoing.

I sat in my office with my HR rep across from me. We had the States and Thailand on the phone. My functional manager walked through the review with military precision. He said that while I made progress, it was impeded by my lack of good relationships with the leadership team in the States (aka the "real" leadership team). The bully in the States must have been dancing a jig.

Repeatedly, my functional manager asked my operational manager if he had any comment. Each and every time he said "no." His excuse was that he had not witnessed my day-to-day interactions. Exactly, and neither did my functional manager or anyone else. It was me, myself and I doing this job without support, without supervision, without anyone watching my back. I was set up to fail and, despite that very obvious fact, I succeeded. And somebody, or several somebodies, felt threatened.

I arrived in China with a team of zero. In 20 months, there was a team of nearly 50 working together across time zones, cultural differences, language barriers and without any tangible support from the North American Functional Leadership Team. Looking for your goat? There she is – the girl two grade levels below the leadership team working her ass off for you – she's expendable.

My operational manager took a hands-off approach, which until the moment of my performance review was expressed as a vote of confidence. I was managing the issues, keeping the programs on track, dealing with the challenges and managing the team. The objective "pulse" scores were a proof point that I am a good manager as was my 360 review, but facts would just get in the way and clutter the path to the real message: No girl is going to tell the boys how to run the business, even if the boys have never stepped foot into Asia Pacific.

I asked for examples. My favorite was that I escalated things unnecessarily. This was so thinly veiled that my dog could have figured out from where this emanated. The bully was upset that I called him out. Again, the truth was of no consequence. Everyone – including the CEO of Asia Pacific and Africa (who put his opinion in writing) – agrees that the failure was in North America and not in China. Further, I escalated nothing. The Asia Pacific CEO escalated it and I was responding and trying to get facts and data from North America, which never came. The email on this is so clear that it is mind boggling how this example could be used to justify this sham of a review. Worse, my operational manager knew this and stayed mute. Disgusting.

Still, I could have withstood that storm. But, 30 minutes into the review, they dropped the bomb. Everyone on this call, except me, knew this was coming. They had to have known for months. Yet, I had no warning. Nothing. Indeed, the opposite. Just months earlier, I was asked to consider extending my assignment from 3 years to 5 years. Now, I was told that I was repatriating to the States no later than February 1st. Less than 45 days.

Everyone on the call also knew that I was meeting my family for an extended holiday in Hawaii in 5 days. I was not due back in China until January 8th. I have three children – all school age. From a logistics perspective, this was insanity. The Salt Mine did not care: "This is a business decision. Your family doesn't factor into it."

Let that settle in for a moment. "Your family doesn't factor into it." Really? The family that I dragged around the world for the Salt Mine and my career. The family that sacrificed while I worked 12- and 14-hour days. The family that had just adjusted to China, that finally feels settled, that has overcome so many hurdles. That family? Well, screw you! No. We will not be getting on a plane on February 1st. End of conversation.

I saved the "screw you" sentiment until after I hung up the phone. The poor HR guy in my office got some of my anger (I apologized later), but all in all I handled it well – all things considered. Then I got in the Transit with Mr. Cao and drove to Baker & Spice and ran into the shop where Jack was sitting with Sue, Nigel and Scott (our closest friends) and I wept.

Jack took me to the therapist and 90 minutes later I was back at the office. Smile plastered to my face. The HR guy was stunned. "Why are you still at the office?" he asked me. "Where else would I be?" I responded. Did you really think I was going to crawl into some corner? Oh, no, this isn't over. Not by a long shot.

You better get ready because I am pissed off now!

December 16th

2012
Shanghai

When you don't have much time, you get busy getting busy. I had meetings with human resources, found an executive coach and saw my therapist daily. I was not going down without a fight and I was not pulling my children out of school before the end of the term. The Salt Mine would just have to deal with it and, eventually, deal with me.

Tomorrow morning we get on a plane for Hawaii. Things are not settled. A counter proposal is on the table to allow me to stay until April, when the bully from the States is due to visit. If, at that time, I am not sufficiently charming, then I will return to the States and my children and husband will follow at the end of the school year. If, however, my charm quotient improves, I stay until the end of June. I will not press for the third year. Who needs that headache? Not me.

I've agreed to accept an executive coach. It seems the Salt Mine prefers to promote people to executive level first and then work on their deficiencies – that explains a lot. I hired my own. Turns out that I am not the piece of shit that the Salt Mine paints me as; I am smart and talented and intimidating to those who are not as smart and talented. I need to be more compassionate towards these people – which I am happy to do but the bully is not deserving of my compassion and I am not that nice of a person.

Our children know nothing about this situation. They sense that Mom is not herself. They may hear me crying, though I am trying hard to keep it together. My anxiety meds have been increased. My anti-depressants have been increased. My drinking has increased. I am thinking there is a correlation here somewhere.

My compass has been pointing toward tomorrow morning for months. Now, I am dreading it. The Salt Mine essentially shuts down over Christmas in the States, which means I will wait for 3 weeks wondering if my counter proposal will be accepted. I will be left in limbo to try and fake my way through our holiday. Every moment will be a bit less happy because I will be worried, anxious, angry, and lost.

My work is how I define myself. It is how I have defined myself for most of my life. I invested my time in my work, in my mentors, in building something from nothing, and I believed those investments would pay dividends in the form of money, rank and opportunity. A better life for my family. I was so wrong. So very, very wrong.

The question of "who am I" hangs in the air and goes unanswered. My personal despair is overwhelming me to the point of paralysis. Jack is not pushing me forward; he is pulling with all his might. "Do not regret not being present." Jack repeats this mantra several times a day. He says it to me quietly so no one else can hear it. He is trying to keep me moving toward Hawaii. He does not want me to "miss it" in the fog of my despair.

The sun will rise. I am a sunrise girl. But, it is mighty dark right now and the night seems endless.

Isolated . . . sunset on Maui, December 17, 2012

Part Three:
Unravelled & Nearly Broken

Fate & Destiny

December 2012
Maui

Can't sleep, again. This may have something to do with the myriad of time zones travelled in the last few weeks, not to mention that for the last two days we've been stuck on December 17th. There's an 18-hour time difference between China and Hawaii, so we arrived before we left, if you know what I mean.

Maui. Should be bliss. Heaven. Yet, I can't seem to relax. The waves are crashing, the trade winds are blowing, all of the things important to me in life are under a single roof and in a week I'll be joined by a few of those other "priorities," notably my parents, one brother and two nieces.

I am in need of family. The tragedy at the Connecticut elementary school reminds us all how important family really is and how we often take it for granted. We let our children walk out the door in the morning to go to school without ever imagining that they might not return that afternoon. It is unthinkable – or at least it was until recently.

How do those parents get out of bed in the morning now? Family. Their children, their spouse, their loved ones who need them and they need in return. Being needed and needing others in return is part of the human condition and only when you no longer feel part of the human condition can you let yourself stay in that bed and do nothing. I have no idea what makes a person want to take the life of another. But, the desire to curl up under the covers and ignore the world . . . I get that feeling.

My internal compass has pointed to this date for months now. The desire to surround myself with people who love me for me, with all my failings and all my mistakes, and still manage to see my very real desire to be more, do better, be worthy. Now, the date on the calendar is finally here and I am struggling to feel worthy.

I don't really feel the sand beneath my feet yet. It will come. Jack assures me it will come. I am fortunate. I have Jack. I also have my parents and, even at 45, I just want to hug my Mom and cry on my Dad's shoulder and have someone tell me that it will be okay even if it won't.

I hold our children close and tell them it will be okay. I believe it will be okay. I have no idea how or when but I believe it will be . . . I have no other choice. I am a parent. I must believe.

Today, we saw "Crush," a giant sea turtle, swimming in the ocean waters off our beach. Locals said he has lived here more than 100 years, long before any of the condos sprouted up. Our children were mesmerized.

I was mesmerized by the three wonders of my world. And, in that moment, I thought about those parents thousands of miles away. Will they ever feel the earth beneath their feet again . . . I wonder. Who is holding them and telling them it will be okay even when it won't?

I won't sleep for days. Fate seems to have fallen out of my grasp and until I manage to pull it back some, I will not sleep. I will, however, treasure each moment I am given with those who give me so much each and every day and ask for so little in return.

> I am the master of my fate and the captain of my destiny.
> ~ Nelson Mandela

China is hard. China is isolating. China is polarizing. China is galvanizing. China is contradictory. China is discovery. China is courage. Connecticut is harder, and has the potential to be even more polarizing and galvanizing. What will we discover, what do we want to discover and do we have the courage to face whatever is discovered? Courage is a choice. A choice made by children and parents, by citizens and subjects, by politicians and dictators. Courage is not often popular. And popular is often over-rated.

We have a voice. And, thus, we have a choice. Whether you are protecting a band of five in China, restoring faith in a community or protecting a nation or a world of innocents, you — no, we — are the masters of our shared fate and the captains of our collective and evolving destiny.

Note: In an eerily similar incident in China, a mentally ill man walked into a middle school and attacked the children and staff. 22 were injured. No deaths. He didn't have a gun, though — gun ownership is illegal in China. He had a knife. We have a shared destiny . . .

Simple Pleasures

December 2012
Maui

When the day is done and I come home, it is the simple pleasures that make the rest of the world fall away. A glass of wine with my beloved. The tight hug from our youngest. A kiss from our son. And, the smile from our teenage daughter. The simple things are the most pleasing.

I have found it hard these last months to find pleasure in almost anything. It has been an excruciating long year. Work has been difficult, the travel has been endless and the battle to remain true to myself has been hard fought, if not won. And, yet, I feel as though I have no idea who I am anymore. China seems to have that effect on people. It makes you question everything.

And in questioning everything, you question yourself. In such circumstances, I think it is best to keep things simple. Thankfully, I am surrounded by a wonderful and loving family. I have friends who have supported me through this sometimes wonderful and sometimes painful journey. It has been a shared experience in many ways and, in other ways, it has been isolating.

While I have chosen to write mostly about my own personal journey, our children have experienced both the joy and sorrow of life in a foreign country. Our friends and their children have shared the same experiences and together we have found comfort. Sometimes comfort comes in the form of laughter and tears but, more often than not, it comes in the form of empty bottles after long nights around a table full of food and friendship.

Simple.

Maybe it is my age or my station in life, or maybe it is the Middle Kingdom itself, but I find myself wanting more from life or, perhaps, wanting more from myself. As the year draws to a close, I find myself both disillusioned and enlightened. How long I will remain in this cocktail shaker looking for my answer? I don't know. I do know that I am capable of more and that I want more. I want to do more. It is simple, really. I want more for my daughters and my son. I want to contribute in some way to making more possible. Somehow, I thought more was already possible, for myself at least, but I was wrong. Very, very wrong.

Being a woman is a great gift. You have the ability to create, carry and nurture life. You are not less than; you are so much more. And, yet, for most of this year being a woman has been a great struggle and an impediment to achievement. No, that isn't right. It isn't being a woman that impedes me; it is the view of women still held by the majority that impedes me. A far, far different thing.

I fought the urge to be "liked" in order to do the job. I was the dissenting voice in a room where it was not valued or wanted from a woman. It certainly wasn't valued like it was by this once young lawyer looking to save a client from the electric chair. In those circumstances, a life may hang on a phrase in a dissenting opinion. Dissent is not necessarily bad; indeed, it is necessary to achieve any meaningful democracy.

At the end of the day, I find myself wondering if this is still what I want. Frankly, I am not sure I know what "this" is anymore. What was I trying to achieve with all of "this" — recognition, money, fame? It is hard to remember. I wonder if I ever really knew or if I just got on the treadmill and kept running, increasing both the speed and the incline to prove that I could do "it."

I will need stronger armor if I want to continue this battle. Perhaps this is the reason there is but one woman sitting at the Salt Mine's big kids' table: Do women just burn out? Do we make a conscious choice to exit the race because the sacrifice is too great? Is it the constant drum beat in our heads that we aren't good enough or don't measure up? (And, who are we measuring ourselves against?)

I don't know the answers. Today, I only have questions: Am I putting my family and myself through too much for something that I may no longer want? If so, what do I want to do?

On the Saturday before we left for our holiday, we decorated cookies and ate cookie dough with friends from around the world. All of us in one kitchen filled with far too many bottles of wine and even more friendship. It was pure joy. In that moment, I didn't question myself. I did not seek more. I was simply me.

Like any human being, I am a complex and confused creature. I seek out wisdom from others, particularly this group around the cookie decorating table. And, I am capable of reflection and introspection. It slows the rhythm of the cocktail shaker and I begin to hear myself again. Soft whispers. But, I know she is in there trying to reach me.

I am, it seems, in search of me. I am in search of the project, the job, the thing that will allow me to be me full time. No apologies. No excuses. Maybe I have grown, or am beginning to grow, into myself. Either way, it seems that I have my New Year's resolution . . . to find and *be* me.

Searching . . .

My Favorite Things . . .

December 2012
Kauai

While work has been challenging, personally our family has enjoyed an amazing year. My husband keeps telling me to focus on the things we've done as a family — he's right, as usual. We've had a great year.

The year is going to close out well because more family is on the way. Tomorrow, Christmas Eve, my parents will arrive in Kauai. Then, we will close out the year, with them and also my older brother and his wonderful daughters. Really, what could be better? (The rest of the gang being here too would be, but I'll take what I can get.)

Looking back on 2012, there is a lot that I can be proud of in both my professional and my personal life. If others don't see it in the same way, then they don't. We'll have to agree to disagree, and take that up in 2013. For now, I am in one of the many versions of paradise that I've had the good fortune to experience during the last year.

If I am honest with myself, I am disappointed in 2012 because I am disappointed in myself. I have many regrets. Most are very personal. It has been a struggle to be the professional person that I want to be and also be the mother that I need and want to be to our

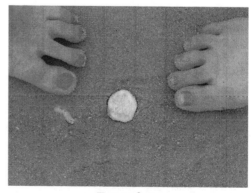

Toe-gether.

children. Finding a way to balance these competing desires is harder than I ever expected. Still, I do not regret coming to China. I do not regret trying to achieve as much as I believed myself to be capable of achieving. I would regret not having tried.

If I hadn't tried, then my list of favorite things would never have included some of the following:

- We celebrated Chinese New Year on the beaches of Phuket, Thailand. Thai food and hospitality and elephant riding. This, after monkeys in the Malaysian rain forest. A great start.

- Watching Henry and Jane on stage in *Oliver Twist*. I was so nervous!

- Henry playing incredible baseball in an International Baseball Tournament. Boy, that team from Hong Kong was amazing!

- Celebrating 20 years of marriage by taking our children to Europe for the first time. Beer in Munich. Touring Salzburg while singing along to the Sound of Music. London just before the Olympics. The kids really loved that Harry Potter walk! And, of course, Paris!

- American football in Shanghai. Henry played center and defensive tackle. Of course, he was the BEST player out there or at least my favorite player. And, it cured my football fix. Sunday football, complete with a grill and a bar on the sideline. That's football.

- Rooftop evenings with Jack and friends. Late evenings on the rooftop deck, Sherpa's delivering lamb chops and tzatziki along with wine (or ice if we were drinking bourbon).

- Watching Bella discover that not only does she love swimming but she also is a very good swimmer. And, gaining a training partner . . . a shared love of the water.
- Trekking the Great Wall of China with William Lindesay. The pre-dawn hike to the Wall was transformational for me. I still can't quite put it into words.
- Driving in India and surviving. I love India. I love the food, the people, the colors, the chaos. It can be totally overwhelming but, at the same time, it's on the edge, about to emerge and it's very exciting.
- Australia Girls' Weekend with Sarah. Touring the vineyards of Yarra Valley and exploring Melbourne. And, following it up the next weekend, in Sydney. Just unbelievable.
- Turtles and whales in Maui. Rainbows and surf. Black sand and waterfalls.

I have no idea what 2013 will bring. While this is true for all of us, it is truer this year for me than almost any year that I can recall. I do know that no matter what lies ahead, it can't take away any of the joy, any of the discovery or any of the love I've been fortunate to enjoy in 2012.

I am grateful for all of the wonders of this past year. The 'hard' makes it better in some way, I suppose. The contradictions and the extremes of 2012 are not something I want to repeat in 2013, but I wouldn't mind a return to Europe or another amazing island.

Is it too late to send my letter to Santa?

Time

December 2012
Kauai

I recently read an article by Andy Ellwood of *Forbes* — *"Add 15.2 Days to Your 2013."* It blew my mind because time is the theme that I settled on for my New Year's blog. Ellwood sent out a Tweet asking if you could find 15.2 days in 2013. I responded to the Tweet saying that in 2013 — just like 2012 — I purchased extra vacation from the Salt Mine. That's when it hit me: Time *is* an investment.

Time with family . . . flying over Kauai.

The Salt Mine's benefits package includes up to two weeks of "purchased vacation" each year, with your supervisor's approval. I started purchasing vacation as soon as I was eligible to do so. I use it to attend school field trips, stay home when one of our children is sick, play hooky with my husband or make cookies at Christmas. I use it so that I can have more time with my family without feeling guilty about taking that time. I pay a fair chunk of change to be guilt-free.

Ellwood's article forced me to look at how I invest my time, including the "extra time" that I purchase every year. I realized that if I am not reaping the rewards of my time at the office, then that is a poor investment. However, when I invest time in my daughters, my son and my marriage, I reap rewards far beyond my expectations. I had to learn this the hard way by coming to China. But, I did learn the lesson.

In 2013, I will be the person that I have always wanted to be by investing my time in things that truly matter *to me*, where I can actually make a difference. Further, I will stop investing my time in things that are not worthy of my investment, which includes things like late night meetings, unnecessary travel and an obsessive attention to detail. I will be happier, more fulfilled and a better human being because investing my time in what matters to me will pay dividends directly back to me. It is the most selfish of New Year's resolutions, I suppose. Still, I am making it.

I will still purchase vacation because time is the greatest gift (and the cruelest task master) and I won't let that gift go unwrapped. I have been fortunate to spend this holiday season with my parents, my husband, our children and my brother and his daughters. When it is over, I will have invested 23 days. The rewards are already rolling in.

The benefits just roll in with the tide.

The Winds of Change

January 2013
Hawaii ("The Big Island")

The sea is nearly navy blue with abundant caps of white. The sky is, well, sky blue. And the sun is shining hot and bright. The wind is fierce, however. The green palms are swaying dramatically and scaring even the hardiest of golfers back into the club house. But it is still a picture perfect day in Hawaii.

On this last real day of our holiday, I am feeling a bit melancholy. How do you leave paradise and not feel a twinge of sadness? How do you leave your family that you've seen twice in the last year and not shed a tear? Sad blue eyes, slumping shoulders, and small quiet tears give the children away. My heart breaks. Ice cream won't make this better; though, they'll still have ice cream. Maybe two ice creams.

Leaving family is the hardest part of the adventure. Getting back on the plane and wondering when or if you will see them again. Could this be the last time I see my parents? The question is always in the back of my mind. I push it aside and move forward. At least, that is what I have always done. Pushed my personal anxiety aside and moved forward. But, the winds are changing and my ability to just push the anxiety aside is dwindling.

They say that struggle should not be confused with failure. I think this is true — but when you are struggling, it sure as hell feels like failure. I watch our three children struggle to hang on to the last moments with their cousins and grandparents and wonder if I have failed them. I feel the uneasiness in my own mind and wonder if I have failed myself or, worse, all of us.

As I write this, the wind is growing stronger. It feels as though it is speaking to me. Gather your strength, hold your head high and step into the wind . . . it will take you where you need to go. Believe in yourself and ride the wind.

Wave crashing on the lava rocks of the Big Island, Hawaii.

Time is my resolution. The wise and thoughtful investment of time in that which makes me happy and allows me to be the person I want to be; not the person others expect me to be. Yes, the wind is growing stronger.

I need to let the wind carry me for a bit. It is going to be bumpy. On the eve of 2013, nearly everything is uncertain except the most important thing — the love of my family. So, once more, I will push aside the anxiety and the voices in my head telling me it is 'my fault' and hold my head high. I will not brace myself against the wind, I will not merely step into it, I will embrace it and use it to lift me up and carry me to the next adventure, the next chapter, the next stop on my journey. Damn the non-believers.

Believe

January 2013
Hawaii

Before he got on the plane, he hugged me tightly and whispered in my ear, "Believe." I was suddenly 12 years old again. He stepped back and looked at me, lovingly but sternly, as only a parent can. Tears ran down my cheeks. He smiled. "Believe."

One last hug. A kiss. And he walked away never looking back. Even this was a message to me. Time to move forward. Believe.

I find it hard to believe in God. I find it hard to believe in people. I find it harder still to believe in me. I wasn't always this way. It took years, more like decades, to hone this fine sense of non-belief. I've had many tutors along the way teaching me: You can't . . . you won't . . . you shouldn't . . . . At some point I started believing the nay-sayers and stopped believing in me. Why?

I likely know the answer to that question — it is the secret that I have kept for 30 years and is the source of my insecurities — and it haunts me. Literally, haunts me. Wakes me up at night. Sends shivers down my spine. Raises the hairs on the back of my neck. Sets off alarm bells in my head. Leads me to expect disappointment and, yet, I am always surprised by how disappointed I am.

Believe.

So, the seemingly lone voice that from the beginning always told me I could, said it again just before he got on the plane. And I cried. He says I have a steel core. Strong and unyielding. He says that I have proven it over and over. I will withstand the attack, weather the

Dad, who always believes.

storm and move forward. It is what I do. No matter the internal struggle, the rising tide of self-doubt, the overwhelming desire to run and never stop, I have stood my ground in whatever form that has required.

How many times can a person do that before it becomes too much? What is too much? What is too little?

Believe. Believe in *me.*

I am fortunate. I am not alone. I am surrounded by people who believe in me, love me, trust me. They can't take my place, however. I must hold my head high, walk firmly in my stilettos and move forward. The fact is I have exceeded the Salt Mine's expectations on this work assignment, and virtually every assignment I have ever been given. The fact is I am gravely disappointed in those in whom I once believed. The intersection of these two facts has left me at a crossroads. I was always headed here, I realize that now.

Believe.

The next chapter begins tomorrow. The process of preparing myself has already begun. Undoubtedly, I will confess my self-doubt in the dark while being held by the man I love, who has loved me all these years. He knows. He has seen the demons. He is the demon-fighter. In the safety of his arms, the steel core melts and I allow myself to be vulnerable, to be afraid, to be . . .

The first page of life's next chapter is blank. But, if I could write it, it might start with:

"She wore her black leather boots, adding 4 inches to her 5'5" frame, and her slim grey skirt that stopped an inch above her knee. This left just enough bare leg to reveal her well-tanned skin. Her black shirt draped perfectly across her body and her black jacket was neat, well-tailored and strictly business. Her boots, however, announced that she wasn't going away easily, she would kick-ass if necessary even if she had to walk through some shit to do it. She is, after all, a woman."

Believe. Believe in me.

Nothing is insurmountable . . . if you believe.

Resurrection

January 2013
Shanghai

For a non-believer, resurrection is hard to fathom. Yet I feel that I have returned from the dead. Or, at least begun to dig out.

It took weeks, not days, but I am back. I feel it deep within my soul. I no longer feel that I have failed. I have done nothing wrong. I have no reason to feel ashamed. Indeed, the opposite is true. To be strong in the face of adversity is difficult. To remain steadfast while others levy slings and arrows in your direction is difficult. To give up on yourself, however, is unthinkable. So you must move forward.

Just 24 hours ago, I didn't think I could do it. But today in the elevator on the way to the 31st floor, I decided I could. No discussion. No debate. I simply decided I could. I would. I will. Today. Now.

Resilience. Why do people bounce back? I have no idea, but they do. I do. Time and again. Wiser. Stronger. More determined. And, angry. The kind of anger that makes you want to change the world.

I am, in so many ways, my Father. For this, I am grateful because without his tenacity and fighting spirit, I likely would not have survived, let alone achieved. His reminders to believe in myself, to keep moving forward, to ignore the nay-sayers awaken my fighting spirit. It reminds me that others do not define me. I am the person I choose to be. And, whether anyone else likes me or not, I do.

I have no idea what tomorrow will bring. I do know that I will handle it. I may grieve. I may scream. I may jump for joy. But, I will do it on my terms. I will do it with dignity. I will not allow others to take what does not belong to them — me.

It may be just two weeks into 2013 but keeping that New Year's Resolution is looking pretty good. Time wasted worrying about things I cannot control is time I cannot get back and time that would be better spent playing cards with the kids or drinking wine on the rooftop.

I am back. I am unsteady, but I am determined. It's a good start.

Conquering my self-doubt one wave at a time.

Homesick

January 2013
Shanghai

I finally got on Facebook. It was a Christmas gift to my husband, who was tired of me ghost writing on his page. Fair enough. I thought it was great when I was in Hawaii. But back in Shanghai, I find it makes me homesick. A feeling I really was not expecting.

I expect the children to be homesick, particularly around holidays and birthdays. But, for the most part, I have not felt homesick until that damn Facebook. Am I missing something at home? Not really. I mean time is passing, nieces and nephews are growing, my parents are aging but, all in all, life at home is as it was before we left for Shanghai. Great, but the same.

Today, though, I wanted to pick up the phone and call my friend Maya. I just wanted to talk. Girl talk. Old friend talk. Her Facebook page is great but it isn't the same as hearing her voice. But, it's 4:30 a.m. where she is and I can't just dial her up.

And, you know what, I miss my Mom. Maybe it was being in Hawaii. Sitting around the table with my parents and talking about nothing, watching them play cards with the kids and reprimanding my Dad about of the abundance of ice cream he gave them during the card game.

You just never know what the next day brings. On December 11th, I thought I was doing a great job at the Salt Mine and I was looking forward to a wonderful beach vacation in Hawaii. On December 13th, I didn't want to get out bed. I wanted my Mom and Dad to hug me and tell me it would all be okay. And, today, I wonder how much longer I will have with my parents, my husband, my children. They say tomorrow is promised to no one and that is certainly true.

I can't remember the last time I was homesick. I wasn't homesick at summer camp, at college, in Los Angeles or Chicago or even when I lived in Belgium. I don't think I've ever spent so much time thinking about home and where it is, what it is, what it means to me. It took modern technology in the form of a "social network" designed to connect people to make me miss home. Ironic?

I think my Mom would call this progress. It may have taken nearly 46 years but I am finally — once and for all — homesick. She always seemed to think that I was running away. And, for years, that might have been true in a way. Now, I feel the strings pulling me home.

I think I'll go back to ghost writing on Jack's Facebook page. I just can't take all this "connecting" long term. It's too much of a commitment.

Don't tell the kids their Mom is homesick. Because that is the same as saying I'm ready to leave . . . and I'm not ready . . . not yet.

On The Clock

January 2013
Shanghai

The NFL Commissioner: "The New York Jets are on the clock."

"On the clock." The three words that strike both fear and exhilaration in the hearts of most NFL owners, coaches and, when the Jets are on the clock, most college players. Everyone is thinking it — the thrill of having the first pick and the fear of blowing it . . . again. I feel a bit like the New York Jets. I'm on the clock.

All those young, fresh-faced boys with their amazing stats and large pectoral muscles. The quarterbacks are particularly hard to resist. So good looking. Six-pack abs. But, an offensive lineman can be so appealing when looking for protection. Then again, the speed, agility and strength of the linebacker is equally enticing. These choices are just so hard.

So much riding on this pick. The franchise is on the line here. The fans, the analysts, the pundits and the owners are all watching. Have to make the right pick. Or do I trade the pick, move down in the draft and get two or maybe three picks in the next round? My head and heart are pounding.

In the war room, the strategy sessions have ended, the donuts eaten and the coffee spilled across the player stat sheets. All that remains is the decision. The room is silent but the silence is deafening. The clock is ticking down and the decision is no clearer now than when they first called our name. The New York Jets are on the clock . . .

We are not the New York Jets. We aren't the New England Patriots either. But we are on the clock. The Commissioner is counting down the seconds. The owners are weighing their options. The coaches don't like the choices on the board and are considering a bold move that could change the nature of the game completely. We are making a trade.

The New York Jets — aka Five for Chinese — are trading their 2013 draft pick for . . . well, no one is sure yet. The fans are stunned. The owners are secretly thrilled. The Commissioner is reviewing the rules with the lawyers and the coaches would be giddy if they weren't scared to death.

Welcome to the new season . . . the new year . . . the new next best thing . . .

Forget Jesus, What Would You Do?

January 2013
Shanghai

After wallowing for days in my misery, it is time to stop. I took a step in that direction this evening by reaching out to a woman who is accomplished, wonderful and makes me feel worthy. After several martinis, she told me about a game she plays with her husband (get your mind out of the gutter) — if money and health were not an issue, what would you do, where would you go, how would you live?

And then she said to me, "If money were no issue, what would you do?"

With a few martinis in you, it is easier to be honest about the answer than you might think. I made a list on my iPhone. It wasn't a list of things or accomplishments. It was a list of what I want — no, it's what I need — to feel fulfilled. Money did not appear on that list. In part, because it was put aside for the exercise and, in truth, I only need enough money to allow me to fulfill my role as a parent. The question was about creating the perfect environment in which to thrive. If I were creating the recipe, what ingredients would I choose?

And, that was Step One. I have a checklist against which to measure whether I am doing what makes me happy. Or, at least, what I think would make me happy after a few martinis and some discussion about how, even at the highest levels, women are still "less than" on any measuring device employed by the status quo to rate their potential, performance or capability. It was, in some respects, shocking to have my fears confirmed. But, then, I wasn't really surprised. Admitting a problem exists may be part of Step One too.

I take inspiration from those who blaze the trail that I only wish I could travel. I do not believe you can have it all. I never have really believed that to be true, it just isn't logical. If I have it all, what do you have?

Disappointment has been my companion these past several months, nipping at my heels and chipping away at my self confidence. It is a process, I suppose. Grieving. Disillusion. Disappointment. Anger. It takes time to really feel these emotions, wrestle with them and, hopefully, defeat them or beat them back long enough to move past them on your way toward something better.

My family and dearest friends have given me the luxury of space and time to go through this process. But, at some point, it's time to move forward. With my list in hand, I am preparing to move forward. I hope to discover that I am. Am what? Just that . . . that I am.

I Want To Tell You A Story . . .

January 2013
Shanghai

She was a happy and contented child. She laughed. She played. She loved her family and they loved her. Then, when she was 16, it all changed. It changed in a single night. She would not talk about what really happened for another 30 years. But, that night would define her for the rest of her life.

When she was 18, the girl fell apart. She didn't know why exactly and she would forget the events almost entirely. She was thin. Maybe 90 pounds. She was confused. She was lost. Her parents took her home and saved her life. But, they had not saved the child she had once been or the woman she may have been. That girl was gone. Forgotten. Thrown away. But, still hiding in the corner of the girl's mind.

When she was 21 she met a man. He was kind and gentle. He loved her. He knew somehow that she had secrets. Deep, hurtful, unspoken, ugly secrets. He never asked her. He waited. He was patient and he too saved her life. He kept her moving forward.

When the girl was 30, she had a child with this man. They were happy.

When she was 31, they bought a house and a dog. The girl compromised and quit her job for one more suited to a mother. Or, so she told herself. They were still happy, if less so.

At 35, she gave birth to their second child and, at 36, their third. She loved her children. She still loved the man. She wasn't sure she loved herself or the dog. Darkness crept into the tiny spaces left open by the secret and waited there, along with the young girl thrown away 20 years earlier.

When the girl was 38, she beat back the body invaders and reclaimed her health. She didn't think of herself as a survivor or lucky or anything really. Still, she bought a bright pink raincoat to remind herself that there is always a rainbow after the rain.

But still the darkness grew. Resentment now crawled into bed with her, taking up the space between her and the man. She had to remind herself that she loved the man. She had to remind herself to live. She didn't love herself. That was too much to expect.

When the girl turned 40, the man quit his job for her. Resentment sat at the breakfast and dinner table and gloated. The girl worked, struggled to move up the ladder. She took every assignment, worked every hour asked and more. The girl never moved up, only over. The man warned her. She would not listen.

The girl's first daughter turned 10. The girl felt uneasy, struggled to sleep and started seeing the once forgotten young girl in the corner of her mind again. But she never spoke of it for she knew people would think she was crazy.

Lurking darkness . . .

She wasn't really there. She was a myth, a demon, a foreboding.

When the girl turned 44, she moved her family to China. She believed that this assignment was the payoff for all of her hard work. She was happy but lonely. She loved her children. She loved the man even though it seemed hard to remember and even harder to give him a reason to love her back. It is hard to love when you are numb. They had a new dog.

The girl's first daughter turned 14 and the darkness spread. The girl no longer slept and often did not eat. She worked. Harder and harder, longer and longer. The girl avoided her oldest daughter, unaware it was happening. The girl's daughter felt her Mother's rejection. The darkness saw opportunity and seized it.

The girl took a trip the States in winter. It was cold. The man kissed her when she left and told her it would be okay but she knew that wasn't true. It had never been true. At least, it had not been true for almost 30 years. She felt it but could not say it. She could say it was cold but could not feel it. The girl was quiet and slowly smoldering.

When the girl was in the States, she cried. The man had been right. Hard work and long hours would not pay dividends. Not for the girl. They did not want girls. She would be thrown away in the same way she had been before. She knew it. She felt it. The smoldering in her soul continued, increased and was at risk of becoming a raging fire.

The girl took a trip to see her parents. She let her father hold her. Her mother stroked her hair. They talked about ambition, strength, power. Her father told her to press on and believe in herself. He told her she was bright and talented. The girl went back to China believing she was a failure.

The man met the girl at the airport and held her close and she cried. Resentment was not allowed in their bed that night. Sorrow and compassion took its place. The girl felt safe but insecure. She cried often now in the arms of the man. The man held her, kissed her and told her he loved her. The girl felt worthless but grateful.

When she was 45, the anger overtook her. Worse, the darkness overtook the girl's first daughter. The girl knew she was responsible. It was the secret, though the girl did not know this yet. Afraid and angry, the girl worked harder, longer. She avoided her daughter and then her son and then her younger daughter.   Happiness seemed impossible.

The girl was lost. The man worried. Their children were confused. The ticking of the clock grew louder inside the girl's head.

Anger replaced resentment in the bed of the girl and the man. The passion was intense and intoxicating but passion from anger is not the same as passion from love. The girl was searching. She loved the man, she knew it, but she often behaved as though she hated him. In bed, hate and love exploded and the darkness and the secret plotted.

Her guardian angel watched over her, protecting her from the demon in the night.

The girl was 45 and 16 at the same time. The man loved her more each day than he had the last. He would not let her throw herself away. And, so the man marched her to the medicine man.

The medicine man forced her to accept help not for herself but for her first-born daughter. The girl was hurting her, though she didn't intend to or even realize that she had. The girl loved her children. The girl's daughter grew older, increasingly closer to 16. As she did, the secret grew more powerful and an alliance was struck between the darkness and the secret.

The darkness moved out of the tiny spaces and overtook both the girl and her daughter. The child in the corner of the girl's mind taunted her. Crazy. Crazy angry. Crazy scared. Crazy, maddening sorrow, disappointment and regret.

The man sat in the waiting room. The girl slowly confided in the medicine man.

After, the man took the girl to lunch. They drank beer and held hands. Eventually, the girl confessed her secret to the man. The man cried. Slowly, the child in the corner of the girl's mind retreated along with the darkness and the secret. Not gone completely, but caged to protect the girl and her daughter.

Jane and me in Paris.

The girl turned 46. Her first-born daughter was happy again. But the girl was still a girl. And, though she did what they said could not be done, she was a girl and so she was forced to the back of the line. The man let her cry, but not for long.

Though disappointed by the boys club, the girl was in love again. That made her happy. And, her happiness made the man happy and their happiness made their children happy.

The man saved the girl. Again. Resentment, anger and the secret no longer lived in their bed. Passion, love and forgiveness took their place and filled their bed, their lives and moved them forward.

The girl, the man and their children survived and were stronger, better, tighter, closer. China was the greatest, hardest experience of self-discovery the girl ever endured. It was so great that the girl even learned to love the dog.

Random Thoughts of Despair & Anger

February 2013
Shanghai

Ever sit on a plane and think to yourself that the best outcome would be for the plane to go down? I know, pretty dark. I found myself on a virtually empty Air China flight tonight — which is rare in China — and that was exactly what I thought and thought and thought. I decided it would be best to get some sleep. I shut my eyes and may have slept some but I'm not sure, really.

Of course, now its 1:20 a.m. and I can't sleep. I landed at 10:30 p.m. and as I turned my phone on it rang. Call from South America asking me if I was okay. Well, if thinking about plane crashes means you are okay then, yes, I am great! Made my way out of the airport to see my greatest supporter waiting for me. And, by the time we got home, I managed to pick a fight with him. Stellar!

An "old" friend suggested I just get it all out but I really can't talk about it. Or, rather, we don't want to talk about it with the children just yet. No one is dying or anything tragic. It will be fine. It is always fine whether it feels that way or not, whether you believe it is or not — if you have kids, then it is always fine and always going to be fine. And, so it is.

When I arrived in China 20 months ago, I didn't think I could be any more lonely. I was wrong. So very, very, very wrong. China has, in some respects, been one of the most isolating experiences of my life. And, in other ways, I have never felt closer to my husband, our children and my family. I can't reconcile these emotions in my own head other than to acknowledge that my personal life seems to be getting back, if not staying, on track — despite this evening's fight — and my work life is a mess.

I know I have to take ownership of my failings. And, hard as it is to believe, I have acknowledged that I could have handled some things better. But, I also did what everyone said could not be done, would not be done and, now, I find myself sitting on the outside looking in and not understanding what happened. And, try as I might, I don't seem to be able to fix it. Hell, I can't even get the same answer twice.

Today was hard. Very hard. I have refused to defend myself because there is nothing to defend. I've been over this with my consigliere (aka Dad) and there is nothing to defend. But, in doing so, I had to let others define me, define the situation and the next steps.

The communication about the change in leadership in Asia Pacific began today. An email went out to the global team advising of the changes to the organizational structure, including my move back to the States. I, of course, was not told when this would be done. In fact, I was on a plane to Beijing when it was delivered.

After landing, I went straight to the office where the China regulatory team is located. We had meetings scheduled with our joint venture partner to review changes in China's regulatory standards affecting our industry. Awkward does not begin to describe the scene. Shock. The faces looking at me as I unpacked my laptop from its bag were shocked. I smiled. It's all good and I apologized: "I thought I would have a chance to tell you first. I am sorry you found out this way."

Questions. The team had questions that I could not answer. Or, at least, I didn't think I should answer at this point. I had no idea what the email said – I still had not seen it. There would be a meeting the following morning with the new senior executive (a member of the "real" leadership team) in charge of Asia Pacific, who would remain located in the States, when everyone would learn more

Teams gathered in conference rooms across Asia Pacific to listen to our new senior executive. The exact words escape me but the message was:

> *Jennifer is returning to the States after doing a great job in Asia Pacific pulling the team together and laying a strong foundation for growth. The Interloper (my word) will be taking over to allow Jennifer to return to the States. Her experience in Asia Pacific is needed to help get Europe and North America aligned to the new global structure. In addition to the Interloper and myself (the senior executive), Asia Pacific is now also supported by a global manager located in Europe . . .*

I sat at the table in the Beijing conference room trying to keep my composure. I knew this would happen but I was under the impression that we would resolve the issue of when I would actually repatriate before making an announcement. But, no. Effectively, at that moment, I was out of the job. Tossed aside.

I interjected and thanked the team, gave my support to the new leaders and the new structure they would bring to Asia Pacific, and then I excused myself so the team could talk candidly with the senior executive and ask any questions. I almost delivered my brief nod to my successor without showing my pain. Almost. My voice cracked at the end.

Conversations like this were taking place that day all over the globe. One senior executive led the call with the Americas and another handled Europe. I only participated in the Asia Pacific call.

My counterpart in Brazil called me this evening. The phone literally rang as I was getting off the plane from Beijing. She told me about the conference call with the Americas. They heard a very different story than the one told in Asia Pacific.

Within the hour, a friend in the States who attended two meetings — one for the Americas and one for local North American mangers – called and relayed another version that had been told in the smaller group meetings. In that version, I was incompetent. And, as was told in Europe, I requested to return home. None of these stories — not the one told in Asia, Europe, Brazil or the States — represents the truth. At least not from where I sit. I don't recognize those stories. I am angry. I am hurt. I am disappointed. I am lost for the moment.

Isolated.

When you no longer recognize yourself in the person others describe, have you lost your sense of self, have you lost perspective or are you the person you believe yourself to be despite the chatter? Standing alone for what you believe in and think is right is not only hard, it is isolating, sometimes heartbreaking and, for me, it will come with a degree of humiliation as I try to hold my head high and find my way back.

I think the first step is the one up the stairs to find my husband . . . maybe I can get lucky!

Big Girl Pants

February 2013
Shanghai

I have to put on my big girl pants, as a friend of mine kindly reminded me.

Each Monday, I lay in bed clinging to my husband wishing the morning away. But, children must be woken, fed and put on the school bus. And, a woman must grab her big girl pants, her stilettos and go to the Salt Mine. I feel humiliated and I have to keep going to the very place and see some of the very people who make me feel this way. It is much easier to tell someone that they have nothing to be ashamed of than it is to be the person shamed. Still, I hold my head high, smile and pretend that all is well with *Five for Chinese*.

What else do you do?

Fact is, we have very little information about what is happening to us, our family or my career. My career is the least of our concerns, though it is the source of immeasurable misery lately. My own fault. Too many years defining myself by my career and not by the things that actually create a life worth living — family, love, forgiveness, personal values, me. I am on the road to changing that dynamic but it will not happen overnight. Old dog that I am. Still, I intend to honor my New Year's Resolution — to invest my time more wisely.

What keeps me up at night is the uncertainty. The looming separation. And, the sense of responsibility I feel for those I love and who have sacrificed for me, my career, the Salt Mine. There is a silver lining, though. Our children have seen the world. We have seen the world. More of the world than most humans ever have the opportunity to see. I am grateful. But, I also earned it.

So, in the mixing bowl of emotions, which is what I am these days, I put on my big girl pants and my lipstick and greet the day. This does not mean that I am not grieving. I am. I have lost my identity, or what I thought was my identity. And, again, it is my fault for allowing others to determine my value and believing their assessment. What was I thinking?

When will the grieving end? When I have concrete information, facts, data, timetables and every excruciating detail about the next steps, including the care of my family. I cannot complete the grieving process without this information and the Salt Mine seems unmoved by my requests even when made as a desperate mother worried about her children. Instead, the cycle keeps repeating itself with each new or updated piece of information that drips from the Mothership like the last drops of syrup from the bottle.

So each Monday, I put on my big girl pants and I go on with my life, our lives. But, armed with no information, my better half and I have had to keep this secret from our children. And, this secret is hard, destructive and will bring a mix of joy and sorrow. We will focus on the joy and work to minimize the sorrow. But, we can't do that yet. Stuck.

I wear my big girl pants during the day and weep in the darkness of the night. My emotional roller coaster is extreme. Fortunately, extreme emotion seems to focus me. Maybe only great loss can focus you in the way that I feel focused. Great loss and fear.

I am — in some very strange way — grateful for the opportunity to focus. I am more aware of who I am at the core, what my value system is and how I want to invest my time — more than I have ever been before. I hired an executive coach to help me, to challenge me and to force me to keep my focus and not allow me to

Courtesy www.keepcalm-o-matic.co.uk

fall back into the pattern that has defined me up until now: the pattern of a workaholic.

Really big shoulder to cry on — got that too. I am a lucky girl, after all.

27 Days

February 2013
Shanghai

I saw that movie *27 Dresses* the other day.   When I woke up this morning, I realized that I may have only 27 days left in China. I still cannot confirm whether I have 27 days, 47 days or 10 days. The details of my life are unimportant to the Salt Mine.

Being on the clock, however, did require us to make some choices. Each day has been a series of choices. This morning, we made another choice. We told the kids. We told them what we know, which is that Mom has a new job and it is in the States. They get to finish the school term in China. Mom is not sure when she is leaving but she will not be away more than a few weeks at a time (even if it bankrupts us). And, it's all good. It's really great news. Time to go home.

And, that is true. We've had a great adventure over the last two years.   You almost could not plan a better ending, actually. An amazing production of *Grease*, football drills with Ndamukong Suh on the Saturday before the SuperBowl and a couple of

Ndamukong Suh in Shanghai.

gold medals in swimming. Not such a bad send off.

I'll admit it would be nice to know what the hell is actually going on with our lives. But when you are just a little family of five trying to make your way in the world, you don't attract much attention. All you are to the Salt Mine is an employee with an identification number who happens to have three kids and a large husband and a dog. What's the big deal? How hard can it be to move a family back — oh, no, my mistake — how hard can it be to leave a family behind, while the employee ID number returns to the States? But, I digress.

Jane as "Principal Lynch" in *Grease*.

Bella winning medals and learning discipline.

In truth, in the end, it won't be that big a deal. We'll manage it. Ironic, really. Doing the impossible, my boss used to say, was what I did best. So, it's not a big deal. I mean it isn't impossible.

Our children are citizens of the world because they have lived and played with other world citizens. Their horizons are broader, wider and deeper and more colorful than they ever would have been without this experience. Still, a twinge of bitterness remains. A twinge that I likely will carry with me for some time. Never mess with a women's kids. Never.

At this point, you have to make some plans. Forget manning up. Women plan better, particularly when planning their revenge. It took about 2 hours and the plan was complete.

If you may, or may not, be leaving in 27 days for a job that may, or may not, be your stepping stone to oblivion or redemption and you may, or may not, be separated from those you love most in the world for 4 months and you are a stiletto and wrap dress-wearing woman, then you do what every good woman does: You pull out your credit card and book a trip to Cambodia. Isn't that the obvious solution?

Forbidden holidays are so much more fun, more memorable and far sexier than those taken at appropriate times. My revenge is happiness.

Being happy. The first step in my revenge plot is to celebrate. And, the best celebrations are spontaneous, unexpected and without excuses. We'll be playing hooky. Skipping school, skipping the Salt Mine and skipping town for a few days. We are headed to Siem Reap and Angkor Wat and Bayon Temple. We'll be 4-wheeling, taking tuk-tuk rides and sipping cocktails by the pool at a place called Navatu Dreams Resort & Spa.

A woman spurned needs a holiday at a resort with the word "dreams" in it. A woman I know is taking that holiday. She is taking it with the man of her dreams and the three little Defectors. She is taking it because she deserves it, they deserve it and she isn't going to let anyone or anything spoil it. Her Daddy is right. This woman is made of steel and she is gonna walk tall and, eventually, she will be 'more than' or at least 'equal to' but she will no longer be 'less than.'

27 days — maybe a few more or a few less. At the end of the day — whether it is 1 day, 27 days or 270,000 days — all you really have is your family and a few true friends. In addition to being the opportunity of a lifetime, it has also been an opportunity to discover, if not confirm, who is family and who is friend.

Tail of the Dragon

February 2013
Shanghai

We are in the final days of the Year of the Dragon here in the Middle Kingdom. The tail of the dragon is taking its final swipes at me before it finally leaves. It hurts.

Someone once said you come into this world alone and you go out alone. I have no idea who said it, when it was said or why they said it, but I've been thinking lately that there are many, many, many things in life that you must do alone. You must do them alone no matter how much others may love you or want to help you. You have to walk some roads alone.

He bought me tulips today. My favorite flower. They are next to me now as I am writing this. What is this? My midnight confession. I can't sleep, again.

He held me, told me it would be okay while I wept into his chest. It won't be okay for a little while yet. Before then, there are some things I must do alone. Things I don't want to do. Things I am not sure that I still have the strength

Tulips at the Shanghai flower show.

to do. But do them I must and I must do them alone.

I don't know if it is irony or just bad luck but this all started with me getting on a plane alone and it will end that way too. I don't know when exactly. The Salt Mine is still mulling it over — it is just my life — no reason to rush to any decision. It may, in fact, be a good sign that I am still waiting for the official order. I am stalling for every week, every day, every hour, minute and second that I can. I do not want to get on that plane and leave him and them behind for even a day. I am not sure I can bear it but I must. I must get on the plane and go alone.

Years ago when I was a new lawyer, I had the opportunity to work on a team of lawyers representing clients on death row in Illinois. I could not imagine what these men went through waiting to learn if they would be spared the sword. Someone else holding your life in their hands. Unable to control any aspect of the process and not knowing exactly when the final day might arrive. These men were literally and figuratively isolated — alone. Working on these cases leaves an indelible mark on you. It is a powerful and humbling thing to end or save a life.

I am not sure why that occurs to me now other than it is hard to imagine a more lonely time than your last moments on death row. Although, as a parent, I have felt extreme loneliness when I have been separated from my children. I have felt alone in their presence when they have been in physical or emotional pain that I cannot fix no matter how much I love them or want to fix them. A mother's love can be comforting but it cannot fix everything.

It is not loneliness that I feel now. It is aloneness, which is not the same thing at all. I am surrounded by people who love and care about me. My family and friends have been wonderful throughout this roller coaster ride. In the past few days, I've learned that my team at the Salt Mine had too many drinks at lunch and started speaking their minds. While there has been no protest march, there has been an out-pouring of support for me that I never expected. Certainly, not in this culture. Not in Asia Pacific.

At Chinese New Year, red envelopes containing money are given as gifts. It is a very significant tradition in China and this is how the Salt Mine bonuses are delivered. While delivering my red envelopes, I received gifts, was hugged and even had an employee cry. The Chinese do not hug and, if one has 'lost face,' then the practice is to physically distance oneself from the outcast. It is not to embrace them. I know this should make me feel better but somehow it has made me feel even more alone.

It gets harder every day to go to the office and it will be harder still when I return to the States. I know this and I am trying to prepare myself. I tell myself that I have only until March 1st and then I will be on the plane alone. I tell myself that I will have 4 to 5 months without him and without the children. I tell myself that I can walk into the building with my head held high. I tell myself that I am smart, good and important. I tell myself I can do it . . . alone.

As Bonnie Raitt sings in *"Silver Linings:"* "Help me Lord, help me Lord, I'm feelin' low." Of course, I don't believe and I don't pray, so mercy seems unlikely for me.

We come into the world alone and experience life alone. We share moments and experiences with others, make connections, find love, joy, despair and sorrow but really we are alone. In our heads and our hearts, we are alone. There is no one with you. Some may say that God is with you but I have never believed or felt that in any way that I can remember. It is you — alone.

I have filled up the spaces in my life with wonderful people and experiences and, for the most part, when they surround me I don't feel alone. It is the gut-check moments when you are reminded that you are alone and that no one can walk in your shoes but you. I am loved. I know this; I do. But, I will have to get on that plane and go back to the States — for months — home to an empty house where I will not just feel alone but be alone.

The Salt Mine is spiteful, vengeful and without remorse. It will have its pound of flesh.

And, so at 1 a.m. on a newly minted Friday — the last of the Dragon — I am alone at the table with my tulips and my thoughts (which will not turn off and allow me to sleep). Upstairs, in my bed, is the man who is desperately trying to keep the pieces of me together. He knows I slipped out again and that I am likely sitting at the table with the tulips. But he also knows it is best to *leave* me alone so that I can prepare myself to *be* alone.

Burned by the Dragon, I am hopeful that the Snake will charm and not bite me in the ass. I will celebrate the coming year, with my family here in Shanghai. We have planned a surprise and it will be wonderful. We are taking the kids to the Shangri-La on the Bund for the Chinese New Year's Eve. The kids love hotels and room service! I will be surrounded by my three wonders and the love of my life and I will be happy. It will lurk in the darkness and in the recesses of my mind. I know it is coming.

But, Saturday night is New Year's Eve and I will not be sitting at the table with the tulips. I will be watching fireworks until I can't stand it anymore and then, with any luck, making some fireworks of my own with him.

Lanterns at Chinese New Year.

Throw Away People

February 2013
Shanghai

The news came this morning at 8. I've been granted a 30-day reprieve and will be in Shanghai until April 1st. Of course, I will extend the time to include the Easter holiday with our children in an exotic location of our choosing! If they keep moving the date, this is going to bankrupt me.

I was the model citizen, really. I stopped short of being grateful but I offered to provide all the support required to enable a smooth and orderly transition, including playing tour guide to the new guy. My 30-day reprieve will involve a bit of country-hopping. Oh joy! I heard myself say "happy to do whatever is required to make this work," and thought "who is this person?" But, alas, we all do what we have to do when we have to do it.

There was snow. The buses failed to run. The children had a snow day. I was home because my office building was shaking and was "unsafe" for an as yet "undetermined" reason. No avoiding it. They heard me on the phone and now they knew that there was an end date. Mom was leaving. I would rather have had this conversation without the kids in the room listening to every word and watching my reaction.

Put on the happy face, I thought. "We have some extra time together and Mommy will bring your cousin back in May. It actually works out great." Again, "who is this person?" Please, someone, shoot Pollyanna in the head.

Realizing that I was out of anxiety pills and still behaving as though I was fully dosed, I knew I needed to get to the shrink's office. Of course, I dragged him with me to the shrink's office. We stopped at the shaky office building on the way so I could pick up a few things (letting go seems to be an issue) and then we hit the road. I felt fine. I did. I had just been granted a stay of execution. No clemency but a stay. I should be grateful. I **should be** grateful.

There it was "should be" as in I am not grateful. Feel it rise up and push it back down, I told myself trying to keep it together as we got closer to the shrink's office. We were just five minutes late and he was another 10 minutes behind. I was pacing now in the hallway. He was sitting calmly playing 'Words with Idiots' or something on his phone. He hardly noticed me or so he wanted me to think. But, I knew he saw it building. I was not going to sit. I needed to keep moving or I was going to explode.

I heard my name called and I saw Dr. Feel Good motion to me. I was outside the office in the hallway. He got up off the couch and walked back with me. I didn't have to ask him. He knew. He always knows. We sat down and he settled in and placed his arm around me. I sat there, arms folded, clutching a bag. Dr. Feel Good was across from us.

It was maybe 2 minutes at the most before the cork left the bottle. I know I **should be** grateful. I know I should not care what others think. I know that there are more important things in life than this stupid job. I know that I have it better than most people. Yes, I have my health. I know all of this — I am not stupid. I was nearly screaming at the good doctor.

Intellectually, I know all of these things but when I try to put my head on my pillow at night, that is not what occurs to me. What occurs to me is much darker and comes from a place so deep it scares me. I am afraid to close my eyes. It is not about this stupid job. It is about the demons that I have yet to slay. The demons I was battling before I was distracted by the skirmish at the Salt Mine. I am afraid of the dark again. I cannot remember the last time I really slept. And, now, I can't hide it anymore. I am a walking zombie.

Dr. Feel Good would not let up. "You know, some people would see this as an opportunity." "This could lead to something better." "My friend is a writer and he says there is no bad experience just good material." And, on and on and on.

Finally, I could take no more. "I get that everyone wants me to move on. I get that this could be a blessing in disguise. I get that I have a loving family. I get that anyone else would handle this better than I am handling it but they aren't me. And, this isn't about what I know; it is about how it makes me feel. And, really, I don't want to keep apologizing for the way I feel."

Dr. Feel Good couldn't help himself "but you can control your response, control your emotional response." With all the control I could muster, I reminded him that "I control my emotional response for 14 to 16 hours a day. But, when I lay down at night, everybody comes out to play." I was actually pounding on the couch. He was sitting calmly as ever next to me. Patient, loving and non-judgmental. He put his hand on my shoulder and gave it a squeeze.

"What are you afraid of . . . what scares you the most?"

Without hesitation, I looked over at him and then at Dr. Feel Good: "Being thrown away."

It was quiet as Dr. Feel Good took that in for a minute.

"I'm a throw away person."

'That's a rather harsh assessment, don't you think?" Dr. Feel Good poked at me.

I laughed. "I'm garbage. People throw me away. I am always fearful of being thrown away."

It was quiet for a few moments. Then I heard my voice crack and say, "People use me and then throw me away. That is my experience." It was a matter of fact as far as I was concerned. You want examples, try me, I thought. He didn't.

Session over.

He has never thrown me away. I am devoted to him. I have tried to push him away. I have tested him in every self destructive way I could ever imagine but he refused to go. I know the job is crap. I know what is important. I just can't shake the fear of being thrown away, particularly when I am being thrown away again. Yes, this is likely a totally distorted view of myself but it is my view. It has been my view for nearly 30 years. It won't go away overnight even with magic pills.

So, here I am at the table with the tulips less than 24 hours since I was last here. I think it is a good thing that we won't be home tomorrow. Perhaps, the demons and the tulips can battle it out for the night without me.

I think the point of today was to release the anger and say what is really scaring me aloud. I'm sure — like this whole experience — I'll look back one day and **be** grateful. I know I **should be** grateful. Today, though, today I am *not* grateful. I am scared, humiliated, angry and very, very tired.

Tomorrow, though, is another day!

Tangled

February 2013
Shanghai

With some relief, I can finally say that it is the Year of the Snake. Our son, who will turn 12 this year, should have an especially auspicious year as it is *his* year. If I am lucky, some of that auspiciousness may rub off on me.

To celebrate, we took a staycation at an amazing hotel in Shanghai and enjoyed the most wonderful views of The Bund and the city alight. After a great meal, we bundled up and headed down to the river to watch the celebratory customs of Chinese New Year's Eve. We found ourselves quickly wrapped up in the wonder of the event.

While China Police Authorities were busy pushing lantern peddlers along and stomping out lit lanterns set to launch into the sky, we searched desperately for a match to light ours. A group of three policemen stopped and said "Happy New Year," smiled at our vendor who emerged with a lighter and then moved along staring back at the two blonde children with the crazy mother. In China, no one can resist the lanterns' pleasing glow — not even the police.

Each of our children had a lantern, and we added a fourth for the family. As each child lit their lantern, you could see them unraveling wishes in their heads and concentrating deeply on them as the lanterns warmed and began to fill and prepare for flight. Daddy was taking photos and Mom was helping them hold onto the lanterns until they were ready to float. Magic. Pure.

Fireworks, the beauty of The Bund, the river and our children — all together in this wondrous country on a night when everyone is happy, wishful, hopeful and looking forward. Even me.

Gone was the tangled web of emotions running through me these last weeks. Everything became simple in that moment as I hung onto the lantern with our children. That single shared moment, where their desires were the most important desires in the world. And getting that lantern off the ground would determine if those desires would have a chance at flight.

I was completely overtaken by the fireworks last year and still this year, they amaze me. But more striking to me are the beautiful and hopeful red lanterns lighting the dark (if somewhat "foggy") sky.

Let's face it, when you are lighting the fire beneath the lantern of a precious, beautiful 10-year-old, waiting for it to warm enough to float and carry her most heartfelt wishes and desires toward the heavens in the dark of night just as the fireworks begin their tune, how can you be anything but hopeful? How can you not look around and feel the longing we all share as a human race for something better for each of us, for all of us?

New Year's wishes waiting to take flight.

As we launched our New Year's Eve lanterns, I tried to release my disappointment and look more hopefully toward the future. It is often one step forward and two steps back, but I am hopeful that my step forward is getting larger so as to overcome the setbacks. It has been an amazing two years. It was an amazing evening on The Bund.

I am lucky. I am fortunate. I am going to be okay. In fact, we are going to be so much better than we have ever been before . . . I know it.

Everyone is optimistic on New Year's Eve.

Part Four:
Leaning In & Moving On

The Assignment

February 2013
Shanghai

My assignment from my executive coach is to write a stream of consciousness — so to speak — using the following theme written at the top of the page:

"It's been a very good year after all . . . and I am so pleased now that . . . "

You might be wondering why I have an executive coach. I already have a shrink, so why exactly is the executive coach necessary? Because I need a team. A dedicated team of people working to improve me or, at least, to make me believe that I am improved. Yes, it does take a village to raise an adult. Or, at least, a sane adult.

Yes, it has been a very good year after all. We celebrated 20 years of marriage, our children traveled around Southeast Asia and Europe, and I learned that there really are people out there who care about you, and that you can be completely overtaken and surprised by that fact.

I have wonderful friends. I have a wonderful and loving family. I have a job. I may hate my job at this exact moment in time but I have one. I am healthy. My parents, in-laws and children are all relatively healthy and happy. Even the dog seems to be doing well despite the constant barrage of fireworks.

I am so pleased now that I did not quit when I wanted to chuck it all. I am pleased that the plane did not go down when all I could think about was the plane going down and the amazing amount of insurance money Jack would get to start over, better and happier. I am pleased that I have 30 more days with my family before I have to head back to the States.

I am so pleased that I get to be the tour guide for the guy coming to take my job so that I can make his freakin' transition so smooth and easy. I mean, really, who wants to travel to China alone, land in the dark, and be met by a driver who doesn't know you or speak a lick of English while you speak not a lick of Chinese and will almost certainly get lost on the way to your temporary accommodations? Oh right, me.

I must have wanted that . . . because that was my freakin' transition. Hell there was nothing here to "transition." It did not exist. I was blazing a trail. But, we wouldn't want the new guy to be frightened by China or India, now would we?!

I pulled the undisciplined approach to regulatory lobbying and strategy into a process, and I took the heat for certification programs that were mismanaged regardless of the "root cause" of the mismanagement. Blame was not my concern. Everyone was learning. A leader leads and that includes protecting the broader team. I also argued for a work force plan — *actual people to do the work.* I did it and I am now so pleased to turn all of that hard work over to some schmuck who will get far more respect, support, money, stock and other rewards.

I am also so pleased now to return to the States and a dead-end, phony, made-up job that will remind me every day that I am less than all the freakin' men that I ever worked with or for at the Salt Mine. I am equally pleased to know that if I had only gone to charm school or been a member of a sorority, I might have had a better chance at the brass ring. Being courageous, smart and direct are traits we value in our men but not our women. We want our women to behave like the wives of the boys on the executive floor and that ain't me.

I am so very pleased now to know and understand my place in the world, which is under the freakin' rock.

Yes, it has been a very good year after all. I've discovered anxiety pills, Zoloft, bourbon, single malt scotch, shrinks, executive coaches and spent thousands of dollars trying to make myself into the "leader" the Salt Mine wants me to be — all the while leaving tiny little bits of myself, my beliefs, my values, me strewn across Asia Pacific, Africa, Europe and the States.

And, I am so pleased now to be able to say out loud how truly awful I have come to feel about myself. How incredibly angry I am that I have been put through this and that I have allowed myself to be taken advantage of – again. Yes, I am pleased now. So very, very pleased.

I can barely get out of bed some days. I really hate where I find myself. I am pleased to be able to give voice to that, I suppose. But, in truth, I just want out. Off the roller coaster. Stay under the rock and hide.

But, I am pleased now to know that however difficult it might be, I won't give up. I don't know where I am going or how I will get there but getting it done is what I do. So I will do it again. I will focus on getting it done and work on feeling better about it later. It is too much to bite off all at once.

It **has** been a very good year after all because despite all the hell, fire and shit that has come our way, my husband has not only stood by me but held me and done all he can to hold what are now just pieces of me together. Our children have grown closer to each other and to us. We are a family tested under fire. We know so much more about ourselves now than we ever have because of this past year. And, I am so pleased now to try and find a way to hang onto the good and shed the bad so that I, we, all of us can move forward together and be happy.

It's a wonderful freakin' life — most of the time, anyway.

The Assignment . . . A Year Later

February, 2013
Shanghai

I have been asked to look forward now . . . oh, joy. The new assignment is to imagine what might be possible, could be possible, if I apply myself to it. So, let's play pretend, shall we?

"2013 was a very good year after all, and now that it is 2014, I am so pleased that . . . "

In 2013, I remade myself into the person I once believed I could be. I started a blog in 2011 and by 2013 I decided that I do have a voice. A voice that, unbeknownst to me, resonated with others. I wrote that book. (You are reading it.)

My shrink actually said to me in 2012 that there are no bad experiences, only good material. Well, maybe you have to suffer to be able to know and express joy. Are all experiences really meant to teach us something? I don't know. If they are, then I am a slow learner.

2013 was a very good year after all. I conquered it. I left behind the people, places and things that made me feel unworthy. I found happiness in writing and devoting myself to causes that I care deeply about, like women's rights and ending violence against women across the globe, and became affiliated with groups that care about the same things. I traveled the globe with my husband and, at times, our children to understand these issues better and write about them. My writings appeared in my blog, in magazine articles and, occasionally, on stage when I speak on these issues.

It wasn't easy. It was scary. Incredibly scary to leave the security of the corporate world and the steady paycheck of the Salt Mine but, in the end, the Salt Mine was killing me. If you find yourself taking more and more anxiety pills and having to count them to be sure you don't overdose, then something is not working in your life. My life was no longer working for me.

The Salt Mine provided income — a very good income — but it was breaking me into pieces. I was as much a part of that as anyone. I just did not want to play their game. I no longer wanted to be someone else's doormat. But, the ability to walk away required a kind of courage that I was not sure I had inside me.

I found that courage in the form of my family and my friends. I spent 2 years writing a blog about our adventures in China. It turned into a blog about my personal growth and discovery in China. And, people I had not heard from in decades contacted me to say that my blogs meant something to them, touched them in some way, encouraged them, made them laugh or just brought some quiet relief to their day. After hearing again and again that I should write a book, two friends reached out to me. The first offered to help me with an editor. The second is a talented screenwriter. I found the courage to ask for their help.

And now that it is 2014, I am so pleased that I find myself in a place where I have more control over my life. I feel a sense of pride in what I do. I feel that I am making a difference in a small way. I now feel that the struggles I fought have meaning. I have meaning.

Could this year ahead that I imagine in my mind be a real possibility? I don't know. But, do I think about it almost every day and I have 365 days to make it happen. Maybe the shrink is right (and you know I don't want to admit it) — there are no bad experiences, just good material.

The Assignment . . . At The Crossroads

February 2013
Shanghai

I guess this is turning into a series called "The Assignment." My executive coach gave me an assignment — a mission, really. And, I chose to accept it.

First, I had to look back at 2012 and fill in the blanks: "it actually was a very good year after all . . . and, now, I am so pleased that . . ." Yes, it seemed like the perfect opening for sarcasm and drivel but I took the assignment seriously. The result was a fair amount of anger mixed with an attempt to find the silver lining. Yeah, I know. What a sap.

The second assignment was the same as the first except the view is from 2014 and I am looking back on 2013. I approached this assignment imagining what I could do, if I wasn't afraid. I would write. I would try to publish what I write. I would try to be more than I am now.

Well, now there is another assignment and as long as we've gone this far together, why not go a bit further? So, this is the third in "The Assignment" series. Truth is that writing is how I think best or maybe it is just how I get shit out of my head. I don't know really. But, it has fewer calories than french fries, so here we go. The questions below are from my coach — I almost feel like an athlete!

1. What reaction does each assignment evoke in you as you read it? What does that tell you?

Looking back on 2012, my reaction is "WTF?" Seriously, my reaction is "WTF?" And that comes with plenty of anger, fear, frustration and self-doubt. I had extremely high expectations when I came to China, for me and for our family. They weren't realized. I force myself to find the silver linings, intellectually I know they are there but I do not *feel* them. That is not to say that I have not had moments of joy and happiness. But if asked "How was 2012?" I am reminded of my beloved Queen Elizabeth and her "Annus Horribilis."

Looking back at 2013, my reaction is wistful. 2013 reflects what I wish to be not what I am today. My reaction is "pretender." This is what I want to be, what I probably always wanted to be but never had the nerve. A writer. Still, the reaction is more hopeful. Hopeful that I can actually find it within myself to do something so completely out of the box and regain my freedom. But, doubt lingers.

What does it tell me? Not sure. But, clearly, it is supposed to tell me something. These two years represent polar opposites – so does it tell me that I am bi-polar? I think it tells me that, at this moment today, I am able to see only the extremes. I am able to feel only the extremes. The middle ground is not something in my purview ... at this moment. But, it is also honest. Very honest. I don't want to continue on the

2013 was a good year after all . . .

path that I have been on. I want to do something that makes me feel worthy.

2. As you choose where and on what to focus your thoughts, how does that change you?

The obvious answer to this question seems to be that it changes your attitude, your perspective — and in changing your attitude and perspective, you give yourself the opportunity to change.

When I focus on the future and not the past, I am scared. When I focus on the past and not the future, I am angry. I would rather be scared than angry because being scared means that I have the opportunity to be courageous. Being angry means I am stuck. I want to choose to be courageous.

Choosing to face what scares me has the potential to change me, my life, completely. Or, it gives me the opportunity to change myself, or maybe just *be* myself.

3. As you reflect on the "bad" experiences, what happens if you ask "What for?" vs. "Why me?"

You move from victim to champion.

Asking "what for" lets you take back control. In other words, this was meant to happen because I needed to grow in some way, it opened a door that would not have opened otherwise, it gave me the opportunity to overcome, to learn, to share.

Asking "why me" allows me to wallow. I've been doing a fair amount of wallowing recently, though it has been peppered with self-reflection in an effort to determine "what's next?"

4. We judge our experiences based upon how we frame them. More often than not we are totally unaware of that framing process. So we don't get to see that we are making a choice, and that how we make that choice defines the experience for us. Does this resonate with you? If so, what options does that create for you?

I understand that how we frame things often informs our conclusions. I am, or was at one time, a trial lawyer so I've had some practice framing things in a professional capacity. In my personal life, however, it is very different. I am aware of my tendency to frame things in a negative way — I am reminded of that small boy on the back of the Polar Express "Christmas just doesn't work out for me" — I get that.

If I can consciously focus on choosing to frame the experiences of the past year in a more constructive way, then I can learn from them, use them as examples of things that I have overcome, find strength in knowing that I did not only survive those experiences but that, despite the difficulties encountered, I accomplished more than was expected. Indeed, I succeeded.

5. Do you really think you are a slow learner? Or are there a few areas in your life where you have not been paying as much attention as you could? If so, what might be possible if you chose to pay more attention to those areas?

I do actually see myself as a slow learner. Perhaps, the reason I see myself as a slow learner is because I feel that I have allowed people to take advantage of me, my skills, my abilities for their own gain. Fool me once, shame on you. Fool me twice, shame on me.

There are areas in my life that I have not paid attention to for years. I have personal demons I should have dealt with years ago. I am dealing with them now. I have neglected my self worth — actual neglect. In my thoughts about myself and in seeking the financial rewards I believe I deserve, I have done nothing to secure those rewards or change those thoughts. Others ask for rewards and, often, get them. I would never ask; it never even occurred to me.

If I paid attention to these areas of neglect, I could improve my outlook if not my financial circumstances. I am not someone who wants to be a millionaire. I am someone who wants to provide comfortably for her family and also have time to enjoy them. If I focused more on the things holding me back from this, I might be able to find happiness.

6. What would need to change in order for you to pay more attention to those areas? (Be aware of your framing as you answer this one. We tend to frame even our framing.)

Stop defining myself based upon the views of other people. I think this is why I keep repeating the same pattern — being fiercely loyal and helping others advance on my work. I do that because I want them to value me because if they don't value me, then I don't have value.

Lighten up. Just let it go.

7. I see the 2013 version of your looking back framing your options as an "either/or" scenario. Either you continue to evolve your career or you leave and focus on building your voice and reach. Does it have to be "either/or"? Is it possible there could be an "and/with" scenario?

- Extremes. I am at extremes at this point. No denying it.
- Is there a middle ground? Yes, but finding it is harder than I expected.
- I believe somewhere deep down that I can evolve my "career" while building my voice.
- The Salt Mine, though, I think not. I'm not that nice a person or that forgiving.

Now What?

March 2013
Siem Reap, Cambodia

Effective March 1st, I "completed" my assignment in China, 14 months earlier than expected. I guess I was simply too efficient. And, still, I feel so much is not yet done. There is so much to do. So much more that I want to do.

We have been privileged to travel to many beautiful and developing nations. The wonders in these countries are unlike any I have seen elsewhere. Our children have seen more of the world in their short lives than we ever expected they would see in an entire lifetime. And, these countries are truly wondrous. Both in their sites and their people.

I find myself not wanting to leave this part of the world. Not yet, at least. I feel a shift happening here and I want to witness it and even, in some small way, enable it. These countries and their people are moving from centuries-old traditions into the 21st century. But not everyone is prepared, not everyone is able to make the leap, not everyone has the means to make the change.

This is the space I want to play in for a bit. I want to witness that change, participate in it. I have no delusions of grandeur. But I do have Facebook. And, I am impressed with the Gates Foundation, the Clinton Foundation, and organizations like Vital Voices, Women Under Siege and so many others working to make the world a better place.

I have been fortunate. I am not wealthy. I barely have a savings account. We chose to show our children the world and it cost a bit of money. There will be money for college. As my Father says, things have a way of working out. I sometimes worry about not having a designated college fund but I have a house and it can be sold, if it is ever worth anything again. Still, we are privileged, more than privileged compared to most people on this planet.

Now what? For me, it will be about giving, contributing and doing something bigger than myself for someone other than myself. In what can only be described as chance circumstances, an

Could I help this woman in Cambodia?

opportunity to give back presented itself. It is, more accurately, a nugget of an idea that I am nurturing, but an opportunity begins the same way as a tree — from an acorn, a seed, a nugget of an idea. I have created my own opportunities before and I am hoping to do it again.

I am anxious about the next few weeks. It is an odd thing to be asked to spend a month teaching someone to do your job. A job that, in some ways, has been taken from you just when things were clicking. But that is what I have been asked to do, so I will do it and do it well. I will be on the road or in the sky heading to Australia, Thailand, the Philippines and then the States. And, then what?

I don't yet know to be honest. It may not be what I expect or even hope for at this very moment, but in time, I will get to where I am going. I do not want to leave my home and return to my house. Home is where my soul mate and our children rest their heads. One of my next several planes will take me to my house and away from my home but eventually we will come back together.

With some luck, I'll also be able to answer the question: "Now what?"

Choice and Power

March 2013
Melbourne, Australia

I was among my Australia team or, I should say, my former team. My purpose was to introduce the new leader and step off the stage. By late afternoon, the path to my door was worn, and I was overwhelmed. I never expected anyone to take the time to find out where I was sitting in the maze that is the Melbourne office complex, but they did. It required effort. You could not have stumbled upon me.

At some point, I started thinking about these people who were coming to thank me. Thank me for what? Truth is, I am the one who is thankful. The past two years have been amazing and have, undoubtedly, changed the lives of the people I love most.

I am not suddenly in denial of the manner in which this game is ending. I have been treated poorly, used and tossed aside. But, to replace me they needed three men and a complete change in structure and that says more than I ever could or will say.

Most unexpected, however, has been the people who have reached out to me asking to have coffee, dinner, drinks or just a few minutes. Some are Aussies who worked in China and already repatriated themselves. Others are work partners from other organizations who want to say goodbye, talk or share experiences.

I was thrilled to have dinner plans that did not involve the person taking my job (though I did take him to dinner one night). Dinner every night with the Interloper was just a bit more than

I thought I could handle at this point in the metamorphosis. An excuse to get out of dinner was exactly what I needed. And, not exactly what I expected.

I am not alone. In fact, I am just one more member of a club that sadly exists within the Salt Mine. I listened to others — all women — tell me what was happening to them or recently happened to them. I immediately empathized with them. All were in some stage of the grieving process. All of them wanted to know how I was handling "the situation."

I was shocked to learn that so many people in Australia were aware of my circumstances and had heard rumors of how poorly the situation was being handled. Most people at the Salt Mine in China have no idea that I am leaving, let alone the circumstances. But, even more surprising to me, was the reaction among the team here to the way I have chosen to handle these circumstances — playing tour guide to the person replacing me. Most found it confounding.

I recognize the anger and despair in the faces sitting across from me at dinner. I feel the anxiety and the intensity of their emotions. And I realize that I am beginning to move forward. I have been given the opportunity to say goodbye to people I care about but to do that I had to accept the role of tour guide. For me, it was an easy decision — a simple choice. It gives me more time with my family — despite the travel — and I get to go out with some dignity.

I get to choose.

I listened, poured a second glass of wine, picked up the check and left grateful for the conversation. I truly had no idea what I meant to others or, at least, to these others. This is illuminating. You can tell a person that their value is not determined by others and that simply because someone characterizes them in a particular way doesn't necessarily make it true. You can choose to believe it or you can choose to focus your attention elsewhere.

My experience is unpleasant. And, it is not unique. I wish it were. I am saddened that it is not. I am choosing, however, to focus on what the broader experience gave me, my husband and our children. I am choosing to focus on the support that I am now able to offer others who find themselves in similar unpleasant circumstances. I am choosing to conduct myself and the affairs of this transition with dignity. I am choosing to respect myself and, by doing so, sending the message that I will not allow others to determine my worth, my value, my measure of success.

In choosing, I have taken back control. Ironically, it is through shared sacrifice and disappointment that brings me to this point, combined with unexpected gratitude and respect for that sacrifice. The tour continues for the next few weeks but I feel more able to control my emotions and to allow myself to feel whatever emotion I might feel without apologizing or castigating myself for it. Giving myself permission to just let it go, to just feel it, to just be, is powerful. It is a choice. It is a choice to move forward.

It is my choice.

Tour Guide Barbie

March 2013
Adelaide, Australia

We got on the plane headed out of Oz and I could feel the darkness creep back and linger in the back of my mind. It was taunting me. We would land in Shanghai and get home around 8 p.m. At 6:15 a.m., my driver would take me back to the airport to go to Thailand. Less than a 10-hour turnaround. Tour Guide

Barbie back on the circuit and, this time, the mighty and powerful wizard was not coming with me. Jack met me in Australia for some couple time but he would not be able to do that for the remainder of the tour.

On the trip back to Shanghai, I am reading *The Art of Possibility* by Roz and Ben Zander. The book gives you tools to re-frame your life — to discover the art of the possible. While reading it, I start crying. It isn't like I am reading *Schindler's List* here. Why am I crying? Well, that's a bit complicated and also very simple. The book is on-point. It is everything that is wrong with me and my life, my perspective, my frame, my whatever.

One of the concepts is "it's all invented." Everything is invented:

- The standard against which I measure myself;
- The standard others use to measure me;
- The game that I am playing with the Salt Mine; and
- The definition of success, happiness, etc.

Once you realize that it is all invented, then you can re-invent it, ignore it, create a new game, a new reality, anything is possible because the frame in which you place yourself and evaluate your options is likely limited by these inventions.

On one hand, I agree and even like this notion. It allows me to toss out the crap. Yet, the reality is that I am getting on a plane in just hours to play Tour Guide Barbie in Thailand. Do I want to play Tour Guide Barbie? No. Can I just say no? No. Why not? Because I am afraid I will be viewed negatively and I don't need any more of that. But if it is all invented, then I should be able to skip the trip. And, it's my choice. So simple and yet so difficult.

As I sit here reading, I know I will be on that plane. But, I decide to modify the plan. I will not accompany the Salt Mine boys to Pattaya (no one wants a girl with them there anyway — well, not a girl you work with anyway). I resolve to change my return flight and go home on Wednesday.

I cried on that flight back from Thailand as I read *Lean In*.

From the time I was a little girl I was called "bossy." In high school, I was voted something like "most likely to be the boss" and it was *not* meant as a compliment. Now, at work, I am not "charming" and I am "too aggressive." I have been teased my entire life about this quality, which as it turns out would be a leadership quality if I had been born a boy.

It's somewhat comforting to know that even the most successful women in the world — indeed the most powerful — suffer from the same insecurities, are plagued by the same self-doubt and even lack the confidence to believe in themselves. Somehow they overcame it, but I am not sure I will overcome this setback. Not today, at least . . .

Fear is holding me back. I want to chuck the whole damn thing. I do. I want to walk out and leave them to their boys' club. I want to work on women's issues and make a difference for my daughters, my nieces and the granddaughters I hope to have one day. I want to be valued by me — how sad a statement is that? I want to be valued by me . . . which is to say, I find it hard to find value in myself. Why?

Well, many reasons, but my functional manager, who had been a mentor of mine, delivered the final blow by looking at the work I've done and telling me that while I did the work, I failed to cultivate relationships with the boys in the States. I could bore you with the details of evidence that prove some of his specific examples wrong but why? That isn't the point.

The point is I am a woman who was put into a position of authority that required real-time decision making and the exercise of judgment. And, I am ranked two levels below the men in similar jobs. No one likes an "underling" giving them assignments, particularly when that underling is a woman. Set up to fail and, in spite of that fact, succeeding. What else could they do but characterize me as a non-team player?

It is my greatest fear — to be thrown away. It haunts me. It lives in the nooks and crannies of my soul and taunts me. Worse, as I smile and lead not just the Interloper but also the Englishman (who is also involved in replacing me — yes, it takes three men to replace an un-charming woman, including 1 senior executive) around Bangkok, I am reminded that I am emptying the last pieces of me into the trash bin before I am pushed aside like day-old bread.

Even worse, like in Oz, the team in Thailand is far too generous. One of them makes a big speech thanking me and goes so far as to say that they hope I will continue to have oversight of the region. I am sure the Interloper and the Englishman loved that one. And, there was a crisis to manage while I was there, and, yes, I handled it. Idiot.

What would I have become if I had not been riddled with self-doubt, if I had stayed the course, been more steady? What could I have achieved? I will never know. Sheryl Sandberg is right: It begins when we are girls and it is reinforced our entire lives. Even other women will stifle you.

I have daughters. I have nieces. I am haunted by them now too, but also inspired. I must find my course again and believe in me. I am only beginning to peel the onion and the depth of the pain, disappointment and despair is, at times, overwhelming.

And, yet, just as deep is the profound happiness I feel when another woman tells me that I have inspired her, particularly the women who sought me out on the Barbie Tour.

It's there. Somewhere, that new frame, the re-invention of me is there.

I leaned in and felt the backlash. But, I don't want to lean back. I want to lean in further. This will undoubtedly put me at odds with former mentors, even friends, but I am committed to this cause. Perhaps there is a possibility of creating a shared vision but I am skeptical at this moment.

First, I need to commit to myself and restore my faith in me. I must be crazy — okay, we knew that didn't we?

Fear . . . Success . . . Reality . . . Perception

March 2013
Shanghai

In 1991, I was a first-year law student when U.S. Supreme Court Justice Nominee Clarence Thomas was in the midst of Senate confirmation hearings and Anita Hill raised allegations of sexual harassment against him. I remember watching the hearings in the law school common area. What really struck me was the composition of the Senate panel as I watched Professor Hill testify. I also remember the strikingly different tones of Professor Hill and Nominee Thomas.

The Senate hearing made an enduring impression upon me. Recently, I've been thinking about Anita Hill, Hillary Clinton, Sheryl Sandberg and me. Not because I belong in their company (I don't), but wouldn't lunch be interesting? I've been thinking about them and how their experiences influenced me, shaped me and reinforced my internal feelings about myself.

I remember Thomas being demonstrably angry and consistently (and, clearly, effectively) using the term lynching. I recall thinking that the coverage of his "anger" made him seem resolute.

In contrast, Hill tried very hard to remain calm, reserved, if not somewhat demure but in no way embarrassed. She deftly answered *the* question. Senator Biden asked if she recalled the name Thomas used to describe a particular penis. "Yes," she answered. Only when asked specifically to provide the actual name did she give it up: "long dong silver."

I remember thinking, at that time, that if she wanted anyone to believe her she would have to remain calm. She could not play the "lynch" card or she would be characterized as overly dramatic. Her testimony had to be factual, clinical, surgical.

The juxtaposition of her demeanor against his was striking to me. Anger, resolute anger, from a man was acceptable and even admirable, particularly as his wife sat behind him holding back tears. Hill could not play the angry card in the same way. She was the demon, the devil, the spiteful woman coming forward to have her revenge. Anger would not help erase that stereotypical image, which was far too easy to cast. She would be irrational, delusional, scorned. Watching her testify was like watching a tightrope walker work without a net.

I also remember thinking that the hearing seemed like a trial. Except that, if it were a trial, I would have expected to see a woman, an African American man and maybe even an African American woman on the jury. But the panel was composed of white men. White men who had very little life experience similar to Thomas or Hill.

It scared the hell out of me then, and it still does.

How is it that, more than 20 years after Anita Hill, I am still afraid and what exactly am I afraid of?

- Success?
- Being discovered as a fraud?
- The stereotypes that come with being a "successful woman"?

In addition to being afraid of something that I can't quite put my finger on, I also wonder if I am self destructing or trying to self-destruct and, if so, why. Maybe I am afraid of success. Women check out. I've seen it.

- Do they check out because they decide that being home with their children is a better choice (which it is for some women)?
- Do they check out because successful women are perceived as something less than a woman?
- Do women check out by being self-destructive?
- Is it just too hard? And, if so, what is so hard?

The Impostor Phenomenon

In 1968, when I was still just a baby, academics and researchers asked these same questions. [See e.g., *Behavior: Sex and Success, Time Magazine,* 1972]

One of them was a woman named Matina Horner. Ms. Horner was a scholar and administrator born in 1939. She conducted early research into women's fear of success. She later became the youngest president of Radcliffe College during the period when Radcliffe redefined its relationship with Harvard University.

Horner's research concluded that women are conflicted when their competencies, interests, and abilities do not align with the stereotypical and internalized female sex role. But, the desire or motive to avoid success has to be triggered to have an effect on their performance.

To determine if a motive to avoid success existed, Horner had test subjects watch members of their own gender and recorded their comments.   When statements were made showing a degree of conflict about the success or the potential for negative consequences because of success, Horner concluded a motive to avoid success was present. Even statements suggesting the individual was not responsible for the success or denying the success entirely were considered evidence of a motive to avoid success.

A decade after Horner, Paulene Chance and Suzanne Imes coined the term "impostor phenomenon" to describe highly educated women who had significant professional accomplishments yet felt they were fooling people about their brightness.   Four types of behavior were identified with the impostor phenomenon:

- Group 1 lived in constant fear that their ruse would be discovered;
- Group 2 resorted to flattery;
- Group 3 used their charm on superiors, to gain favor; and
- Group 4 feared rejection for appearing too smart and accomplished as a woman in our society.

The concept was extended to men by Manfred Kets de Vries in a *Harvard Business Review* article in 2005.   Kets de Vries introduced the possibility that there are "genuine fakers" – individuals who lack the qualifications and skills to perform. Genuine fakers are different from individuals who are truly competent but believe that they are fooling people.

Not surprisingly, one of the conclusions of the research has been that personal attitudes are not based upon reality but internal psychic inequities. In other words, perception shapes our reality and our perceptions are formed, in part, by our own internal struggle to rationalize our self-talk. A genuine faker may believe he or she is an expert and move up the ranks while another competent individual may believe they are a fraud waiting to be discovered and self-destruct.

In 2006, *International Forum of Psychoanalysis* devoted an entire issue to the subject. The majority of articles were written by feminist authors. These authors placed an emphasis on social attitudes toward women, in addition to psychodynamics.

The various authors acknowledged that attitudes toward women presented real challenges and that the glass ceiling was, in fact, a real barrier. The more important question for the researchers, however, was *how* these very real circumstances were approached by women. The internal struggle going on within each woman determines whether she will fight the injustice or succumb to it. Her choice — to fight or succumb — determines her level of personal achievement. [Source: "Fear of Success," Carl V. Rabstejnek, www.HOUD.info]

I am not an academic but I am fascinated by this research and what I've been able to understand about the phenomenon. Would the researchers qualify me as competent or just a faker? Is my own internal struggle raging on such that I have yet to decide if I will simply put down my sword or fight on? What about the Salt Mine? Would there be a stand-off between me and the Salt Mine like the one between Thomas and Hill? Would I be cast as the woman scorned? Have we grown up since the Thomas-Hill hearings?

Hillary Clinton: The Definition of Success

I am a fan of Hillary Clinton for many reasons, including the fact that she makes it okay for me to be me. Crazy? Maybe. But, that is how it feels when I watch her. She is a role model in some way. I watched her evolve like other women of my generation: The Bill Clinton Presidential campaigns, the health care debate, the Monica scandal, Hillary's own Senate and Presidential campaigns.

Like many women, I wondered why she couldn't beat Barack Obama. Was it that nobody likes a smart girl? Was it that we couldn't take a woman seriously? The media was fascinated by her hair and wardrobe, but her mind?

Now I read that Hillary is "redefining success." The following is an excerpt from Arianna Huffington, *"Redefining the Meaning of Success: Hillary Clinton's Next Great Challenge?"* The Blog on huffingtonpost.com, Feb. 5, 2013:

> "[Hillary's] the most important woman in America," writes Michael Tomasky. "More: she is almost certainly the most important woman in all of our political history." For an entire generation, she's been the foremost example of the successful woman. Here's what *Salon's* Rebecca Traister said about Hillary:

> "I was 17 when Bill Clinton won the presidency. My entire adult political consciousness has had Hillary Clinton, even more than Bill, in a position of public power in one way or another. It's been twenty years, and that twenty years for me has been my adulthood, and I have felt not warmly towards her for a lot of those years and then very warmly towards her in other years but the idea that she was going to leave, I did wake up on Friday morning thinking, hey, it's the end of an era."

And, let's hope, the beginning of another. "In the 20 years she's been on the stage," writes Tomasky, "the country has gone from wondering whether women could handle the toughest jobs to knowing they can."

Have We?

Have we really come to know that women can handle the toughest jobs? Have we come to accept it as the norm? And, many are asking "what is the price we pay for handling the toughest jobs?"

In a profile in *Marie Claire* by Ayelet Waldman (October 2012), Hillary Clinton spoke to at least one part of the problem. "It's important for our workplaces ... to be more flexible and creative in enabling women to continue to do high-stress jobs while caring for not only children, but [also] aging parents." I don't disagree, but that is hardly the biggest problem.

Here, I agree with Sheryl Sandberg. I don't know whether or not Ms. Clinton would agree or disagree on this point. She did say "one part of the problem," which suggests the problem is multifaceted. And, it is.

Sandberg's *Lean In* openly discusses the problem of women's internal self talk. Women's internal self talk holds them back. Their internal self-doubt and conflicts about how they see themselves and how they want to be seen is reinforced by a society that continually characterizes authoritative and successful women as something less than a woman.

Words like "bossy," "difficult" and worse are ascribed to authoritative women. And, when trying to appear more politically correct, we simply put the word "too" in front of the descriptor: "too aggressive." A man that is "too aggressive" is described as driven and passionate. A woman is just "too."

I was thrilled to see Hillary Clinton at the Benghazi hearings displaying every facet of herself: her compassion and empathy, her wit, her intelligence, her anger, her passion and her unwillingness to suffer fools or play games when the consequences of such actions are so very high.

But, we are not all Hillary Clinton or Sheryl Sandberg, are we? And, the consequences for us "normal women" don't seem to have changed all that much since 1991. If I display all the facets of myself — my compassion, empathy, wit, intelligence, anger, passion, etc. — I am neither admired nor liked.

Soul Searcher

I have been reading, thinking, writing and searching my soul.

- Who am I?
- Who do I want to be?
- What does success look like for me?
- What is success anyway?
- Do I want to be successful?
- If so, why?
- What is important to me?
- What should be important to me?
- *What questions should I be asking myself?*

I am down to weeks now. Weeks comprised of too few days that go by far too fast; and, then I must get on a plane and leave my family behind. Not forever, but for weeks comprised of days that go by far too slowly.

I return to a place that I cannot fathom any longer. To a place that makes me feel 'less than' exactly when I believe I am creating more. And, in doing so, I have been called many things but successful is not one of them. No, I am not Hillary Clinton or Sheryl Sandberg.

Alexandra Chang of *Wired* (like many working women) is reading *Lean In*, as am I. I see my own life experiences in the book, as does Chang. Chang writes that to understand her reaction to the book all you need do is look at the "stars" and "exclamation points" in her review copy. [Source: "*Why You Should 'Lean In' to Sheryl Sandberg's New Book,*" Wired.com, March 11, 2013]

Chang writes: "The first of these appears next to a paragraph where Sandberg details the divergent cultural messages directed at boys versus girls. Girls are often, blatantly, encouraged to be 'pretty,' Sandberg explains, while smarts and leadership are left to the boys."

I call this the smart girl syndrome and reflect on the debates between Hillary Clinton and Barack Obama. I recall thinking Clinton should hold back and wait to see if Obama knew the answers or even the correct pronunciation of the new Russian leader's name. She did not wait.

I kept thinking you are smarter than me and, even I know, that if you are seen as a "smarty-pants" no one will like you and you won't win. She didn't. Could she now?

Chang continues by highlighting a piece of Sandberg's book that so many of us can relate to:

"When a girl tries to lead, she is often labeled bossy," [Sandberg] writes. "Boys are seldom bossy because a boy taking the role of a boss does not surprise or offend." This small remark had me spinning. . . . as someone who, like Sandberg, has been called bossy her whole life, I was shocked I hadn't realized this before."

Chang cites this as *Lean In*'s "virtue:"

"Sandberg's 'sort of feminist manifesto' . . . is at its best when it shines a light on sexism's shadowy, more hidden nooks. Another key strength is the advice Sandberg offers, informed by her indisputably remarkable rise through the ranks of politics and business, that you can actually act on."

It is this subtle, shadowy discrimination that I believe is the most insidious. I also believe that women are reinforcing this discrimination either unwittingly or in an attempt to further their own careers. Yes, I have written about being told to be more charming, to not call attention to my differences, to not make the men uncomfortable. Sadly, this advice has come from women more often than men.

In her book, Sandberg talks about a Columbia Business School study that measured "likability" among men versus women in business. Some students were told about an aggressive, successful

Are we really ready for a female leader?
Photos courtesy Associated Press

venture capitalist named Heidi; others were told the same story except that the venture capitalist's name was changed to Howard. Even though no other details were changed, students found Howard the more likable of the "two."

I know this kind of discrimination exists. I know this kind of subtle sexism is continually reinforced in our society, in workplaces both large and small and I know this is happening to me. It is happening and it is making me crazy. Literally. I find myself constantly questioning every decision I have made, re-reading each and every email I have written, replaying every conversation in my mind. And why? Because nobody likes me; I am too ambitious.

In truth, it isn't that nobody likes me. It is a small group of powerful white men that don't like me. But, even if it were true, why do I care? Why should I care? My husband likes me. My kids like me. My dog likes me. Well, I thought he liked me but maybe I am wrong about that too.

So, what am I really afraid of: Success? Likability? Or, telling the truth about what is really happening?

What For?

March 2013
Shanghai

At some point don't we all ask ourselves: What is this for? Why am I doing this? Why am I working so hard? What is the reason for this pain that I am going through?

Do we ever ask ourselves that question when we are in the midst of joy, happiness, or success? No, introspection seems to come only with loss or pain. Is that right? Probably not entirely. I am not in pain 100% of the time, not even 50% really. I am, however, contemplative. What am I contemplating? Honestly, I don't know anymore.

Well, that is not entirely true. I am contemplating fire. Setting fire to bridges and lighting up the sky with my fury. When I ask myself what is this for? What is the point of this journey that I have been on? Maybe it is bigger than me. Maybe it is time to go all in and put my cards on the table.

Tell my story.

What is my story anyway? It is the story of an ordinary woman who took her children and her husband (and an 80-pound dog) to China. In the course of that journey, this woman rediscovered pieces of herself that had been buried for decades. And, from that discovery, she learned more about herself and her family than she ever expected. She also discovered what matters to her, truly, deeply matters to her.

It was a discovery not only of her family but of her social conscience. But, discovery is only the first step is self-actualization. It is one thing to know your own beliefs and to hold them close but it is another thing to defend, to promote and to advance those beliefs. It isn't just leaving work at 5:30 p.m. to spend more time with your family. No, it is so much bigger than that for me. And, it comes from a place deep in my soul, a place I thought had I sealed off years ago.

What for? That is the question that I am asking myself these days? Each experience is for something. What is this experience for? Was it meant to remind me, to awaken me to, to teach me? Was it to kindle the fire that once burned inside me to make a difference? Was it to get me off my ass and take some action?

I think so. Trouble is I have a family and a choice. It is a choice. I can chose to devote myself to the causes and initiatives that mean so much to me but that choice is unlikely to feed my family. That isn't to say that I can't find a way. It just means I can't just chuck it all and start over despite the overwhelming desire to chuck it right out the window. I love my family. They are not holding me back in any way. Indeed, they enable and encourage me.

But, I feel like I am gearing up for a fight. And, the truth is that the fight may very well pit me against friends, mentors, loved ones. It doesn't make the fight wrong. It doesn't make them or me "bad." Rather, it sparks the very debate that we are lacking in our world today. And, it gives voice to the voiceless.

Courage. Conviction. Commitment. Do I have it? I don't know yet but the clock is ticking . . .

Raise Your Hand!

March 2013
Nanjing, China

Today, I traveled to Nanjing, China to speak to a group of women working at the Salt Mine. On my way there, I was reading *Lean In* feeling very much like an impostor. After all, I no longer have a "leadership" job in China. Frankly, I have no clue what job I have these days aside from Tour Guide Barbie.

I fell asleep — thankfully. I hardly sleep it seems and the 45 minutes that I did sleep on the train really made all the difference.

I realized — while sleeping, where all my best thinking is done — that I don't have to have some title to be a leader. I don't even have to have a job. That notion is invented. I don't have to believe it. It does not have to be part of my reality. Hell, at this very moment the most powerful woman in the world is unemployed. Her name: Hillary Clinton.

I just am who I am. Who is that? Well, that is a bit more complicated than just a single blog, which is why I have posted more than 90 of these things. But, I think the 'what for' occurred to me today on the train — what has all of this been for; why am I here; who am I and what do I care about? What has this journey been about, what has it been for?

It's about the same things that I've always cared about — fairness and equality. Whether that was the size of my allowance or the size of my paycheck. (Ask my Dad!)

Last night, I could not sleep and I was watching the coverage of the Steubenville, Ohio rape trial verdict. To say that it made me ill would be an incredible understatement. I've alluded to some experience in this area in other blogs and there is no real point in telling the details of that long ago story. Except to say that it has shaped every moment of my life since it occurred, whether I knew it or not.

Violence against women is the root, the core, the source of inequality. Gloria Steinem said you can't have a real Democracy if you don't first have democracy in the home. What she was saying is that if women aren't equal in their relationships with their mates, how can they expect to be equal in the workplace? Worse, until only a couple of decades ago, spousal abuse had no name other than marriage. Domestic violence is a fairly new term in the American lexicon. Giving it a name was a huge step forward in women's rights and most people have no idea or, at least, no idea why it is so important.

Americans think we are enlightened. We watch Syria and India on the news and find the rapes of these women repulsive. We condemn the marriage of young girls, trafficking of women and girls, and we make speeches and promises and then, in our own backyard, we condemn the young woman raped by "promising young students" who had "promising football careers." Hey, I like football as much as the next Notre Dame graduate but seriously?

What does this have to do with my trip to Nanjing? Everything. This is China. You are allowed one child. Your thoughts, dreams and ambitions are to a large extent controlled and limited by the government, your station in life, your history and location of birth. Your ability to move, to better yourself, to think, to grow and become what you want to become is limited by strict protocols and rules.

Certainly, it is less limited now than it was in prior decades. But, make no mistake, we are still talking about a country where government officials forced a woman to abort her baby at seven months because she already had one child and she could not afford to pay the fine. The most fundamental of human rights — to create life — is controlled in China in a way far beyond Roe vs. Wade. And, yet, the women I see at work are remarkable.

Their concerns are no different from yours or mine. They want to raise their child to be strong and productive but worry that their child is spoiled by grandparents who have *only* one grandchild.

They worry about proper socialization. Will their child be able to survive in a world where they will first encounter other "children" as "adults?" The pressure on these women to give up their careers and stay home is significant. Their ability to cope with the stress associated with raising only one child upon whom an entire generation's hope rests and "balance" a career is marginal at best.

Doctors in China tell women to cut their hair because long hair steals nutrients from the baby. They are told not to have sex for the duration of the pregnancy and then even beyond. They are afraid of everything because they have no experience, no frame of reference, nothing to help reassure them. And, yet, despite all of this they want to work. They want to raise a child who can face the world, negotiate society and be productive. They believe in themselves but support from parents, spouses and even co-workers is lacking.

"How did you do it?" It's a question I am often asked. Today, I told this group that I did it with a great deal of help. First, my mother and my mother-in-law. My youngest sister. My husband. I did it by owning who I am and knowing that I like *and* want to work and that Jack is a better parent than me. I am not a bad parent but I am a better parent when I work.

And, yes, until Jack and I made the decision for him to stay home, it was expensive. But, I decided not to consider the cost of childcare, good childcare, a burden. I decided it was an investment — in our children and in me. I wanted to work and it required an investment in myself. So, we both kept working until we decided that my traveling internationally was becoming an issue that even the best childcare could not solve. We needed — I needed — Jack.

I was also asked "What would you tell a new leader?" Simple, really.

"I would tell a new leader the same thing I tell my 10-year-old daughter. Raise your hand." They looked at me and I explained. From the day you are born you have the potential to lead. The question is do you have the courage? And, if so, then do you have the desire? Don't sit in the back of the room. Don't wait to be noticed. Raise your hand and offer a point of view. Take a position, right or wrong — decide. Start from your first moment. Leadership is making music and the best music is made by musicians who constantly practice, make mistakes, and practice more. Observe, listen without judging, and practice.

We need these women in China, India, Syria, Cambodia and so many other places to raise their hands and offer their point of view. Ask their questions. We need them more than ever because it seems women in America and even Europe have stalled.

We have fallen down in our quest for equality. Why? Because we want to be liked? Because it is too hard? Don't quit because it is too hard. Quit because the work is no longer compelling or fails to align with your core values and principles as a human being but not because it is too hard or you think you aren't good enough. Don't listen to that voice in your head that keeps telling you that you are less than. You are more, so much more.

Subtle, shadowy sexism. I think those are the words Sheryl Sandberg used to describe the way we often evaluate women in the workplace. It is also the way we evaluate women and their value in the world. Ask yourself why, in America, we still focus the blame on the raped and lament the lost promise of the rapist. The fundamentals have not changed. Not yet.

What Questions Should You Be Asking Yourself?

March 2013
Shanghai

It has taken many years and yes, a lot of expensive therapy, to realize that the question I should be asking myself at all times is what will make me happy, *not* what will make me successful. 'Success' is a trap. It's what we believe will make our peers respect and even envy us. But that definition can be changing and elusive, and most of all, unrelated to happiness.

Excerpted from *"The Truth About Super Women,"* Melissa Francis, published on huffingtonpost.com, March 25, 2013

Is that the right question? I wonder. Maybe it is the right question for Ms. Francis but does that make it the right question for you or me or anyone else?

And, what is wrong with success? I don't understand the notion that women who are "successful" can't also be happy. Who made that rule? And when did the pursuit of success or, said differently, the pursuit of excellence, become a "trap"?

I wonder why women are so upset with Sheryl Sandberg. What did she do that is so terrible? Did she suggest ways in which women might help themselves? Did she cast a light under the bushel of gender bias that so many of us experience in silence throughout our careers? Did she admit that it is a constant struggle even for a woman who has an incredible support system? Yes, she did. And, again, why is any of that so terrible?

"Unfortunately, in the stumble that has become women talking about powerful women, you only get to the reasonable part of the conversation after you go through every possible iteration of figuring out how terrible all the powerful women are," wrote the *Atlantic Wire's* Rebecca Greenfield in "*What Your Reaction to Female Executives Says About You,*" March 1, 2013. (Some more interesting reading: "*Maybe You Should Read the Book: The Sheryl Sandberg Backlash,*" The New Yorker, post by Anna Holmes, March 4, 2013.)

Is that really the problem? Are we comparing ourselves now to Sheryl Sandberg and finding that we come up short? It was suggested to me by someone I consider to be wise where I am blind that a more helpful distinction is "me vs. my peers" rather than "success vs. happiness." Indeed.

Isn't that the point, really?   Frankly, isn't that Sheryl Sandberg's point? Maybe you don't like her method — *Lean In* — maybe that's just not your style but don't let that cloud the message. Could she have written more about the role her husband plays in making her work-life balance work? Maybe. But, isn't the point to think. And, think for yourself. Pick and choose what works or resonates with you and leave the rest on the table for others.

My friend commented that "whether we use happiness or success as the measure, I think it is more helpful to ensure it's our own assessment, and not the assessment of others. If we try ourselves in the court of public opinion, we give away our power of choice." Exactly.

Look, I am writing this after midnight because I can't sleep. Melissa Francis would point to her blog and say that this is one of the problems with trying to be a super woman. Maybe. Or maybe, I just have insomnia. I suspect that if I had no job at all, I would not be able to sleep. I would find some reason to be up at night pacing the floor. It's me.

The truth is that I am not trying to be Wonder Woman. I am, however, trying to be happy, which for me includes a dynamic, challenging career. It is part of what makes me tick. When I had my third child, my oldest daughter was 6 and she could not wait for me to go back to work. Happiness, for her, was a working Mom because a working Mom was a happier Mom. I don't aspire to be Sheryl Sandberg necessarily. I aspire to do the best with what I have; I believe I have something to offer and I want to share it.

I am choosing to have a career and a family. I have a husband who chose to take the harder job and stay at home so that I can pursue my career interests *and* be a Mother. Open and honest communication over a number of years made this possible and ended the "constant fighting" or the "constructive friction" that enabled us to make a decision together that we both could embrace and was in the best interest of our marriage and our children. This is not what works for other women and men. It is what works for me and my partner.

This is not to say that I am not frustrated by what I perceive to be inequality in the workplace. I am. I am also outspoken about that perception, which has career consequences. Much

> "Probably my worst quality is that I get very passionate about what I think is right."
>
> ~ Hillary Clinton

like Sandberg, I choose to speak up and I am prepared to take the backlash. I may not like it. Who likes being called ugly names? But, I choose to do it because it is something I believe in and it matters to me. While it makes me sad at times, it also makes me happy. I just need to choose to focus more on the moments that make me happy than those that make me sad.

I have made a difference for other women where I work. I know this because they have told me and because I have seen them take advantage of opportunities where they otherwise would have sat quietly in the corner waiting for someone to notice them. I am thrilled by their growth and their success. I view it as a collective success.

"Leave the door open and the ladder down!" In other words, help your fellow woman. Or risk the fires of hell, as Madeleine Albright forewarned. [Source: *"Leave the Door Open and the Ladder Down,"* Stacey Gordon, *Forbes* contributor, March 18, 2013.]

I am flabbergasted by women who refuse to engage in a meaningful discussion about gender issues. I am even more perplexed by the complacency of the few women who have made it up the ladder.

I applaud Sheryl Sandberg for sharing *her* story. She is propping open the door and offering you a hand as you climb the rungs. She is not, as far as I can tell, admonishing you if you choose to jump to another section of the jungle gym and climb that for a bit, even if that climb is lateral or down. The point is *choice*. You can choose not to take the hand.

Choosing to climb or not is yours and it should not matter what anyone else thinks about your choice. What does matter is that if you make the choice to climb, you deserve to be treated equitably. I think it helps if you have a bit of inside information on what works and what doesn't – at least until we have a level playing field. Personally, I am grateful to know that I am not going crazy and that someone like Sheryl Sandberg thinks the same things I think, including the nagging self-doubt that constantly derails me. It is communal — better to be crazy in a group than alone, I say.

I am a feminist. I am a mother. I am a wife. I am a triathlete (well, I try). I am a lover. I am a complex human being just like you. And, finding happiness can be a struggle. No one single thing makes me happy. Sorry Virginia, there is no secret to happiness.

My career is now among the things that contribute to my level of happiness but it no longer *defines* it for me. That did take some therapy and honest conversation and soul searching, but it doesn't mean that success and happiness are incompatible. It only means that my definition of me was a bit out of whack. Perspective was needed, sought and found. Nothing is easy. Even choosing to do nothing is not easy. And doing nothing does have consequences.

Recently, Nike came out with a new advertisement for Tiger Woods — "Winning takes care of everything." Maybe it does for Tiger Woods. Maybe winning is his definition of happiness and success. Maybe winning, for Tiger, is a like a salve and all his troubles fall away when he wins. I have no idea. I am not Tiger Woods. But, this advertisement sparked a backlash of its own. And, I was actually surprised.

> "Nike is causing a social media storm with its latest online ad showing a picture of Tiger Woods overlaid with a quote from him, "Winning takes care of everything."
>
> The ad, posted on Facebook and Twitter, is supposed to allude to the fact that the golfer recovered from career stumbles to regain his world No. 1 ranking on Monday, which he lost in October 2010. But some say it's inappropriate in light of Woods' past marital woes. It's the latest controversy from the athletic giant who has recently had to cut ties with biker Lance Armstrong and runner Oscar Pistorius due to separate scandals.
>
> Woods has long used the phrase — at least since 2009 — whenever reporters ask him about his or other golfers' rankings."
>
> [Source: " 'Winning Takes Care Of Everything': Tiger Woods Ad Under Fire," Mae Anderson, Associated Press, published on huffingtonpost.com, March 26, 2013.]

I just don't care about Tiger Woods marital problems or dating status or even if he wins. If it works for him, great. Winning does not take care of everything for me. Even if I did "win," and I am not sure what that would even look like in my current circumstance, it would not "take care of everything." It would be nice but it isn't everything to me.

A good hair day, a wrap dress and great pair of stilettos coming together on the same day that I am making a speech on an issue that I care passionately about and then coming home to my husband and children for pancakes for dinner is "winning" and "winning big" for me. It would be nirvana. But, I'd take the good hair day too. Hillary Clinton likely requires a bit more — world peace, maybe. But I am not Hillary Clinton; I am me.

The Semantics of Equality

April 2013
Shanghai

Irene Dorner, CEO of HSBC USA, says women of her generation should have done more to help women coming behind them, and she is right.

You already know that I believe Madeleine Albright when she says "There is a special place in hell for women who do not help other women." No, Irene Dorner should not go to hell. Why? Because the next generation has the same responsibility and that includes reaching forward and not just back.

I actually read *Lean In* by Sheryl Sandberg, unlike many who have criticized her and stopped at the cover because they preferred to talk about the "sticky floor." This debate over what lean in means vs. the realities of the sticky floor are not helpful to me. And, frankly, I just don't care what label you place on the problem. The semantics of equality are holding us back.

I'm a lawyer. Words matter and I have spent days and weeks arguing over the placement of a comma let alone word choice. But, here and now, on this topic in 2013, I no longer care what you call it. Because my reality is that I am the sole breadwinner for our family of five. My husband is a full-time father.

We made that choice together and it empowers me to do what I do and it empowers him as well. But, the fact is that by making that choice, we may have cut our income by 33% because I may only earn 77 cents for every $1 my male counterparts earn.

What does that mean? It means our children have less opportunities, I will have to work longer to close the gap before I can retire and it means I am growing more bitter and resentful by the minute, which is unhelpful to all of us. So, does it matter if a woman finds herself "behind" because she did not have the confidence to lean in early enough, long enough or hard enough or because the forces conspired against her creating a sticky floor? No. The root of the issue is extraordinarily complex and simple at the same time.

Do women lack confidence to lean in and are they, therefore, stuck to the floor? Yes. It starts early in our lives.

Every woman (and man) has a story. I have mine. It isn't a story most people know and I've only recently begun to talk more honestly about it.   I suspect I am doing that because I am now angry enough not to care how others judge me.

Like Irene Dorner, I know other women of power who failed to do more to help the next generation of women. It broke my heart to be told by a senior female executive that I needed to be more charming or risk being labeled a bitch. I'd been hearing this from my human resources rep — also a woman — for some time, so I knew it would eventually be said by others but when it happened, I came unglued.

Irene Dorner told the *New York Times* recently that she wishes she'd worked harder to change the "status quo" while breaking through glass ceilings on Wall Street.

> "I've always felt that satisfaction with the status quo has always been a recipe for disaster. In today's world, it's like raising the white flag of surrender."
>
> ~ Ursula Burns
> CEO of Xerox

'The women at the top of organizations that I know will tell you that we think that we've made it because we were born the way we are and can play by these rules without feeling damaged by them,' Ms. Dorner said. 'Or, we've learned how to play by these rules and use them to our own advantage. I suspect that we were simply not very good role models,' she added. 'And there aren't enough of us to be visible so that people can work out how to do what we did.'

Like Sandberg, Dorner too thinks women hold themselves back. But she also urges the next generation of women infiltrating the executive suites to do more. She told the *Times*:

> "I only realized what was happening when I was 50, because there I was, making my way in the unconscious rules. . .
> I really do think the next push has got to come from the senior middle-management women who must stand up and be counted on this earlier than I did."

[Source: "*Woman in a Man's World*," Andrew Ross Sorkin, *New York Times* Financial Blog, DealBook, April 2, 2013]

My mentor's parting words of advice, after seven years of dedicated service to her, were that I should expect to be the only woman in the room and to blend in — "don't highlight your differences" meaning everything from being a lawyer (most of the men are engineers) to wearing too much bling (aka my wedding ring). The goal was to avoid making the men uncomfortable. She was serious. I was at risk of being labeled a bitch.

I was crushed. Most of my career I have been uncomfortable. Uncomfortable trying to play a game that I know I cannot win. Uncomfortable sitting through performance

> "You show people what you're willing to fight for when you fight your friends."
>
> ~ Hillary Clinton

review after performance review being told that no one gets the work done like I do. "The difficult she handles in a minute; the impossible takes a few minutes longer" was a favorite phrase of one of my mentors — an African American man — and, yet, being passed over for promotion because I was "too aggressive" or "too" something. Another favorite: I need to learn to "let others catch up." Really? WTF?!

I was unglued, literally. I had leaned in, asked for and taken an assignment in China. After 2 years of incredibly long hours, a grueling travel schedule and little support from the "home team" in the States, I accomplished the goal of building from scratch an organization, laying the foundation for process discipline, growing the local national talent and empowering the team to make decisions because I would support them and, if necessary, take the heat if things went wrong. My role made me responsible for all of our organization's deliverables across all of Asia Pacific and Africa.

There was no specific team when I arrived. I built it by negotiating the transfer of heads and budgets from other organizations within the Salt Mine. The men leading those organizations were reasonable and happy to have the help. They were even more eager to give me the responsibility and accountability of assuring product certification.

In fairness, Asia Pacific and Africa is a small operational team compared to the North American and European operations. It certainly is far less political or territorial than North America or Europe. Working together is all that matters. Nothing gets done if each one of us doesn't pull our share and then some. Help, in all forms, is welcome.

I was the lowest ranking member of the Asia Pacific and Africa Operating Committee by two grade levels. A middle manager reporting out every week to the CEO of Asia Pacific and Africa of a major multi-national corporation. One of three women in the room but not a direct report to the CEO, though I did report directly to two Company Officers. One located in the States, who reported directly to the Salt Mine CEO, and the other in China who reported directly to the Asia Pacific and Africa CEO.

Only one of the women at this table was at the "executive" grade level. Not surprisingly, she led human resources. (When the second woman left the Salt Mine for health reasons, she was replaced with an executive level woman, who coincidentally had worked directly for the Salt Mine CEO for several years.) Despite my status or lack of status, I was the "executive sponsor" of our "women's organization." This only reinforced my feelings of being an impostor. And, I hated being "dressed up" as something I was not, most notably an executive.

Still, despite all the accomplishments and leadership, I am being called back to the States because I can't get along with the predominantly white male leadership in the States. The entire leadership team is male. Even the person replacing me is male. There are no women at executive grade level in my current organization and there are none in the grade level just beneath it either. You must go two levels deeper to find a woman. And you won't find many women there either.

Saying that I have poor relationships is simply another way of saying that I am "difficult," "too aggressive" and "lack charm." I took the news like a man, so to speak, and held my ground. But I signed my performance review like a lawyer, adding my dissenting opinion. Then, I left the building and found my husband and wept.

I blamed a woman who, like Irene Dorner, failed to do enough to change the perception of women in the boardrooms of America. Who, in my view, hurt us by pretending to be just like the men and denying their very womanhood. The single most important thing about them, the one thing they offer that the men cannot offer, is their experience as women. And, it is a powerful experience. Why did they deny it?

After some careful reflection and therapy, I no longer blame women like Irene Dorner, who climbed the ladder and didn't look back. Their accomplishments are inspiring. They had no rulebook or map. They climbed the ladder using their skills and the methods available to them. But, before they all retire and leave a gap in female power in these halls of commerce, they owe it to themselves and us to challenge the gender bias that keeps us "stuck to the floor" even when we do "lean in."

Gender bias is real and it makes you doubt everything you are, everything you have accomplished, everything you believe. It makes you wonder if it is "all in your head" or if you have a warped perspective of who you are, what you stand for and how you lead. This gives rise to tremendous self-doubt. At best, you find yourself stuck to the floor and, at worst, you give up entirely and find yourself broken and, if someone loves you enough, in therapy.

I don't care what you call it. The debate is healthy. But, whatever you call it, I've gone all in. I've put gender on the table where I work and readied myself for the storm. In the end, I know the truth. I am kind, I am smart and I am important. I just might not be popular.

Global Identification Number

March 2013
Shanghai

So, the time has come. Finally, time to go home. After protracted negotiations with the Salt Mine, the children and Jack will remain in China to complete the school year. I will return to the States "no later than April 1st." Uh, no.

First, April 1st just doesn't work for me. Second, who made you the boss of me? Third, uh, no.

The first email suggested not so subtly that I had been given a 'gift' of an extra month in China while I played Tour Guide Barbie to the Interloper. Are you kidding me? Seriously, dragging my ass around Southeast Asia as the opening act for the Interloper is not exactly a gift. I am working my tail off (when I am not drinking too much wine in Australia) and I am not seeing my kids or Jack. Gone for 9 days, land at 10 p.m. on Sunday night and back in the car at 6:15 a.m. the next morning to head to Thailand for 4 more days. Joy.

My reply was not charming: "I understand that I am just a Global ID Number to the Salt Mine but I am a mother to my children and a wife to my husband and a human being. We are taking a family vacation April 1 to 8 for Easter Break. I will be in the office no later than April 15th. I find it hard to believe that the Salt Mine can't live without me for a few days."

The second email came from human resources reminding me that the "terms" of my repatriation required my return by April 1st. Wrong.

My reply was even less charming than the first: "Technically, I am not repatriating until June 30th. My family will remain in China based upon my China work visa. Accordingly, I remain an employee of Salt Mine, China Limited until June 30th. Nothing requires me to return to the States by April 1st. Furthermore, the 'terms' of my original contract state that my assignment is for 3 years not 2 years. Again, I will be in the States no later than April 15th."

The third email suggested that I take the extra days after my family vacation as more vacation. I decided not to respond. I made my point.

The Salt Mine no longer dictates to me or controls my life. It is ridiculous that it ever got to this point. I am responsible for teaching the Salt Mine to treat me this way. I failed to set boundaries, or honor the boundaries that I tried to set. Why? Because I didn't think I was valuable unless the Salt Mine decided that I was valuable. Unsettling to say the least.

To be honest, I could not believe that I had the courage to push back so hard. But, I guess I have just reached my limit. Well, I reached it some time ago and, now, I just don't care. I really don't care what anyone thinks about me any longer. It has taken me 30 years, therapy, medication, and two "break downs" but I am finally beginning to feel like "me" again.

And, my soul is on fire.

Pool Talk

April 2013
Cebu, Philippines

You never know where opportunity will find you or you it. Today, opportunity was talking to our children at the infinity pool under the Cebu sun. Two amazing women just chatting with our son and daughter. Next thing you know, I have met two amazing and incredibly accomplished women who are in the Philippines with the organization Opportunity International. They are here to change lives.

The title of Opportunity International's fundraising campaign speaks volumes: "Invest in one woman. Empower many." They "provide microfinance loans, savings, insurance and training to over four million people working their way out of poverty in the developing world." Now, that is something worth doing. Don't you think? [Check it out: www.opportunity.org]

What really intrigued me is the notion that by investing in one woman you will empower many. Investing in women means that you are investing in their children and their communities. When you give women a loan, they use it differently than men — a higher percentage of women than men will use the proceeds to benefit their families and communities, making the world better for all.

It was just yesterday that I was writing about the semantics of equality and not letting that stop progress. Debate is great. I love debate. Hell, I'm a lawyer. I live on debate. But, filibuster I don't love. Opportunity International has a "one woman" philosophy that, frankly, makes the business case for women. What do I mean?

Often when you talk to multi-national corporations about investing in women or empowering women, whether it is within their halls or via funding for outside organizations devoted to developing and empowering woman, you hear that it is "something that is nice to do" but not essential or core to the business. In other words, where is the business case? Women *are* the business case.

If you require proof, take a look at the research. Large businesses with women on their board of directors outperform business that have all male boards. Outperform. By how much? By 26%. [Source: "Gender Diversity and Corporate Performance," a report by Credit Suisse Research Institute, August 2012]

Women have different life experiences than men. Women have a wider lens than men. Women care about issues that men don't care about, or don't care about in the same passionate way that women care about them. Women share in a different way. Women care about the economy and can debate the nuances of the North Korean rhetoric as well as any man, but they also care about children, human trafficking, and poverty in ways that men do not and this perspective is important for every business.

Businesses that continue to believe that empowering women is "nice to do" but not a "must do" will lose. It may not happen in the next 10 years but it *will* happen. Why? Because women are becoming more empowered across the globe and they will remember who helped them. Invest in one woman, empower many. Don't get left behind.

Cebu in the Springtime

April 2013
Cebu, Philippines

Me, the sun and the waves. French music playing (I Love Paris . . .). A slight breeze off the ocean brings the smell of the sand and salt. The sun has just risen and there is no one here but me *and you.*

The sun brings with it the final day of our springtime holiday in Cebu and the start of the transition back to our reality. Spring is a time of renewal. I am hopeful that it will bring something new. But, hope alone won't make that happen any more than the turning of the page on the calendar will make the snow stop falling in Minnesota in April. If I want my spring to flourish, I must toil in the dirt, water the planted seeds and pick the weeds that inevitably will seek to strangle this new growth.

In front of me is an endless sea with no shore in view. We are far from family and friends. And, yet we are closer than we have ever been to each other. Looking out over the seemingly limitless ocean, hope swells. A sea of opportunity perhaps? Like my garden, sailing that sea will require focus and dedication. Rough waters, unpredictable winds and a disgruntled crew can easily sink a ship.

Our view in Cebu, Philippines

Uncertainty.

Few of us like to face the future without a map. We like to know where we are going, our course charted. I am mindful that our children have been living with a level of uncertainty and change for many, many months now. The winter was cold and unkind. We step into spring in a sort of paradise, abundant with sun, water and natural harmony. Enjoying each moment as it comes. Still, the hard work of spring remains ahead.

I will till the soil and watch over my seeds. Will the seeds yield an abundant harvest? Eventually. I must be careful to balance my desire for renewal with our children's desire for certainty, stability.

I feel in some way that we have come full circle. Our journey began with tremendous uncertainty, trepidation and excitement. We are ending this chapter and beginning the next in the same way. We are all brimming with fear and excitement, disappointment and expectation, sorrow and yearning.

The winter was colder and longer than we expected. It left scars on each of us. Cebu has warmed our bodies and thawed much of the ice in our hearts. Our scars are fading and transforming into lessons. We are ready, if not prepared, for the journey ahead. We will take the next steps together, and now we know what together means. We are undaunted by the journey because we know — we are certain — one of us will carry the other when necessary along the way. From our perch in paradise, the sea appears calm but we know storms lie ahead. Still, we press on.

Perhaps *you* will press on with us. I hope so.

———————————————

EPILOGUE

Tempest: *a violent storm with high winds, especially one accompanied by rain, hail, or snow; a violent outburst; tumult. An old poet might say "to agitate violently." And, of course, Shakespeare put a human face on the storm.*

I believe we all have a rising storm inside of us. Every individual cares passionately for and about some thing, some issue, some cause, some person, some something. My journey over these past 24 months has led me to that something. It has awakened the inner tempest and I can feel the gathering storm swell within me. Sometimes, the tempest will not stir until poked. Poking the tempest can be a dangerous game to play.

Once awoken, the tempest can be unpredictable. I feel the swirling winds inside and around me. The storm that has been brewing within me also seems to be brewing within others. And now, the storm is rising, elevating and preparing to overwhelm those who fail to see her growing strength. Poking the tempest can be a noble cause.

The conversation has started, the debate begun. But where this particular tempest will finally land is yet to be determined. It can be exhilarating to watch the storm roll in over calm, safe and distant waters. It is safer on the shore. There, the storm is nothing but a beautiful confluence of color, light and sound.

Though seemingly safe, the shore can be nothing more than a harbor for complacency, or worse. Those on shore often watch the tempest swirl and fail to catch the wind themselves. Others try to fight the tempest, out-maneuver her, protect against her or capture her and put her in a teapot.

The tempest within me cannot be tamed so easily. The tempest will not settle; she will not calm herself. She wants to rage, to fight. The friction of the storm, while often seen as destructive, can indeed bring new life. I am hopeful that the tempest raging within will reveal a new path, ignite a new light.

The constant battle within soon will cease. The raging tempest is taking flight. She will wander the world as she has these past months gathering her courage, finding her voice. The path cannot be predicted and, even if it could, I would not ask for the map. It would destroy all the fun. A tempest once poked is forever undone.

My journey continues. You can find me, wherever I may be, at www.pinkstreakink.us

ACKNOWLEDGEMENTS

How do you say thank you when words are too clumsy a tool to convey the depth of your emotion? You pay it forward. For all of those who have helped me along the way, I will pay it forward. The joy found in paying it forward will make me smile, laugh and rejoice in the journey, which each of you played a part in making possible for me.

"Jack, Jane, Henry and Bella" made the journey possible by keeping me whole when I was dropping pieces of myself all over Southeast Asia, and providing so much useful material. Mom and Dad, I don't want to say beyond Mom and Dad — you help lift me up. Bill and Nancy, you raised a man capable of loving me and I will be forever indebted to you.

Deirdre Joy Smith started a chain reaction of connections that gave me the courage and inspiration to share my story. Thank you, Deirdre. And, thank you to Gail Evans, Selena Rezvani, Gail Romero and John Williams.

Bob Kantor shook me by the shoulders (virtually) and knocked sense back into me when I needed someone not related by blood or marriage to tell me that I was worthy. You helped me find my voice and push out the clutter that kept me from taking the first step. Thank you for your honest and candid feedback and for pushing me beyond my self-imposed limits.

Whitney Foard Small inspired me to write by showing me that it could be done. Everyone needs a buddy. Thanks for being my buddy and guiding me through a difficult transition. You have the potential to be a world-class mixologist (if you desire to follow that path) and you are already a mighty fine human being! I love you.

Janet Hanson gave me a voice by sending my blog to Forbes. com. As I write this, I have not come face-to-face with you, which is a testament to the pay-it-forward concept. You offered a helping hand simply because you could and you chose to help me. Madeleine Albright would be so proud of you, Janet. You are an inspiration and the best example of how women can help empower other women. Grateful is an understatement.

Tim Quinlan. Shared experience. Thank you for taking my call and providing such great advice — legal and otherwise. Paolo Mazzucato. A voice from my past, an inspiration and a friend who can never be replaced. Thank you for telling me I had a voice.

Killeen Mullen — Big girl panties. Barbara Lentz — amazing weekends in Winston Salem filled with wisdom, margaritas and s'mores. Andrea Ferrard — from Belgium to Atlanta — you've been there for me. Love you all. And, I love you Ben and Harry too. I didn't forget you, Mike Smith, thanks for lending me Barb, cooking, making a "camp fire" and letting me hang out!

Sue and Scott Radeker introduced me to the wonders of Bourbon on the rooftop deck and showed me how to navigate IKEA. What more can you ask? Nigel and Joanna Price listened to me complain and drank good wine with Jack and me. Nigel, thanks for all those wonderful meals. Time around the table with food, wine and friends was never as good as with all of you — thank you!

Lisa Wilder, my editor, thank you for your patience and keen eye. Randa Mansour, my illustrator — WOW! Roman Jeil, my ebook expert, I would have been lost without you and Whitney Foard Small. Technology is not my thing.

A special thanks to Dr. Liqun Hu, Yolanda Wang and the women in Nanjing. Thank you Kim Bowden-Adair, Donna

Crawley, Sarah Harty, Susie Bradfield, Sophia Chong, Ronna Luo, Yota Baron and Mag Dvonch. JMo, KShaughn & Sullivan, there are no words. You helped me see that I have a passion, that I am worthy, that I am more than what others would have me believe. Thank you for letting me into your lives and sharing yours with me.

Fife — thanks for documenting our journey in China and in life. You are my world.

And, finally, Delta Airlines. While that first trip was difficult, you carried me and our family around the globe countless times. And despite a rough start, you were on-time, your pilots and crew were professional and helpful, and we arrived at every destination safe and sound. We still fly Delta today!

Locked together forever . . . Jennifer, Jane, Bella, Henry & Jack